PRIVACY AND THE PRESS

PRIVACY AND THE PRESS

JOSHUA ROZENBERG

OXFORD
UNIVERSITY PRESS

OXFORD
UNIVERSITY PRESS

Great Clarendon Street, Oxford OX2 6DP

Oxford University Press is a department of the University of Oxford.
It furthers the University's objective of excellence in research, scholarship,
and education by publishing worldwide in

Oxford New York

Auckland Bangkok Buenos Aires Cape Town Chennai
Dar es Salaam Delhi Hong Kong Istanbul Karachi Kolkata
Kuala Lumpur Madrid Melbourne Mexico City Mumbai Nairobi
São Paulo Shanghai Taipei Tokyo Toronto

Oxford is a registered trade mark of Oxford University Press
in the UK and in certain other countries

Published in the United States
by Oxford University Press Inc., New York

© Joshua Rozenberg 2004

The moral rights of the author have been asserted

Crown copyright material is reproduced under
Class Licence Number CO1P0000148 with the permission
of HMSO and the Queen's Printer for Scotland

Database right Oxford University Press (maker)

First published 2004

British Library Cataloguing in Publication Data

Data available

Library of Congress Cataloging in Publication Data

Data available

ISBN 0–19–925056–1

1 3 5 7 9 10 8 6 4 2

Typeset in Bembo by
Cambrian Typesetters, Frimley, Surrey

Printed in Great Britain
on acid-free paper by
Biddles Ltd., King's Lynn

Preface

This was never meant to be a book about the Royal Family. When I started writing in the summer of 2001, it seemed sensible to begin Chapter 1 with a famous breach-of-privacy case involving the Queen and one of her servants. Now, as the book is at last completed some two-and-a-half years later, I find myself writing about the Prince of Wales and his inability to prevent the invasion of his privacy by those who once were loyal to him.

It came as little surprise that Prince Charles and his sons decided not to take legal proceedings against Paul Burrell, the former butler who published confidential letters from the Royal Family in the *Daily Mirror* and then in his book, *A Royal Duty*, in October 2003. As I shall explain in Chapter 1, we do not currently have a law in this country that effectively protects personal privacy. When another former royal servant, Michael Fawcett, sued the *Mail on Sunday* at the beginning of November 2003 to prevent publication of allegations relating to himself and the Prince of Wales, the case was brought not in privacy but in libel. And yet in the United States, where the libel laws are notoriously weaker than they are in England and Wales, we find lawyers who specialize in invasion-of-privacy claims, boasting of their prowess in 'policing' the use of their clients' images throughout the world.

Is that what we want to see here? Should public figures be able to keep their private lives, and their private faces, out of the public eye? At first sight, the answer seems obvious: why should we have any interest in—still less, any right to know about—the sexual conduct of a head teacher, a sports personality, a television performer, a Cabinet minister or the Prince of Wales? What they do in bed is no business of ours.

Or is it? Surely we are entitled to know a little more about those who hold positions of authority in society—if only to decide whether they are fit to remain in office? Surely we should not give young people the impression that adultery or sexual profligacy are to be admired in those they respect? Can we really trust the word of a public figure who has been deceiving a spouse or partner?

A privacy law in Britain would undoubtedly stop reporters telling the truth. When Andrew Morton first published his book, *Diana: Her True Story*, in 1992, chronicling the Princess of Wales's estrangement from her husband, her eating disorder and her suicide attempts, he was attacked for invading her privacy. It emerged only much later that his book was based on tape-recorded interviews with the Princess herself, checked and corrected by her before publication. Of course, her book invaded the privacy of Prince Charles and his companion Camilla Parker Bowles. But would it really have been in the public interest for us to have been as ill-informed about the Prince of Wales's affair with a married woman as we were when just the same thing was happening in the 1930s?

Before we decide what a privacy law might sensibly say, we should make some effort to decide what the concept means. This will not be easy. Is privacy the right to do what we like in our own homes without being seen by others? Or perhaps being heard by others, because the walls are too thin? Is it the right to enjoy a quiet meal in a restaurant without being photographed? The right to walk down the street or sunbathe on a beach without finding our pictures in the newspapers? To visit a prisoner without being strip-searched? Is it the ability to share information in confidence with one's secretary—who, as the name suggests, was originally a person entrusted with a secret? Or with another employee, such as a nanny or a butler? Or with a fashion designer who has signed a confidentiality agreement?

Is privacy the right to prevent others from taking photographs of us without our permission—perhaps because we were doing something disreputable, like visiting prostitutes, or something personal, like celebrating our wedding? Or is it indeed the ability to prevent newspapers from reporting our visits to a brothel, or a drugs rehabilitation centre? Is it the right to conduct a lawful but unpopular trade, such as running an abattoir, without being filmed by intruders? Or simply to preserve trade secrets, such as a new invention? To cheat on one's wife without being exposed as an adulterer? To live one's life without being identified as a child killer? To control the image we present of ourselves to the public?

As far as this book is concerned, the answer is all of the above. They are just examples of the privacy claims we shall encounter in *Privacy and the Press*. Not all were successful, of course, and quite rightly: in certain cases, it may well be in the public interest to deny a claim to privacy. And that is where the newspapers come in. More often than not, there is a conflict between freedom from intrusion and freedom of speech—between privacy and the press. Where should we draw the line? How do we reconcile freedom of expression—guaranteed by Article 10 of the Human Rights Convention, and considered in Chapter 3 of this book—with respect for a person's private and family life—protected by Article 8 of the Convention and explored in Chapter 4?

In defining our terms, it is customary to start with the dictionary. 'Privacy', according to the *Concise Oxford*, is the state of being private and undisturbed, or a person's right to this; it also means freedom from intrusion or public attention; or avoidance of publicity.

'Private' also has several meanings. These include belonging to an individual; one's own; personal (as in 'private property'). The term may also mean confidential; not to be disclosed to others (as in 'private talks'). A further meaning is 'kept or removed from public knowledge or observation'. The word reaches us through Middle English from the Latin *privatus*, 'withdrawn from public life', from a root meaning to bereave or deprive.

In their comprehensive textbook, *The Law of Privacy and the Media*, Tugendhat and Christie point out that these definitions encompass two separate concepts: information that is secret and information that is personal. For example, my computer password is private in the sense that I keep it secret; its disclosure in a newspaper, though destroying its secrecy, would not embarrass me on a personal level because I could easily pick a new one. On the other hand, I would not particularly like a newspaper to publish the photograph of my children that greets me when I turn my computer on; there is no secret about the fact that my wife and I have a son and daughter, but we would prefer not to share our personal family photographs with strangers. Both concepts may be covered by a privacy law.

Although some redress may be granted by the courts in specific circumstances, there is—at least at the time of writing, as I have said—no overarching principle of English law that will protect us against invasion of our privacy. That leaves the press relatively free to keep the public informed, a state of affairs that, naturally enough, I welcome. There is, however, the law of confidence, whose origins I shall trace in Chapter 1. This would have been the first legal weapon that Prince Charles's lawyers might have aimed against Burrell the butler. As we shall see, however, he would have had an important defence: if the information is deemed to be in the public interest, a claim will fail.

In the absence of a privacy law, it is still possible to take action under the law of copyright if a 'substantial part' of a private document is published without permission. Burrell's memoirs contained extracts from letters written by Diana, Princess of Wales, her brother Earl Spencer, Prince Charles, Prince Philip and even the Queen. However, most of the extracts were too short to be 'substantial', and so probably not covered by copyright at all. There is also a statutory defence of 'fair dealing', allowing limited extracts to be published for the purpose of reporting current events.

Is a disloyal former royal servant such a bad thing? It all depends on how we regard the Royal Family. If you think that the hereditary principle requires the accession to the throne of whoever happens to be heir apparent, then you may not worry too much about his personality and his weaknesses. On the other hand, if you consider that a constitutional monarchy depends for its survival on public support, then you will want to know everything you can about those close to the throne in order to decide whether your support is merited.

Take another example, current at the same time. In August 2003, the Attorney General, Lord Goldsmith, announced that he had appointed Ken Macdonald, QC, as Director of Public Prosecutions—DPP—making him head of the entire Crown Prosecution Service in England and Wales. He would be taking over in November, the Attorney's office added, and in the meantime he would not be giving media interviews. Shortly afterwards, the *Daily Telegraph* revealed that Macdonald had been fined as a student for possessing and procuring cannabis. Despite his self-denying ordinance, he promptly gave an interview to *The Times*—thus creating the impression that we could no longer rely on Lord Goldsmith's word. The Attorney General insisted he had known all along of Macdonald's criminal convictions for drug offences, and that it had always been intended that we, the public, should be told about them. But not yet.

Other newspapers then waited patiently until November when Macdonald was expected to give his inaugural news conference. In late October, his press office revealed that the new DPP would not, after all, be speaking to the media until January at the earliest. There would not even be an interview until then in his carefully controlled staff newsletter, *CPS News*. It was a complete reversal of the policy adopted by Macdonald's predecessor, Sir David Calvert-Smith, QC, who had encouraged chief prosecutors to become widely known in their communities by working closely with the local media.

There must be plenty of people in their fifties who used cannabis in their youth; some, no doubt, must have been convicted of supplying it to others or attempting to do so. Most of them could argue that this was the sort of incident they might reasonably be allowed to keep private thirty years on. But the DPP is in a different position. It was clearly in the public interest that we should know that the country's senior prosecutor had himself been prosecuted. The crucial question, entirely unanswered in the *Times* interview, was whether his criminal record would have any effect on the way he did his job. Would he have more sympathy for those, like him, who had admitted possessing and supplying cannabis? Would he exercise his ultimate discretion not to prosecute them, thus effectively decriminalizing the use of a powerful illegal drug? Or would he be tougher than his predecessor, simply in order to avoid any suggestion that he had been influenced by his own breaches of the law? These were the questions Macdonald was unwilling to answer during his initial two months in office, a crucial period when he had to win the support of beleaguered staff and public alike.

He presumably regarded his convictions as a private matter; otherwise, they would have been mentioned when his appointment was announced. But it would have been appalling if a privacy law had prevented the press from raising legitimate questions about Macdonald's suitability for office. The new DPP appeared to have forgotten that one of his predecessors resigned immediately he was stopped by the police and questioned about an alleged offence, even though no prosecution was ever brought.

Although I consider that the press had every right to delve into Macdonald's past, I make no attempt in this book to defend every example of press intrusion. According to the judges, certain newspapers have come very close to derailing a number of high-profile trials by publishing information about defendants that could prejudice the jury. But, just as I have adopted a broad definition of privacy, I am taking an all-encompassing approach to free speech. In the end, it may come down to a clash between 'the right to be left alone' and 'the public's right to know'. By the end of this book, there should be little doubt about where I stand.

However, my aim is to entertain and inform rather than to badger and persuade. Privacy is one of the most interesting legal topics around at the moment, if only because nobody knows where the law is going. As we shall see, some judges have been trying to use the Human Rights Act to create a fully fledged privacy law. Others say it is best left to Parliament, although they must know that the Government is unwilling to act. In October 2003, the Department of Culture, Media and Sport published its formal response to the Commons select committee report on *Privacy and Press Intrusion*, discussed in Chapter 8. 'The Government strongly believes that a free press is vital to the health of our democracy,' it said. 'There should be no laws that specifically seek to restrict that freedom, and Government should not seek to intervene in any way in what a newspaper or magazine chooses to publish. We therefore support self-regulation.'

That was not to say that the Press Complaints Commission—the body through which the newspaper industry regulates itself—was not capable of improvement; as we shall see in Chapter 5, everyone agreed that it could be made more effective. But, as the Department rightly said, 'more legislation is not only unnecessary but undesirable'. First, the Government explained, there was already legislation in existence, such as the Data Protection Act (discussed in Chapter 2). Then, of course, there was the right to respect for private life granted by the Human Rights Act. But section 12 of that Act provides protection for free speech (as we shall see in Chapter 4) and, as the Government accepted, there was a balance to be struck between freedom of expression and the right to privacy. Ministers believed that that balance would not always be found at the same point because some people could be said to have invaded their own privacy by, for example, granting access to photographers, and thereby making public details of their private lives. As the Government said, 'the weighing of competing rights in individual cases is the quintessential task of the courts, not of Government, or Parliament. Parliament should only intervene if there are signs that the courts are systematically striking the wrong balance; we believe there are no such signs.'

In the Government's view, 'privacy legislation would pose a particular problem for those not normally in the public eye because the mere fact of seeking a remedy in the courts can, of itself, lead to a further loss of privacy. The provision of an effective, informal remedy through self-regulation can protect against the exacerbation of any harm.' Ministers accepted that people in public life were also entitled to a private life, but it was for the courts to decide to what extent individuals had consented to the infringement of their privacy through their engagement in public life. 'There is not one rule for celebrities and another for members of the public; the rule is the same, but the current situation allows individual circumstances to be taken into account.'

With no legislation in prospect, it will be for the judges to decide how far press freedom should extend. From the newspapers' point of view, the prospects are not at all bad. In Chapter 6, I shall explore how the courts of England and Wales have demonstrated their support for responsible journalism, following the lead set in the 1960s by the United States Supreme Court. No doubt some of my readers will consider 'responsible journalism' to be as much of an oxymoron as 'government organization', 'healthy tan', or 'airline food'; Chapter 7 will show you what it means. In Chapter 8, I shall explore privacy laws in other countries before seeing what the law has in store for us and tying up some loose ends.

But writing a book about privacy law is like firing at a moving target. At some point in 2004, the law lords will rule on Naomi Campbell's plea for a privacy law that would have prevented newspapers from revealing details of the therapy she was receiving for her drug addiction. Also in 2004, the European Court of Human Rights will decide whether Princess Caroline of Monaco has the right to stop photographers from taking her picture as she walks down the street. Whatever next?

★   ★   ★

This book originated, like so many fine things, over a table in the Garrick Club. When John Louth and I sat down for pre-dinner drinks, I had no intention of being seduced and flattered by him into writing another book—not even for OUP. By the time we reached coffee, we had agreed the synopsis and I had mentally spent the advance, thus ensuring I had to deliver. John knew just how much pressure to bring over the months that followed, appearing entirely relaxed when I explained, shamefacedly, that the book would be delivered a year late. (A year! When I worked in broadcasting, being a minute late would have led to disaster: I don't think it ever happened.) John and his admirable copy-editor, Dominic Shryane, have seen my words through the press with skill and efficiency.

It is also a pleasure to thank two friends who looked at an early draft of the book and made many helpful suggestions. Jonathan Coad, over and above the call of duty, took it with him on a family holiday. Even more extraordinarily, David Pannick, QC, read it during his honeymoon.

Needless to say, the errors that remain are my own. Readers who spot them are encouraged to get in touch with me through my website—www. rozenberg.net—on which I hope to post clarifications and occasional updates. However, I do not practise as a lawyer and cannot give advice in individual cases. While every care has been taken, as the lawyers say, no responsibility can be accepted for errors or omissions.

It was not a very good idea to have taken on this book within a year of starting my first job in print journalism for the *Daily Telegraph* and to have written it during a period when our home was a building site. While I was at the BBC, there seemed plenty of time to write on the days when there were no stories. In newspapers, there are no such days. As a result, I found myself writing this book during weekends and, workmen permitting, during what were meant to be holidays. For this reason, the book is dedicated—in what I hope will be an appropriate thirtieth wedding anniversary present—to Melanie, my long-suffering wife. And if that revelation isn't an invasion of our personal privacy, I don't know what is.

JOSHUA ROZENBERG
NOVEMBER 2003

Contents

CHAPTER I

Confidence or Privacy?

The Queen was livid. Her Majesty's private family pictures were being hawked around London for all the world to see. There were portraits of the Prince of Wales, the Princess Royal—even pictures of their favourite dogs. Her advisers told the Queen that the only way to stop further publication was to take legal action. A claim was duly lodged at the High Court—but in her husband's name, because the Queen cannot sue in her own name.

His Royal Highness said in evidence that their pictures must have been copied surreptitiously. They had been kept securely in the Queen's private apartments in Windsor Castle, and although the Royal Couple had occasionally given copies to some of their personal friends they had never agreed to any wider publication. Who, then, had leaked them?

The Prince pointed the finger at William Strange, a publisher, who was said to have been offering the pictures for sale from an office near Fleet Street. This, he said, was 'in the highest degree offensive' to the Royal Couple. They asked the court for a temporary injunction to prevent Strange from copying or publishing them. The judge agreed.

Strange then appealed. He denied obtaining the pictures surreptitiously. They had come from a man called Judge, who in turn had bought them from a middleman called Middleton. How had Middleton got hold of them? It turned out that the Royal Family used to send their pictures to a Mr Brown, of Windsor, to be printed. Middleton was one of his staff, and had simply run off some extra copies without permission.

Confronted with the evidence, Strange said he had not thought for a moment that the Royal Couple would have been offended by publication of their pictures. Now he knew how they felt, he had—of course—abandoned his plans. He asked for the injunction to be lifted. Any other outcome, argued his lawyers presciently, 'would interfere with one of the most valued rights of the people of this country—the freedom of the press'.

The courts were in some difficulty because there was no contractual relationship between the Royal Couple and Strange. That meant the Prince had not been able to sue him for breach of contract in the normal way. However, Strange had obtained the pictures through a breach of trust—not by him, but by Middleton. In the court's view, that was enough. The wrongdoer should not be allowed to benefit from his actions.

It was on that basis that the Vice-Chancellor—the senior Chancery judge—was persuaded to continue the injunction. Since the pictures had been made for the private use of the Royal Couple, he concluded, they were entitled to keep them 'in a state of privacy'. It did not matter that they had given copies to a few friends, the judge added. 'They alone are entitled to decide whether, and when, and how, and for whose advantage, their property shall be made use of.'

Some of this may sound strikingly familiar, though you could be forgiven for not remembering the details. It all happened more than 150 years ago, in 1848. The Queen, of course, was Victoria and her husband was Prince Albert. Their pictures were etchings rather than photographs, and Strange was planning to display impressions of them at the Egyptian Hall ('or at some other public institution of equal respectability') rather than to publish them in a tabloid newspaper. It was the catalogue he published that had led to the legal action: no etchings had yet seen the light of day.

The case of *Prince Albert v Strange* could fairly be described as the first successful claim for personal privacy. But that is not the label lawyers give to it. They regard the case as a major step on the road towards the *law of confidence*. We are about to discover whether that classification makes any practical difference.

The prospects for privacy

In English law, the story of Queen Victoria's etchings is more than just a historical curiosity. Until Parliament passes legislation on a particular topic, the law is what the judges say it is. In a series of decisions over the past century and a half, the courts have built on *Prince Albert v Strange*, little by little, so that we now find ourselves with a set of legal principles that may go some way towards protecting our personal privacy. But most judges still classify these principles under confidentiality rather than privacy. Although the law is in a state of flux, and changing even as I write, we do not yet have a pure privacy law—in legal terms, a 'tort' or civil wrong—that we can use whenever we believe our private lives have been invaded.

Nor is there any prospect in the near future of Parliament creating one by statute. 'The Government has no plans whatsoever to legislate in this area,' it told the Commons Media Committee in 2003 (as we shall see in Chapter 8). There are already several laws on the statute book that may be used to protect our privacy, notably the Data Protection Act 1998 (see Chapter 2), the Protection from Harassment Act 1997 and the 'doorstepping' restrictions in the Criminal Justice and Police Act 2001 (both discussed in Chapter 3). The Sexual Offences Act 2003 makes it a crime punishable with up to two years' imprisonment for a voyeur to seek sexual gratification by watching someone else doing what is defined as a 'private act' (we shall take a look at this, too, in Chapter 8). Much more importantly, there is now the Human Rights Act 1998. This unique legislation, which came into force in October 2000, may be the catalyst for a law against intrusion—though it does not create one itself. For this reason, the higher courts will have to perform some subtle alchemy if the Human Rights Act is to lay the golden egg of a privacy law. Some, in any case, would see that outcome as fool's gold.

Ever since 1966, people have had the right to complain to a judicial authority in Strasbourg that the British Government—or some aspect of the legal process for which the Government is ultimately responsible—has breached the rights granted to people in the United Kingdom when the European Convention on Human Rights came into force in 1953. Since 2000, however, there has been little need to go to Strasbourg: generally speaking, people should get the same results from our own judges. Under the Human Rights Act 1998, courts in the United Kingdom are required, as far as possible, to give effect to all other legislation in a way that is 'compatible' with the European Convention. That document contains two 'Articles', or sections, of fundamental importance to free speech. Article 8 begins by asserting that 'everyone has the right to respect for his private and family life'. Article 10 begins by acknowledging that 'everyone has the right to freedom of expression'.

We can see immediately that these two provisions may conflict with each other. How can I enjoy my right to write about you if you can require me to respect your privacy? How can you insist that I show respect for your family life if I have the right to say what I like about you in public?

Significantly, both Articles contain several exceptions. Article 10, for example, allows restrictions on free expression 'for preventing the disclosure of information received in confidence'. Article 8, to take another example, allows interference with the right to respect for a person's private life 'for the protection of the rights and freedoms of others'. Like Article 9 (freedom of thought) and Article 11 (freedom of association), the rights in Articles 8 and 10 are qualified rather than absolute. All four have a broadly similar internal balance, or tension. In each of them, the restrictions must be no more than are 'necessary in a democratic society'.

On the other hand, we should not assume that privacy and freedom of expression are always in conflict. Shortly before becoming a judge in 2003, Michael Tugendhat, who specialized in media law as a barrister, told the Commons Media Committee that there were many circumstances in which it was impossible to have freedom of expression *without* privacy. 'The most obvious examples of that, of course, are when people give information to newspapers and need to protect their identities,' he said. Another example was of people with unpopular political or religious views that they could express only in private.

As well as obliging courts in the United Kingdom to give effect to the Human Rights Convention, section 12 of the Human Rights Act 1998 requires the courts to have 'particular regard' to freedom of expression. What effect this may have is still far from clear: there is nothing in the legislation to suggest that, as a result, judges must show any less respect to a person's family life.

Later, in Chapters 3 and 4, we shall look more closely at how the courts have balanced freedom of expression against respect for private life. For now, we need simply note that the existing, judge-made common law has accommodated the Human Rights Convention rather as a sapling will grow round a cable that was once secured to its trunk to give it support. As Lord Woolf, the Lord Chief Justice, said in 2002, the courts have applied the Human Rights Act 'by absorbing the rights which Articles 8 and 10 protect into the long-established action for

CONFIDENCE OR PRIVACY? 5

breach of confidence. This involves giving a new strength and breadth to the action so that it accommodates the requirements of those Articles.' As we shall see, he made those comments in a notorious case brought against a newspaper by a footballer named Garry Flitcroft. We shall tackle that particular case in Chapter 2.

Do we need a new law?

In March 2003, Lord Phillips, who as Master of the Rolls ranks second only to the Lord Chief Justice in the judicial hierarchy, gave a lecture in which he said that debate in the country was 'raging as to whether the judges should develop the common law so as to fashion a tort of privacy'. That debate seemed to be raging not so much in the country as in the corridors of the Court of Appeal. In Flitcroft's case, just a year earlier, Lord Woolf had said in court that there was no need for such a law: 'It is most unlikely that any purpose will be served by a judge seeking to decide whether there exists a new cause of action in tort which protects privacy,' the Lord Chief Justice explained. 'In the great majority of situations, if not all situations, where the protection of privacy is justified, relating to events after the Human Rights Act came into force, an action for breach of confidence now will, where this is appropriate, provide the necessary protection.'

It was a stark illustration of the issues at the heart of this book. Should the courts of England and Wales use the powers they undoubtedly have to create a new privacy law, protecting individuals from public scrutiny? As we shall see, that seems to be the view favoured by the dynamic Lord Phillips. Or should they follow the more cautious, conservative approach espoused by Lord Woolf, redefining the existing law where necessary but doing little to restrict freedom of expression by newspapers and others? Lord Woolf's decision to postpone his retirement, planned for the end of 2003, may slow the movement towards a privacy law in England and Wales—particularly as Lord Phillips was seen as a potential successor.

Striking the right balance between privacy and free speech must be one of the hardest things a judge has to do. What makes it a little easier is that the courts do not work in the abstract: they make law by deciding actual cases. That is why this book is jam-packed with judgments, rulings that make more sense and become more interesting the more you know about the facts that inspired them. Since we do not have a Privacy Act, reading the cases is the only way to find out the law. But, paradoxically, people who claim their privacy has been breached must bare their secrets when they give evidence in a public court. For this reason, privacy cases are among the most entertaining around.

It was instructive to watch privacy enthusiasts like Lord Phillips trying to morph the staid, Victorian law of confidence into a turbo-charged, twenty-first century law of privacy. What appeared to stand in his way was the well-established need for some sort of relationship between the parties: traditionally, the existing law of confidence applied only to information given 'in confidence' by one person to another. But, six months after Lord Woolf's ruling in Flitcroft's case, Lord Phillips and his fellow judges tried to steer the law towards a less restrictive definition. 'The development of the law of confidentiality since the Human Rights Act came into force has seen information described as "confidential" not where it has been confided by one person to another, but where it relates to an aspect of an individual's private life which he does not choose to make public,' they said. 'We consider that the unjustifiable publication of such information would better be described as breach of privacy rather than breach of confidence.'

That was said in a case brought by Naomi Campbell, the model, against the *Daily Mirror*. When hearing the newspaper's appeal, the Master of the Rolls sounded quite disappointed to be told by counsel that his court would not 'have to consider whether there was a tort of privacy in English law following the coming into force of the Human Rights Act'. So in March 2003 the Master of the Rolls found another opportunity to lay the groundwork for a new law—the Bentham Club presidential lecture given at University College London. In it, he was careful to say that he had not 'expressed any personal views on the desirability of the development of a tort of invasion of privacy'. There was a good reason for this, he explained. Lord Phillips did not wish to disqualify himself from sitting on any appeal there might be from the then imminent High Court ruling in another key privacy case, this time brought by the Hollywood stars Michael Douglas and Catherine Zeta-Jones.

But a careful reading of his speech showed exactly what Lord Phillips thought of the existing law. He went out of his way to point out that his own ruling in the Naomi Campbell case, which did not address the question of whether a privacy law had yet come into existence, had been 'criticised by some as being over-conservative'. It looked as if he was blaming himself for ducking the issue. Certainly, he believed, the courts' refusal in 1990 to grant a privacy claim brought by the actor Gorden Kaye—as we shall see later in this chapter—represented the 'nadir of the seeming impotence of our common law'. Indeed, he believed, there was 'revulsion' at the decision. But that case had been heard a decade before the Human Rights Act had come into effect. Was this legislation, he mused, 'a skeleton key which opens the door to the development of a right of privacy by the English judiciary'?

A later case, involving the Earl and Countess of Spencer, certainly suggested to Lord Phillips that 'the Government was leaving it to the judges to use the tool of the Human Rights Act to build a law of privacy on the foundations of the law of confidentiality'. Finally, he noted, the European Court of Human Rights had recently ruled in favour of Geoffrey Peck, a man suffering from depression who was filmed on security cameras carrying a kitchen knife in a town centre one night, just before attempting to cut his wrists. The Court's finding that Peck had been denied a remedy for the subsequent broadcast of these pictures suggested to Lord Phillips that 'either the courts or the legislature are going to have to establish a tort of invasion of privacy if this country is to comply with its . . . obligations' under the European Convention on Human Rights. There was little prospect of legislation—as we shall see in Chapter 4, the Government considered it unnecessary. So it seemed clear that Lord Phillips was keen to build his own tort. The only question was whether an even higher tier of judges would get there first: unusually, the law lords had agreed in 2003 to hear an appeal by Naomi Campbell against the decision handed down by Lord Phillips.

As we shall see when we examine these cases more closely, they all raise the classic dilemma. When should the judges try to stop me from writing—and you from reading—about someone else? Should it make any difference if that person has sought fame like Naomi Campbell, or found it thrust upon him like Geoffrey Peck? Should it make any difference if the celebrity has behaved disreputably? Or are there none so disreputable as the newspapers? Ought we to stop them prying into our affairs?

My not-so-private view

You, dear reader, will have your own answers to these questions. My first job in writing this book is to set out the law, as objectively as I can, so that you can test your own views against those of the judges. But this is not a textbook: I am a journalist and commentator, not an academic. If I am asked to choose between freedom of expression and personal privacy, however defined, my instinct is to come down on the side of free speech. I do not want the courts to develop what has been called a 'blockbuster' tort of privacy; still less do I want Parliament to pass a Privacy Act. You would probably expect those views from a reporter, especially one who chose to sacrifice some level of personal privacy by working in television news (and, yes, I still find myself being recognized by total strangers, more than three years after I left the BBC). I shall try to explain my views more fully in Chapter 5, and at other suitable points throughout the text.

That said, this book is not a polemic. After putting both sides of every argument during my twenty-five years in broadcasting, I have not found it particularly easy to come down on one side of the fence rather than the other. My aim is not to persuade you that we in the press are necessarily right, although declaring my hand at this stage should at least help you weigh up your own opinions against mine. But before we can discuss the future we have to study the past.

The law of confidence

In the century and more since the case of Queen Victoria's etchings, breach of confidence has been developed by the courts into a cause of action that can be used to prevent the damage caused by the disclosure of private information that had been entrusted to someone who is obliged to keep it confidential. By 1968, Mr Justice Megarry was able to sum up the case law on confidence into this classic three-part test (the italics are mine): 'First, the information itself . . . must "have the necessary *quality* of confidence about it". Secondly, that information must have been imparted in circumstances importing an *obligation* of confidence. Thirdly, there must be an unauthorized use of that information to the *detriment* of the party communicating it.' We shall consider what this means in a moment.

On the basis of his newly minted test, the judge ruled against a designer named Marco Paulo Coco. He had designed a new moped and shown his plans to a company called A N Clark (Engineers) Ltd—only to find that the manufacturer then brought out its own model, called the Scamp. The designer failed to obtain an interlocutory injunction to halt production of the Scamp as he could satisfy only the second of Mr Justice Megarry's three conditions. Coco might have felt better about it if he had known that mopeds—which, as the name suggests, were motor-assisted pedal-bikes—would soon become museum pieces.

How easy would it be to transform confidence, as defined by Mr Justice Megarry, into the modern privacy law that some campaigners and judges want to see? The need for courts to find that information has the 'quality of confidence' about it should not tax their ingenuity too much: the definition is almost circular. And there should be no difficulty in finding some 'unauthorized use' of the information—if the use was authorized, there could hardly have been a breach of privacy—although detriment may be harder to prove. The real challenge is in finding what Mr Justice Megarry called 'circumstances importing an obligation of confidence'—in other words, some sort of relationship between the parties. A privacy law would not be much use unless it could be used against complete strangers.

In *Coco v A N Clark (Engineers) Ltd* the parties' relationship was commercial. The case was, of course, about the confidentiality of trade secrets, and most of the decided cases in confidence deal with commercial information such as customer lists and product specifications. The law also covers government secrets, such as the diaries of a Cabinet minister: in *Attorney General v Jonathan Cape Ltd* Lord Widgery, the Lord Chief Justice, held in 1975 that 'when a Cabinet minister receives information in confidence the improper publication of such information can be restrained by the court'—though some ten years after they were written he concluded that Richard Crossman's diaries were no longer confidential. 'I cannot believe that the publication at this interval of anything in volume one would inhibit free discussion in the Cabinet of today, even though the individuals involved are the same, and the national problems have a distressing similarity with those of a decade ago,' the judge said. The law of confidence was also relied on by the Government in the *Spycatcher* case, discussed in Chapter 7. By 2003, as Robin Cook demonstrated when he published his memoirs in October of that year, the interval between resigning from the Government and publishing details of Cabinet discussions was down to about six months.

Another line of cases dealt with personal and non-commercial relationships—although the same information may have both commercial and private value. The courts are not particularly censorious: *Argyll v Argyll* (1964) decided that confidences must be preserved between spouses, even after a divorce and despite the fact that the claimant, the Duchess of Argyll, had indulged in what the divorce judge a year earlier had called 'disgusting sexual activities to gratify a debased sexual appetite'—a reference to her infamous sexual liaison with a man, generally believed to have been Douglas Fairbanks Jr, who was photographed 'headless'. In *Stephens v Avery* (1988), the court allowed Rosemary Stephens to sue her former friend Anne Avery under the law of confidence, despite the nature of the information Stephens had given her and which Avery, in turn, had passed on to the *Mail on Sunday*: it related to Stephens's lesbian relationship with a woman, Mrs Telling, who was killed by her husband after he found her in what newspapers used to call a 'compromising position' with Stephens. In *Barrymore v News Group Newspapers* (1997), Michael Barrymore obtained an injunction in confidence against the *Sun* after a man called Paul Wincott told the newspaper about his homosexual relationship with the television personality: 'The fact is that when people kiss and later one of them tells, that second person is almost certainly breaking a confidential arrangement,' said Mr Justice Jacob in an extempore judgment. And in *Archer v Williams* (2003), the wife of the disgraced peer Jeffrey Archer was granted a permanent injunction to prevent her former personal assistant from disclosing any more details about Lady Archer's facelift or other aspects of her private life. Mr Justice Jackson said that Jane Williams, in breach of her contract of employment, gave confidential information in substantial quantities to the publicist Max Clifford and to journalists from the *Mail on Sunday*, the *News of the World* and the *Daily Mail*. Ordering Williams to pay Archer £2,500 in damages, the judge rejected her argument that Article 10 of the Human Rights Convention gave her the right to freedom of expression.

How far will the courts stretch the law of confidence to protect a claimant's privacy? In a case that could go either way, the claimant's personal conduct may well tip the scales. We have seen that the courts have no problem with adulterous or homosexual relationships. But unattractive figures like Garry Flitcroft, the footballer caught 'playing away from home' with a lap-dancer and a nursery school teacher, and Jamie Theakston, a children's television presenter photographed in a brothel, found the courts less accommodating in the spring of 2002 than did Naomi Campbell, the model who argued that her attempts to overcome drug addiction had been thwarted by unwelcome publicity. Later, in the Court of Appeal, even she lost out because she had lied about her drug addiction. 'Where a public figure chooses to make untrue pronouncements about his or her private life,' the appeal judges said in ruling against her in October 2002, 'the press will normally be entitled to put the record straight.'

It is not so much that the courts look down on lap-dancers and prostitutes, more that fleeting relationships are less likely to be respected by the judges. As Lord Woolf, the Lord Chief Justice, said in Flitcroft's case (which, because the footballer was not initially named, appears in the law reports as *A v B plc*), 'whether a duty of confidence does exist which courts can protect, if it is right to do so, will depend on all the circumstances of the relationship between the parties at the time of the threatened or actual breach of the alleged duty of confidence.'

We should not be surprised to find the courts treating an individual's conduct as an important factor. The law of confidence has been developed over the centuries by the Chancery courts when applying the rules of equity, which are binding on the conscience of an individual. Historically, a remedy would be granted only if it were 'equitable' to do so. The Statute of Uses 1535 is framed in terms of 'use, confidence or trust'; and a couplet, attributed to Sir Thomas More, Lord Chancellor from 1529 to 1532, says: 'Three things are to be helpt in Conscience; Fraud, Accident and things of Confidence'. Let us see how well the law has adapted to modern needs.

The quality of confidence

To come within the first of Mr Justice Megarry's three indicators of legal confidentiality, information must have the 'quality of confidence' about it. Like an elephant, this concept is easier to recognize than to define: perhaps judges simply find it whenever they want to allow a claim and deem it missing when they think the case is without merit.

As we shall see, details of Naomi Campbell's attendance at meetings of Narcotics Anonymous were said by Mr Justice Morland to have had the 'badge or mark of confidentiality' because 'they were obtained surreptitiously, assisted by covert photography, when Miss Campbell was engaged deliberately "low key" and drably dressed in the private activity of therapy to advance her recovery from drug addiction.'

Similarly, the wedding of the Hollywood stars Michael Douglas and Catherine Zeta-Jones was said by Mr Justice Lindsay to have had the quality of confidence about it because of the elaborate steps taken by the couple to preclude unauthorized photography. 'Such images as were, so to speak, radiated by the event were imparted to those present, including [the paparazzo] Mr Thorpe and his camera, in circumstances importing an obligation of confidence. Everyone there knew that was so.'

The obligation of confidence

When, for example, will the courts conclude that a person receiving confidential information is—to quote the second of Mr Justice Megarry's three tests—under an 'obligation of confidence'? In the past, such a relationship has been held to exist between doctor and patient, journalist and source, husband and wife, and cohabitants—either same-sex or heterosexual.

Fortunately, there are limits. The brief encounter Jamie Theakston had in a brothel—where, as he explained, a girl 'performed a sex act on me'—was not considered to be a relationship for the purposes of the law of confidence by Mr Justice Ouseley in 2002. Refusing to grant the *Top of the Pops* presenter an injunction against the *People*, the judge said: 'If this sexual activity in that fleeting relationship were invested with confidentiality, the concept of confidentiality would become all-embracing for all physical intimacy' unless a line were drawn. The judge found it 'impossible to invest with the protection of confidentiality all acts of physical intimacy regardless of circumstances'. To do otherwise would have been to concede the existence of a free-standing privacy law, an issue on which the judge was unwilling to be drawn.

Illogically, though, the newspaper was prevented from publishing pictures of Theakston in the brothel. Mr Justice Ouseley held that 'publication of such photographs would be particularly intrusive into the claimant's own individual personality. They could still constitute an intrusion into his private and personal life and would do so in a peculiarly humiliating and damaging way.'

Lord Phillips, in his Bentham lecture, explained why he thought Theakston had been granted an injunction preventing publication of the pictures. 'The claimant had not agreed to being photographed. There was no public interest in the publication of the photographs. The courts had consistently recognised that photography could be particularly intrusive,' he said. Finally, to restrain publication of the photographs 'involved no particular extension of the law of confidentiality.'

Less fleeting sexual relationships can be protected by the law of confidence, as can sensitive medical conditions and artistic confidences. Since the law is judge-made, it can be shaped and fashioned by the judges to meet what they see as the needs of the time. We have seen already how judges can negate an existing relationship by describing it as 'fleeting' and therefore non-existent. But what happens if there is no relationship at all between the parties or, at least, no relationship of which they would have been aware? Simple: the judges simply 'deem' the relationship to have existed. Thus Mr Justice Morland decided that the editor of the *Daily Mirror* and his journalists were 'clothed in conscience with the duty of confidentiality' when they received details from an undisclosed source of Naomi Campbell's attendance at a meeting of Narcotics Anonymous. It did not matter whether that source was a fellow drug addict receiving therapy or a member of Campbell's entourage: both owed her a duty of confidence. The same applied to *Hello!* magazine when it published unauthorized wedding photographs of Michael Douglas and Catherine Zeta-Jones: the defendants' consciences were 'tainted', according to the trial judge.

Does there even need to be a relationship at all now? Dame Elizabeth Butler-Sloss, President of the High Court Family Division, was the first judge to decide that a duty of confidence could exist independently of any transaction or relationship between the parties. Her ruling, in *Venables v News Group Newspapers*, caused grave concern to news organizations when it was delivered in January 2001. It meant that the media as a whole could be prevented from disclosing information about specific individuals—a law of privacy for them, at least, in all but name. Justifying her decision to extend the law of confidence in this way, the judge said: 'A duty of confidence does already arise when confidential information comes to the knowledge of the media in circumstances in which the media have notice of its confidentiality. An example is the medical reports of a private individual which are recognised as being confidential.'

In May 2003, Dame Elizabeth granted a similar injunction protecting the child-killer Mary Bell and her daughter, who by then had reached the age of 18. Like the *Venables* order, it was broadly defined, applying to the 'whole world'—or at least, as Dame Elizabeth pointed out during the hearing, that part of the world which came within the jurisdiction of the courts of England and Wales. Although the case turned on the Human Rights Convention, the judge made her ruling under the law of confidence—despite the suggestion by Lord Phillips in *Campbell* that unjustified publication of information about an individual's private life 'would be better described as breach of privacy'. The case is explored more fully in Chapter 4.

In *A v B plc*, the case in which the footballer Garry Flitcroft tried to prevent a Sunday newspaper from writing about his affairs with two women, Lord Woolf laid down a number of guidelines for breach-of-confidence actions. While acknowledging that a relationship would normally be required, he said 'a duty of confidence will arise whenever the party subject to the duty is in a situation where he either knows, or ought to know, that the other person can reasonably expect his privacy to be protected.'

Other comments by Lord Woolf in the same case appeared to move the law even further. We have already noted his remark that 'in the great majority of situations, if not all situations, where the protection of privacy is justified . . . an action for breach of confidence now will, where this is appropriate, provide the necessary protection.' This seems to mean that there is no longer any need for a claimant to establish that a duty of confidence existed before the claimant's privacy was allegedly breached.

'Where an individual is a public figure he is entitled to have his privacy respected in the appropriate circumstances,' the Lord Chief Justice added. 'A public figure is entitled to a private life.'

Strictly speaking, these remarks by Lord Woolf were *obiter dicta*—incidental observations not material to the court's judgment, and therefore not binding on other judges. They were also too vague and subjective to be of much use in predicting when the courts would intervene. After all, what are the 'appropriate circumstances' in which a public figure's privacy may be respected?

The trend, though, is clear. The need for a formal relationship between two parties has become attenuated almost to the point of non-existence. Where information has the necessary quality of confidence about it, the courts are more than willing to infer an obligation of confidence from the surrounding facts, the second of Mr Justice Megarry's three conditions. That means they will hold that someone who has received confidential information is bound by a duty of confidence. Put bluntly, if the judges think something ought to remain private then they will find a way of making it so.

Going all the way

Why 'infer' a relationship that does not exist? As we saw earlier, Lord Phillips was in favour of grasping the nettle. Where the information had not been confided by one person in another, he thought that unjustified disclosure would be better described as 'breach of privacy'. That was in the Naomi Campbell case, in October 2002. In his Bentham lecture the following March, Lord Phillips pointed out three practical problems in building a law of privacy on the foundations of confidentiality, using mortar to be found in the Human Rights Act.

'The first is that the Human Rights Convention imposes duties on public authorities, not on private individuals or corporations. How can the courts use it to restrain, for instance, over-intrusive journalism?' True, the so-called 'horizontal effect' of the Human Rights Act may allow one individual to sue another, though the Master of the Rolls was careful not to say whether this would work. The horizontal effect is another of the topics we shall come to later.

The second problem that Lord Phillips identified is the one to which we have just alluded. Confidence, he said 'usually arises out of a relationship between two people. "Confidential" does not naturally describe an unauthorised photograph.'

Finally, there is the problem of information about a person's private life that is simply untrue. It may not be defamatory but, said Lord Phillips, it may still be highly offensive. On the other hand, if it is fabricated it can hardly be confidential. German law provided a remedy, he noted, but he did not see how the English law of confidence could logically embrace publication of intimate-but-untrue personal details.

An example of this emerged shortly after the death of Princess Margaret in 2002. It was reported that her son, Viscount Linley, wanted to use the law of confidence against an author who claimed his mother had been a drug addict. Clearly, he could not use the defamation laws, since nobody can sue for libel on behalf of the dead. But how could Lord Linley claim that information was given in confidence to the author's source when he was asserting that the source simply made it up? Nothing more was heard of the claim. (Incidentally, if a statement about a living person is untrue but not defamatory—because it does not damage that person's reputation—the victim may still be able to bring a claim for malicious falsehood. Claimants have to prove that the untrue statement of fact was published spitefully, dishonestly or recklessly, and that it caused financial loss.)

The reason for inferring a relationship—or simply 'deeming' it to exist—now becomes clear. Without it, the judges cannot use the existing law of confidence for the wider purpose of protecting privacy. Whether they would be wise to do so is another matter.

Misuse of information

To satisfy the third of Mr Justice Megarry's tests, there has to be some unauthorized use of the information to the detriment of the person imparting it. That, in turn, depends on the purpose for which the information was imparted in the first place. Since the law of confidence is derived from equitable principles, it comes as little surprise to find the courts emphasizing fairness and conscience. As Lord Justice Brooke explained in the initial proceedings brought by Michael Douglas and Catherine Zeta-Jones against *Hello!* magazine, 'if information is accepted on the basis that it will be kept secret, the recipient's conscience is bound by that confidence and it would be unconscionable for him to break his duty of confidence by publishing the information to others'.

That test was affirmed by Lord Justice Simon Brown in a curious case from 1999. It was brought against the Department of Health by Source

Informatics, a company that sold information about doctors' prescribing habits to drug companies so that they could target doctors who were prescribing too many pills from a rival supplier. The Ministry tried to stop this happening, fearing that targeted marketing would persuade doctors to prescribe more expensive products. Instead of simply banning it, however, the Government advised doctors and pharmacists that patients might be able to sue Source Informatics for breach of confidence if the company found out what was going on behind the scenes.

The crucial point was that the information was 'anonymized', at least as far as the patients were concerned. Pharmacists kept a record on their computers of the drugs they dispensed, together with details of the doctor and patient. When that information was passed on to Source Informatics, all details that could identify the patients were removed. The Court of Appeal decided that participation in the scheme would not amount to a breach of confidence.

'The concern of the law here is to protect the confider's personal privacy,' said Lord Justice Simon Brown. 'The patient has no proprietorial claim to the prescription form or to the information it contains . . . If, as I conclude, his only legitimate interest is in the protection of his privacy and, if that is safeguarded, I fail to see how his will could be thought thwarted or his personal integrity undermined'. The 'touchstone' was the confidant's conscience: in the court's view, 'pharmacists' consciences ought not reasonably to be troubled by co-operation with Source's proposed scheme. The patient's privacy will have been safeguarded, not invaded. The pharmacist's duty of confidence will not have been breached.'

In the public interest

The law of confidence has never been a trump card. News organizations may be allowed to publish information obtained through a breach of confidence—but only if the public interest in publication outweighs the public interest in preserving confidentiality. In Naomi Campbell's case, for example, the High Court decided that the public interest permitted the newspaper to reveal the fact of her drug addiction and therapy, though not the details. The Court of Appeal took a broader view: 'provided that publication of particular confidential information is justifiable in the public interest, the journalist must be given reasonable latitude as to the manner in which that information is conveyed to the public.'

The public-interest rule proved to be crucial when the Jockey Club, which regulates British horse racing, tried unsuccessfully to stop the BBC's *Panorama* programme from broadcasting confidential information 'revealing the existence or apparent existence of widespread corruption within racing'. Documents from a whistleblower related to 'a serious criminal said to be involved in horse-doping, race-fixing and the bribing of jockeys'. Others allegedly involved in corruption included jockeys, trainers and bookies.

Mr Justice Gray ruled in September 2002 that the public interest in disclosing information supplied by Roger Buffham, the Jockey Club's former head of security, outweighed the Club's right of confidence in it. In the judge's view, the information was 'of legitimate concern to a large section of the public who either participate in racing or who follow it or who bet on the result of races'.

True, there was no hard evidence of criminality. True, some of the information dated back years. True, the Jockey Club had only limited powers to protect racing and was doing its best. But it was a public authority, not an individual seeking to protect private information or a company trying to preserve commercial sensitivities. 'In a proper case,' said Mr Justice Gray, 'the conduct of a public authority may be more readily open to scrutiny by the media, even in cases where the scrutiny is based in part on confidential documents belonging to the authority concerned.'

This was heady stuff. The judge made it clear he was following a case decided a year earlier by Mr Justice Sullivan, in which London Regional Transport had tried to prevent Ken Livingstone, the Mayor of London, from publishing a report by accountants on plans for a 'public–private partnership' to develop the London Underground. The judge decided that it was in the public interest for an edited version of the report to be published. Later, the Court of Appeal held that Mr Justice Sullivan had been correct in trying to balance 'the desirability of the public interest of upholding confidentiality agreements and the public interest in freedom of access to information', even when the information had been disclosed by a former employee of the claimant.

To be protected by the law of confidence, information must, of course, be confidential: once the information is in the public domain, it loses its confidentiality. This exception is particularly important now that material may be published instantly on the Internet, although there may be scope for arguing that documents on an obscure website are not in the public domain if they cannot readily be found.

Only significant information will be covered: the law does not protect gossip or, in Mr Justice Megarry's phrase, 'mere tittle-tattle'. Other exceptions or defences include the claimant's consent, either express or implied, and waiver of the claimant's rights. Waiver was referred to in the Garry Flitcroft case, reported as *A v B plc*. Lord Woolf, in the twelfth of his fifteen guidelines, said: 'If you have courted public attention then you have less ground to object to the intrusion which follows.'

Consent was an issue in an entirely different case, confusingly called *A v B & C*, which was decided by Mr Justice Mackay in March 2001— although, sadly, it does not seem to have found its way into the law reports. It concerned a well-known pop singer and former lap-dancer who sought an injunction to prevent publication of pornographic pictures of her which had been taken with her permission but before she became famous. Granting an order, the judge found that she had consented only to the use of pictures for promotional purposes—and then only after she had approved the shots.

'Allo, 'Allo

The low point in the campaign for a privacy law came in 1990. Gorden Kaye, the actor who played the café owner René in the television series *'Allo, 'Allo*, was in hospital after a serious accident. He had been driving his car during a violent gale when a piece of wood that had broken off an advertising hoarding came through the windscreen and smashed into his forehead. The actor was still recovering from emergency brain surgery when two men walked into his private ward, ignoring notices which said that visiting was restricted. They turned out to be a reporter and photographer from the *Sunday Sport*, a tabloid newspaper renowned for its far-fetched stories.

Kaye apparently agreed to talk to them and seemed not to object when they asked if they could photograph the cards and flowers in his room. In fact, they took pictures of the actor himself, showing his severe head wounds. There was medical evidence that he was in no fit state to give informed consent, an opinion borne out by the fact that a quarter of an hour after the journalists had been ejected by security staff he had no recollection of the incident.

The journalists had been sent by Drew Robertson, editor of the *Sunday Sport*. Having achieved what he called 'a great old-fashioned scoop', Robertson wanted to publish these pictures and his 'interview' with Kaye, such as it was. Kaye's close friends were horrified by the prospect and obtained a temporary injunction from the High Court. After an appeal by Robertson, the injunction was overturned by the Court of Appeal. 'It is well known that in English law there is no right to privacy,' said Lord Justice Glidewell, 'and accordingly there is no right of action for breach of a person's privacy.'

Andrew Caldecott, Kaye's counsel, made no attempt to persuade the Court that he could base his claim on the law of confidence. The case had come to court with some speed and perhaps nobody had thought at the time that the argument would succeed. The judges certainly did not work it out for themselves, though it was clear they would have welcomed any clay that they could mould into a privacy law. That job seemed beyond them: in their view, such an edifice could be constructed only by Parliament.

Not that the judges were unsympathetic. 'If ever a person has a right to be left alone by strangers with no public interest to pursue, it must surely be when he lies in hospital recovering from brain surgery and in no more than partial command of his faculties,' said Lord Justice Bingham (as he then was), adding that the invasion of Kaye's privacy, however gross, did not give him a remedy in English law.

In a lecture six years later, reprinted in his book *The Business of Judging*, Lord Justice Bingham explained why he thought 'a claim for breach of confidence could not have been successfully made, at any rate without doing impermissible violence to the principles on which that cause of action is founded: the complaint in this case was not that information obtained or imparted in confidence was about to be misused, but that Kaye's privacy had been the subject of a monstrous invasion but for which the interview would never have been obtained at all'. That argument seems unconvincing: if Mr Justice Morland could infer a duty of confidence towards Naomi Campbell, surely Lord Justice Bingham could have pinned a duty towards the ailing Kaye on the 'No Visitors' signs fixed to his door.

It was the third judge in *Kaye v Robertson*, Lord Justice Leggatt, who pointed out that the American courts had managed to develop a law of privacy over the past hundred years, using raw materials that were readily available in England. He even cited a curiously similar case decided by the Supreme Court of Missouri in 1942 about a hospital patient whose privacy was invaded by a reporter and photographer. Dorothy Barber, of Kansas City, suffered from a rare eating disorder that caused her to lose weight while eating 'enough to feed an entire family'. She was awarded damages against *Time* magazine over an article headlined 'Starving Glutton', illustrated with a head-and-shoulders picture of her in a long-sleeved hospital gown and captioned 'Insatiable-Eater Barber' and 'She eats for ten'. As the US court said, 'it was shown that [Barber] not only did not consent to the publication of any article or picture in connection with her illness, but protested against any publicity to the reporters who interviewed her, and that her picture was taken by one while the other was trying to persuade her to consent to such publicity. Certainly if there is any right of privacy at all, it should include the right to obtain medical treatment at home or in a hospital for an individual personal condition (at least if it is not contagious or dangerous to others) without personal publicity . . . While [her] ailment may have been a matter of some public interest because unusual, certainly the identity of the person who suffered this ailment was not.'

Lord Justice Leggatt pointed out that celebrities in the United States had an additional right, the so-called right of publicity, as illustrated by a curious case from 1983.

Here's Johnny!

The claim had been brought by Johnny Carson, whose television appearances on the *Tonight* show had been introduced for more than twenty years with the irritating catchphrase 'Here's Johnny!'—the first word being prolonged by the announcer into a distinctive crescendo.

Carson sued a small Michigan company that hired out portable lavatories to shows and fairs: 'portaloos' as we would call them here. In North American slang, toilets are 'johns'; hence the company's name, Here's Johnny Portable Toilets. Just in case the penny hadn't dropped, and with a sly dig at Carson's own soubriquet, the company advertised its product as 'The World's Foremost Commodian'.

Carson himself well understood the commercial value of his resonant catchphrase: he had licensed it for use in advertising a chain of restaurants, a range of menswear, and even soap. Toiletries were one thing though, toilets quite another: even for him, the door had to be bolted somewhere.

By a majority, the US Court of Appeals held that the portable toilet company had violated Carson's 'right of publicity', despite the fact that neither his name nor his likeness had been used. This right had been developed, the court explained, to protect the commercial interest of celebrities in their identities. 'The theory of the right,' the judges said, 'is that a celebrity's identity can be valuable in the promotion of products, and the celebrity has an interest that may be protected from the unauthorized commercial exploitation of that identity.' As the Court had said in a previous case, 'the famous have an exclusive legal right during life to control and profit from the commercial use of their name and personality.'

That right has been recognized in the English courts, but in defamation rather than as a right of publicity. Cyril Tolley, a well-known amateur golfer, opened his *Daily Mail* in 1928 to find his image had been used without his permission in an advertisement for Fry's chocolate. A caricature had been drawn of him in golfing costume with the product sticking out of his pocket and captioned with the following dreadful limerick:

> The caddie to Tolley said, Oh, Sir,
> Good shot, Sir! That ball, see it go, Sir,
> My word how it flies,
> Like a cartet of Frys,
> They're handy, they're good, and priced low, Sir.

Tolley sued the manufacturer for libel, claiming that the advertisement implied that that he had 'prostituted his reputation as an amateur golf player for advertising purposes'. The law lords agreed, though they thought the jury's award of £1,000, a large sum in those days, was excessive.

However, libel is a poor substitute for a privacy law. As we shall see in Chapter 6, an author or publisher who can prove the truth of what has been written will have a complete defence: publication of true but private facts will not lead to a claim for defamation. Secondly, information or photographs may breach an individual's privacy but not damage that person's reputation; again, a libel claim would not be possible.

In 1816 Lord Byron successfully prevented publication of a bad poem that had been falsely attributed to him by a publisher named Johnston. Byron being abroad at the time, his agents gave evidence in the High Court 'both as to their belief and also as to circumstances rendering it highly probable that the work was not his Lordship's'. Johnston was given the chance to prove that it was; when he declined to swear that he believed the poem genuine, the Lord Chancellor, Lord Eldon, issued an injunction to restrain Johnston from publishing the poem as Byron's. Such cases are referred to as 'false light' claims. Again, though, they are little use in protecting privacy.

What can you do if you find that a legitimately taken photograph of you has been used without your permission? In 1992 the *News of the World* published pictures that appeared to show Ian Smith and Anne Charleston, the actors who played Harold and Madge Bishop in the Australian television series *Neighbours.* Under the headline 'STREWTH! WHAT'S HAROLD UP TO WITH OUR MADGE?', the couple were depicted in what appeared to be an act of intercourse or sodomy (as it was described in court). However, the newspaper article made it clear that the actors were unwitting stars of a 'sordid computer game': their faces had been superimposed on the near-naked bodies of porn stars. Although someone who merely glanced through the newspaper might have got the wrong idea, the 'ordinary reader' would have understood that the actors had become involved in something that was beyond their control and would have thought none the worse of them for that. On that basis, the law lords held in *Charleston v News Group Newspapers Ltd* that the article was not capable of being defamatory.

On Tony Blair's fiftieth birthday, in May 2003, a photograph of him playing football was used by the manufacturers of Sanatogen to advertise their vitamin supplement for the over-fifties; the caption read, punningly, 'Any chance of a place in the cabinet?' Presumably on legal advice, there was a disclaimer, in impossibly small print: 'The person featured does not in any way endorse the product shown.' At his birthday lunch, the Prime Minister remarked: 'I wasn't looking forward to reaching fifty and this gloom was before I opened today's newspapers and found I was used—without my permission—to advertise Sanatogen.' However, he added, 'it's better than the advertisements Pelé is fronting.' The veteran footballer was promoting Viagra, the anti-impotence drug.

In May 2003, the budget airline easyJet ran an advertisement showing David Beckham with the caption, 'Hair today. Gone tomorrow'—a reference to both his latest hairstyle and to rumours that the footballer was planning to move from Manchester United to Real Madrid. In response, the airline received a letter from his lawyers suggesting that it might care to donate £10,000 to a children's charity. 'We take a very serious view of this type of activity,' said a spokesman for Beckham's management company. 'We have a standard process of taking legal action when companies use images of our clients without our express permission.' Seeing the value of a good publicity stunt, the airline immediately repeated the advertisement and promised to double its £10,000 donation to the NSPCC if Beckham agreed to match it.

As Beckham's lawyers were well aware, there is no such thing as a right to publicity in English law. However, the problem easyJet may have risked flying into was 'passing off', a claim developed during the nineteenth century to prevent one trader passing his goods off as those of another. It was explained by Mr Justice Laddie, rather sweetly, as 'a judge-made law which tries to ensure, in its own limited way, a degree of honesty and fairness in the way trade is conducted'. He was giving judgment in March 2002 on a claim brought by Eddie Irvine, the racing driver, against talkSPORT, a radio station. In 1999, when it was known as Talk Radio, the station distributed a promotional brochure to almost 1,000 potential advertisers. It carried a photograph of Irvine, dressed in his racing gear, in which he appeared to be listening to a radio marked with the station's logo. In fact, he had been talking on a mobile telephone when the picture was taken and the image had been skilfully manipulated.

As Mr Justice Laddie explained, 'the purpose of a passing off action is to vindicate the claimant's exclusive right to goodwill and to protect it against damage . . . If someone acquires a valuable reputation or goodwill, the law of passing off will protect it from unlicensed use by other parties.' Noting that sports stars earn a great deal of money by 'endorsing', or lending their name to, various products and services, the judge decided that the law of passing off should now apply to cases of 'false endorsement'. To succeed, however, a claimant must prove, first, that he or she had a significant reputation or goodwill at the time of the acts complained of; and secondly 'that the actions of the defendant gave rise to a false message which would be understood by a not insignificant section of his market that his goods have been endorsed, recommended or are approved of by the claimant'.

Both those requirements were met in *Irvine v Talksport Ltd* and the racing driver was awarded £2,000 damages, a sum the judge considered to be 'a reasonable endorsement fee'. However, £5,000 had previously been 'paid into court' by talkSPORT as an offer to settle. Since Irvine had refused that offer, he was left facing a costs bill estimated at £300,000. He complained to the Court of Appeal that the damages were too low, pointing out that he had reached endorsement deals with Oakley sunglasses worth £35,000; Tommy Hilfiger clothing worth £125,000; Bieffe helmets worth £85,000; and Valleverde footwear worth £78,000. In addition, he would charge more for endorsing an unfashionable product, in which category he included Talk Radio. In the classic words of his counsel, he would not have got out of bed for less than £25,000. Since that was the sum the radio station would have had to pay 'in order to enable it to do lawfully that which it did unlawfully', the Court of Appeal increased Irvine's damages to that sum. However, it upheld Mr Justice Laddie's conclusions on the facts and law.

Could Beckham have won a passing-off action against easyJet over the use of his picture? The footballer would have had to have proved that the advertisement gave rise to a false message, with a significant number of readers understanding it to mean he had endorsed its flights. Such a claim, though arguable, would be unlikely to succeed. That was because the airline used a recent news photograph of Beckham—a fact that readers would recognize because his latest hairstyle had received much publicity. If the player had agreed to endorse easyJet, he would have been specially photographed with the airline's name visible. Such an impression had been given by talkSPORT—and that was what tipped the balance in favour of Eddie Irvine. By chance, Beckham's name had come up in *Irvine v Talksport Ltd*: during oral evidence, a witness for the radio station told the court that 'if David Beckham said he listened to Talk Radio that wouldn't be a bad thing'.

Passing off, then, is unlikely to be much use as a remedy for invasion of privacy. However, Beckham relied on more traditional legal arguments in the summer of 2001. He and his wife Victoria were granted an urgent injunction to stop the *Daily Mirror* publishing photographs showing the inside of their new home, on condition that they did not allow anyone else to take pictures there for publication. It turned out that the couple were in talks with a magazine that wanted to publish approved pictures of their property. However, they had not decided whether or not to go ahead, security being a major concern for the couple and their family.

The newspaper asked for the undertaking against anyone else publishing pictures of 'Beckingham Palace' to remain as a condition of any final undertaking. Mr Justice Eady refused. The judge said it would place a wholly unrealistic restriction on the couple's freedom of action and their choice in relation to any compromise of their privacy. There was no reason why the Beckhams' freedom of contract should be restricted in order to give the *Daily Mirror* a commercial advantage. As and when photographs of the home came into the public domain, the newspaper would be free to publish its own pictures.

The Royals again

Many years after Prince Albert's case, the law of confidence was stretched almost to the limit by another member of the Royal Family, also over some private pictures. In November 1993, the *Sunday Mirror* published a striking series of photographs, in which the Princess of Wales, at that time separated from her husband but not yet divorced, was seen exercising at a health club. The pictures were taken from above, using a camera hidden in the ceiling, and showed the Princess using a leg-press machine.

What could she do about it? In *Kaye v Robertson*, the Court of Appeal had recently confirmed that there was no right to privacy in English law. However, the Princess's lawyers thought she might have an action for breach of confidence against the newspaper and the gym's manager, Bryce Taylor. It was on that basis that they obtained a temporary injunction from Mr Justice Rougier, freezing Taylor's assets.

He must have known, the argument went, that he was under a duty not to use pictures obtained in confidential circumstances. However, it is by no means clear that the Princess would have won the case if it had been argued in full; she had not, after all, entrusted confidential information to the manager. Geoffrey Robertson, QC, who had been briefed to defend Taylor, maintains that the gym was a public place, like a restaurant. The leg-press machine 'was in front of a vast glass wall looking onto a public thoroughfare: it was like working out in a shop window'.

In his book *The Justice Game*, Robertson notes that the Princess had accepted free membership from Taylor: in his view, 'she weakened her claim that he owed her confidentiality, because she had not paid for any'. On the other hand, Taylor had assured her that her visits would be treated confidentially, and it was on the strength of this promise that her lawyers claimed there was a 'fiduciary relationship' between them, which Taylor had breached by taking surreptitious pictures.

Sadly for us, a settlement was reached before the courts could decide whether they would be willing to row back from *Kaye v Robertson* and build a law of privacy on the back of another royal case. By all accounts, the gym-owner was paid handsomely for his silence. Robertson modestly suggests that the deal was done to avoid any embarrassment that might be caused to the Princess by his planned cross-examination of her—devastating as it no doubt would have been.

Ironically, the law of confidence which may not have been powerful enough to help the Princess was soon to trip up her brother, Earl Spencer, by being too effective. In April 1995, the *News of the World* published an article headlined 'Di's Sister-in-Law in Booze and Bulimia Clinic'. This said that the Earl's then wife, Victoria, had been admitted to a private clinic to be treated for alcoholism and an eating disorder. The story was illustrated with a long-lens photograph of the Countess, captioned 'SO THIN: Victoria Walks in the Clinic Grounds This Week'. Similar pieces were published the same day in both the *People* and the *Sunday Mirror*; the *Daily Mirror* picked up the story the next day.

The Earl complained immediately to the Press Complaints Commission (PCC), an independent body funded by the newspaper industry to deal with complaints from the public about the editorial conduct of newspapers and magazines. As we shall see in Chapter 5, protection of personal privacy is at the heart of the Commission's system of self-regulation and, in due course, it found that the *News of the World* and the *People* had breached its Code of Practice. Both papers apologized.

It turned out that the stories had come from two former friends of the Spencers. Their names were never publicly disclosed, but the Spencers knew who they were and asked them to promise they would not make any further disclosures. When they refused, the Spencers began legal action, seeking an injunction against them for breach of confidence. It was granted, by consent, and the case was settled.

That was not good enough for the Earl and Countess, who lodged an application with the European Court of Human Rights. They complained that there had been a breach of their right to respect for their private and family life under Article 8 of the Human Rights Convention, maintaining that English law had been powerless to prevent publication of the offending articles and photographs. They also complained that they had no right to compensation for their distress.

The Human Rights Commission, which at that time used to filter applications to the Court, held a private hearing in January 1998. It immediately rejected the Spencers' claim as inadmissible because, as the British Government had argued, the couple had not made use of their remedy in the English courts. That remedy was an action for breach of confidence. Giving its opinion, the Commission considered 'that the parties' submissions indicate that the remedy of breach of confidence (against the newspapers and their sources) was available to the applicants and that the applicants have not demonstrated that it was insufficient or ineffective in the circumstances of their cases'.

What this tells us is that, by 1998, breach of confidence was considered by both the British Government and the Human Rights Commission as an effective way of dealing with invasions of privacy by newspapers. Commission members clearly thought that the courts would find a duty of confidence, even though there was no relationship between the parties other than the taking of an intrusive photograph. The Commission's views are not law, of course, but they are persuasive nevertheless. Lord Phillips, in his Bentham lecture, saw it as an indication that 'the Government was leaving it to the judges to use the tool of the Human Rights Act to build a law of privacy on the foundations of the law of confidentiality'.

Lessons from the USA

Although the right of publicity had been violated in the case of *Carson v Here's Johnny Portable Toilets Inc*, there was no breach of privacy on the facts of that case. But that right is certainly recognized by civil courts in the United States—and by state legislatures. In 1999, for example, California enacted a statutory tort to deal with obsessive 'up-skirt' voyeurs: readers who want to look more closely at this phenomenon should turn immediately to Chapter 8. But the Californian legislation merely supplements a common-law or judge-made tort that can be traced back to one of the most influential articles ever to have been published by a legal journal. The young authors, Samuel Warren and his law partner Louis Brandeis, called on the courts to protect what had already been referred to as 'the right to be left alone'. Writing in 1890, they argued that such a right could already be found in the English common law: indeed their main authority for the existence of a law of privacy was none other than *Prince Albert v Strange*, the case of Queen Victoria's etchings. In a demand for greater protection against the 'evil of the invasion of privacy by the newspapers', Warren and Brandeis wrote:

The press is overstepping in every direction the obvious bounds of propriety and decency. Gossip is no longer the resource of the idle and of the vicious, but has become a trade, which is pursued with industry as well as effrontery. To satisfy a prurient taste the details of sexual relations are spread broadcast in the columns of the daily papers. To occupy the indolent, column upon column is filled with idle gossip, which can only be procured by intrusion upon the domestic circle. The intensity and complexity of life, attendant upon advancing civilization, have rendered necessary some retreat from the world, and man, under the refining influence of culture, has become more sensitive to publicity, so that solitude and privacy have become more essential to the individual; but modern enterprise and invention have, through invasions upon his privacy, subjected him to mental pain and distress, far greater than could be inflicted by mere bodily injury.

This much-cited article was prompted by intrusion by the Boston press into the fashionable wedding of Warren's sister. Although the style might strike us as a little arch, the substance could have been written yesterday. 'Since the latest advances in photographic art have rendered it possible to take pictures surreptitiously, the doctrines of contract and of trust are inadequate to support the required protection, and the law of tort must be resorted to,' they said, anticipating in the nineteenth century the arguments to be put by Michael Douglas and Catherine

Zeta-Jones in the twenty-first. 'Instantaneous photographs and newspaper enterprise have invaded the sacred precincts of private and domestic life,' they wrote, 'and numerous mechanical devices threaten to make good the prediction that "what is whispered in the closet shall be proclaimed from the house-tops".'

In the years that followed, some American courts accepted these arguments while others took a more cautious approach to change. By 1960, however, the academic writer William Prosser was able to say that the vast majority of US state courts recognized a right of privacy in one form or another. Drawing on his study of over 300 cases, Dean Prosser identified four privacy torts. They can be summarized as:

- intrusion on seclusion, solitude or private affairs;
- publication of embarrassing private (but true) facts;
- publicity that portrays someone in a false light; and
- appropriation of a person's name or likeness (the right of publicity).

Those four 'civil wrongs' appear slightly differently in the US *Restatement of the Law of Torts*, a codification dating from 1977. That says the right to privacy in the USA is invaded by:

- the unreasonable intrusion on the seclusion of another;
- the appropriation of the other's name or likeness;
- unreasonable publicity given to the other's private life;
- publicity that unreasonably places the other in a false light before the public.

The tort of intrusion is committed by 'one who intentionally intrudes, physically or otherwise, upon the solitude or seclusion of another or his private affairs or concerns . . . if the intrusion would be highly offensive to a reasonable person'. US courts have held that this does not apply in public places.

The American experience was cited by Lord Justice Bingham in the public lecture, referred to above, that he gave shortly before becoming Lord Chief Justice in 1996. Just six years earlier, as one of the judges in *Kaye v Robertson*, he had said that the courts were unable to protect Gorden Kaye's privacy against the tabloids. Now, however, he was predicting that the judges would indeed be able to develop a law to do just that. It should be narrowly drawn, he proposed in his lecture, 'to give full effect to the right of free speech and the public's right to know. It should strike only at significant infringements, such as would cause substantial distress to an ordinary phlegmatic person.'

Lord Justice Bingham said: 'My preference would be for legislation, which would mean that the rules which the courts applied would carry the imprimatur of democratic approval. But if, for whatever reason, legislation is not forthcoming, I think it almost inevitable that cases will arise in the courts in which the need to give relief is obvious and pressing; and when such cases do arise, I do not think the courts will be found wanting.'

This appeared to be a promise—or a threat, depending on how you look at it—of judicial law-making, the centuries-old process by which the judges 'develop' the common law to meet what they see as the needs of society. Only a purist or a formalist would say that this process should always be left to Parliament: the courts generally step in only where MPs fear to tread, and Parliament can always change the law if it thinks the judges have overreached themselves. For their part, the judges say that if they wait for Parliament they will wait for ever: if they sit on their hands in the meantime, individuals will suffer injustice.

How, though, would Lord Justice Bingham construct a privacy law? 'If the judges are, on a case-by-case basis, to extend the protection available under the existing law,' he said, 'it seems clear that this will be done not by introducing a law of privacy so called but by enlarging the boundaries of existing causes of action' (in other words, by extending the law of confidence). He pointed out that some judges had already started down that road. The then Mr Justice Laws had said a year earlier that publishing an unauthorized telephoto picture of someone 'engaged in some private act' would be just as much a breach of confidence as publishing a lost or stolen diary in which the act was described.

'In such a case,' Mr Justice Laws had added in what was to become a much-cited passage, 'the law would protect what might reasonably be called a right of privacy, although the name accorded to the cause of action would be breach of confidence.' He was giving judgment in a case called *Hellewell v Chief Constable of Derbyshire*, although those remarks are not treated as binding, both because they were an aside rather than part of his reasoning and because rulings by a trial judge do not bind another judge sitting at the same level.

As Lord Justice Bingham predicted, some judges have, indeed, tried to develop a law of privacy under the guise of confidence. Just one day after his speech, a strikingly similar lecture was delivered by Lord Hoffmann, one of the law lords. He was later to become known to the wider public for not declaring the close links he had with one of the parties that addressed the House of Lords in the first *Pinochet* appeal in 1998, on which he had sat; his fellow law lords subsequently held that he had been 'automatically disqualified' from sitting on the appeal and decided that one of the most high-profile cases ever to come before the country's highest court should be heard again. Lord Hoffmann never apologized, never explained, and continued to decide cases in the House of Lords.

But all this was in the future. In 1996, Lord Hoffmann noted that 'the right of privacy does not command majority support'. Even so, that did not mean it should not be protected. 'On the contrary,' he said, 'the individual's right to dignity and respect is essential to a civilised community.' He continued: 'If the English judges were to decide that the lack of a right to privacy represented a gap in the law, there are ample materials to hand to enable such a right to be constructed . . . I do not think that one can expect such a right to be created by a majority decision in parliament. But that makes it all the more important that it should be recognised at common law.'

This 'judicial threat to legislate' was understandably criticized by Lord Irvine, who at that stage was still Labour's last Lord Chancellor-in-waiting. 'The general understanding of English law is that it does not recognise a generalised right to privacy,' he told the House of Lords in June 1996. 'Should the judges make one? Only, I would say, if there were a clear community consensus that way. If there is no such consensus—and I am sure there is none—then I say that if the judges invented a law of privacy they would seem to be taking sides.'

All very fine, of course, though once Labour was in power there was no attempt to prevent the judges from taking sides. Even though newspapers were constantly told by politicians that they were 'drinking in the last-chance saloon', there had been no attempt by the Conservative Government to introduce the new eavesdropping offence and infringement-of-privacy tort that had been recommended in a report to the Home Secretary by Sir David Calcutt in 1990. Instead, the Government announced in 1995 that the press would be left to regulate itself.

Two years later, when Labour came to power, Lord Irvine introduced a Human Rights Bill, providing the framework on which the judges could construct a free-standing law of privacy. During a Lords debate on the Bill, in November 1997, the Lord Chancellor said the judges were 'pen-poised, regardless of incorporation of the convention, to develop a right to privacy to be protected by the common law'. This was not him saying so, he explained, but them; and in his view they were free to do so. All he asked was that they waited until the Act was in force. Then, when developing a new law, they would have to give the free-speech provisions in the Human Rights Convention their 'due high value'.

The judges bided their time. It was not until the summer of 2003 that Lords Bingham and Hoffmann were presented with a chassis on which they and three other law lords could construct the superstructure of a privacy law in line with the blueprints they had sketched seven years earlier. But the case of *Wainwright v Home Secretary*—about a woman who was strip-searched by prison staff when she went to visit her son— looked more than a little rusty, dating back to the days before the Human Rights Act came into force. The law lords' ruling, delivered in October 2003, will be considered in Chapter 2.

The Human Rights Act

When the Human Rights Act 1998 came into effect in October 2000, it was seen as the spark that would ignite a new privacy law, consuming freedom of expression in its flames. Three years later, the tinder was barely warm. Judges were certainly not ignoring the human-rights legislation. But they had been approaching it cautiously, sometimes maintaining that whatever decision they took is one they would have reached if they had simply relied on the good old English common law.

The Human Rights Act, as such, was not the basis on which Naomi Campbell's claim and Garry Flitcroft's injunction were originally granted—although, as we shall see, it was fundamental to the decision in the James Bulger case. Whether so many high-profile public figures would have tried bringing 'privacy' actions if the Human Rights Act had not recently been introduced—and whether the courts would have reinvigorated the law of confidence—we cannot tell. Certainly, Lord Woolf said in *A v B plc* that there had been an increase in the number of such applications since the Act came into effect. And the thinking behind the Human Rights Convention, with its respect for freedom of expression, has certainly influenced the approach taken by the judges.

The stars come out

Celebrities did not find everything going their way in the early months of the Human Rights Act. Heather Mills, not yet married to Sir Paul McCartney, was in the process of buying a house in Hove when she discovered that reporters from the *Sun* had been tipped off about her plans. Fearing that she and the former Beatle might be murdered like John Lennon, or attacked like George Harrison, she had bought the property under an alias and tried to keep its address secret. In May 2001, she sought and obtained a temporary injunction against News Group Newspapers, publishers of the *Sun*, to prevent identification of her home. It was lifted by Mr Justice Lawrence Collins shortly afterwards. The judge said there was no evidence that the newspaper had discovered her address from someone who had learnt of it through a confidential relationship or transaction. But that did not matter, in his view: following *Venables v News Group Newspapers*, 'it is no longer a necessary element of the cause of action that the information arises from a confidential relationship'.

So the court was left with the classic balance of the Human Rights Convention: Mills had the right to respect for her private life and her home under Article 8 while the newspaper had a right to impart information under Article 10. In addition, section 12 of the Human Rights Act required the court to pay 'particular regard' to freedom of expression.

The judge took account of the fact that some people would find out Mills's address, simply because she lived in a 'busy and populous town'. The *Sun* had promised it would not be the first paper to identify her home ('last with the news', perhaps?). In the end, Mr Justice Lawrence Collins came down against an injunction, while making it clear that he was 'not permitting, still less encouraging, publication by any newspaper'. This was a wise ruling. Most public figures know that newspapers can usually track down their home addresses with a little persistence. On the whole, newspapers do not devalue this information by publishing it.

Not making news

One early case that might have launched a new privacy law had unfortunately been framed in the wrong way. Anna Ford, the BBC news presenter, complained to the PCC after she and her companion, the former US astronaut David Scott, were photographed on a beach in Majorca applying suncream to each other. The pictures appeared in the *Daily Mail* and *OK!* magazine in the autumn of 2000.

The Commission's Code of Practice on privacy says that 'the use of long-lens photography to take pictures of people in private places without their consent is unacceptable'. However, Ford's complaint was rejected: the Commission said she could not have had 'a reasonable expectation of privacy' on a public beach at the height of the holiday season. So the presenter went to the High Court. But instead of trying her luck with a claim for breach of privacy, she chose instead to challenge the PCC's ruling.

She failed. Refusing her permission to seek judicial review, Mr Justice Silber said the courts should defer to the Commission's decisions, interfering only when it would be clearly desirable to do so. He said: 'The commission is a body whose expertise makes it much better equipped than the courts to resolve the difficult exercise of balancing the conflicting rights of Miss Ford and Mr Scott to privacy and of the newspapers to publish.' In addition, the complaint was time-barred: it had not been brought within the three-month limit specified by the court rules.

Asked afterwards if it had been a mistake to challenge the Commission rather than to sue the two publications, Ford said she believed in using the bodies that were there. 'The fact that we have this weak pussycat of a Commission unfortunately in my case means that I have not got an adjudication which satisfies me, but I think it's proper to go to the proper bodies. I do not wish there to be privacy laws because I believe very strongly in freedom of expression.' But reflecting on the case during an after-dinner speech in November 2003, Ford insisted: 'I have the right to swim in the sea on a quiet beach on holiday without long-lens photographs being taken secretly, and without Lord Wakeham telling me that if I want privacy I should stay off the beach.'

Ford's case was decided in July 2001. A month earlier, the *Daily Star* had published topless pictures of Amanda Holden, an actress, taken while she was at a private holiday villa with her then husband Les Dennis, an entertainer. Instead of complaining to the PCC, the couple went immediately to court. They sought and obtained an injunction and followed it up by claiming damages for what their lawyers called 'breach of confidence and/or privacy'.

Disappointingly—for us if not for them—the case was settled: the courts had no chance to rule on whether the newspaper's actions would indeed amount to a breach of privacy. But though not a precedent, a settled case is something of a weathervane, an indicator of which way the wind is blowing. The *Daily Star* would not have agreed to pay the couple £40,000 plus costs of more than £75,000 if it had not thought they had a good chance of proving their claim and winning even more.

Peter Crawford, the couple's solicitor, said in December 2001 that this had been one of the first cases to come before the courts where damages had been sought under the Human Rights Act for a breach of an individual's right to respect for private and family life. He continued: 'It will serve as a warning to editors to take care not to buy or publish pictures of people in places where they have a reasonable expectation of privacy unless they have either given consent or the intrusion can be justified on limited public interest grounds.'

Not to be outdone, the *People* published pictures in October 2001 of Sara Cox, a Radio 1 disc jockey, and her husband, Jon Carter. Both were naked, although the pictures were discreetly masked. They were photographed on their honeymoon, swimming and sunbathing at a secluded villa on a private island in the Seychelles. The pictures were taken with a long-lens camera by a photographer who had booked himself into an adjoining villa as a guest.

As we have seen, the PCC's Code of Practice says taking pictures in private places is 'unacceptable'. The paper apparently claimed that the pictures were taken from a public place, though Cox said that the island was accessible only to people staying in the villas. In any event, private places are defined in the Code as 'public or private property where there is a reasonable expectation of privacy'. The couple complained to the Commission. It negotiated a 63-word apology that appeared with unusual prominence in the following week's edition of the *People*.

However, this was not good enough for Cox and her husband, also a disc jockey: they decided to sue the *People* and Jason Fraser, the agent who negotiated the picture deal with the newspaper. He was reported as maintaining that celebrities who had colluded with photographers in the past, by tipping them off in order to further their fledgling careers, thereby abdicated their rights to privacy for the future. The litigation was something of a disappointment to the PCC, which had hoped that it might have resolved the matter, but there was nothing to stop Cox taking legal action: the Commission does not ask complainants to waive their legal rights, though its involvement ceases once legal proceedings are under way.

The action went quiet for nearly two years. However, in June 2003 a settlement was announced. Cox was to receive £30,000 and Carter £20,000—slightly more than Holden and Dennis, but then slightly more of them was photographed. Their costs were also paid and all copies of the pictures were to be destroyed. The couple's solicitor, Keith Schilling, was quoted as saying: 'People will now realize that they have a greater chance of seeking damages if their privacy is invaded. Papers should also be aware that they can no longer rely on the defence that the photograph was taken in a public place.'

The settlement was described by one prominent media lawyer as a 'watershed'. But of course it was nothing of the kind: legally speaking, it was no more than another straw in the wind. The *People* presumably thought it might end up having to pay damages of this order if the case had gone ahead but Cox and Carter would have been advised that, as the law then stood, their chances of success were by no means assured. It was extraordinary to see broadsheet newspapers falling over themselves to predict that the settlement would lead to a 'succession of lawsuits' as a result of the settlement. The compromise was described as a 'landmark human-rights victory', as if it had been a court ruling— even though it was no more than the second such high-profile settlement in as many years. All that was unusual about the claim was that Cox had sued in spite of receiving a PCC-brokered apology.

Keith Schilling, commenting after the settlement, said that his clients would have relied heavily on the privacy provisions in Article 8 of the Human Rights Convention (to be discussed in Chapter 4). 'It hasn't set a legal precedent because the Court did not make the decision,' he confirmed. 'However, it provides an indication as to how much newspapers are willing to pay—or will have to pay—in relation to privacy claims and it provides a clear indication that certain types of photos are not acceptable.'

Despite the considerable financial advantages of litigation to Cox and Carter, the chairman of the PCC insisted after the settlement that self-regulation remained the best way for people to seek redress from news-papers. Sir Christopher Meyer said that legal battles against newspapers were 'expensive, slow and uncertain' and thousands of people continued to take their complaints to the Commission rather than to court.

A brief cultural note to end this first chapter: summing up Cox's career after she lost her job as host of the prestigious breakfast show on Radio 1 in October 2003, my esteemed *Telegraph* colleague Matt Born said that 'Cox, together with her friend Zoë Ball, and the television presenter Denise Van Outen, were the high priestesses of the "ladettes"—the female counterparts to the "lad" phenomenon epito-mised by magazines such as *Loaded* and the bad-boy antics of the band Oasis.' So now we know.

CHAPTER 2

Hello! OK?

We should always be grateful when rich people volunteer to spend lots of their money on litigation. Without Michael Douglas and Catherine Zeta-Jones, some of our most imaginative judges would not have had the chance to test the waters of a new privacy law. In the event, there were jellyfish lurking—if not sharks—and other judges proved reluctant to follow their example. But perhaps the beach was not too promising: the first privacy claim to be launched after the Human Rights Act came into force seemed to be more about the right of publicity than the right to be left alone.

Cameras not admitted

Before the two Hollywood stars were married in November 2000 at the Plaza Hotel, New York, they sold exclusive rights to print carefully vetted pictures of their wedding to the celebrity magazine *OK!* In exchange, the couple were to receive £1m. They had turned down an even higher offer from its arch-rival *Hello!* Guests and staff at the lavish ceremony and reception were told not to bring photographic equipment of any kind. Elaborate security measures were in force and a few guests had their cameras confiscated. However, someone still managed to snatch pictures of the wedding and sell them to *Hello!*

The new Mrs Douglas soon heard what had happened and passed the bad news on to *OK!*, which managed to get a temporary injunction to prevent the publishers of *Hello!* from printing the unauthorized pictures. *Hello!* went immediately to the Court of Appeal and eventually persuaded the judges to lift the injunction, allowing the unauthorized pictures to be published in that week's edition. The Court did so not because it thought that *Hello!* had a good defence: far from it. It was simply that if *OK!* and the Douglases were to win when the case was argued out in full, an adequate remedy for the loss of the magazine's exclusive rights would be the damages *Hello!* would have to pay (which one of the judges said were 'likely to be enormous'). The 'balance of convenience' test favoured *Hello!* because it would have been very difficult for the magazine to work out how much money it would have lost if the edition were killed, while it should have been much easier for *Hello!* to calculate the extra profits it made once publication went ahead.

The Douglases and *OK!* had based their claim for a temporary injunction on two main grounds: breach of confidence and infringement of privacy. Giving his ruling in December 2000, Lord Justice Brooke said that, following the case of *Prince Albert v Strange*, it was accepted that the courts could prevent publication of photographs taken in breach of an obligation of confidence. In other words, he said, if people on a private occasion make it clear—explicitly or implicitly — that no pictures are to be taken of them, then everyone present is bound by the law of confidence to comply.

The judge said that could have applied to the unknown person who took and sold unauthorized pictures to *Hello!* When the case was argued out in full at a later date, *OK!* might well be able to establish that there had been a breach of confidence by a guest or staff member. But what if the photographer was an intruder, someone with no relationship of trust or confidence? In that case, the magazine might have to fall back on the law of privacy. Was there such a thing? What about Gorden Kaye's failed case, discussed in Chapter 1?

Lord Justice Brooke remained firmly on the fence. He noted that successive governments had taken the line of least resistance and left it to the judges to decide how the law of privacy and the law of confidence should be developed. In his view, the Court of Appeal did not have to decide, on this occasion, whether to extend the existing frontiers of the law of confidence. He was satisfied, on the present untested evidence, that the Douglases were likely to establish that publication should not be allowed on confidentiality grounds—rightly as it turned out. In his view, therefore, the judges had no need to reach a view on whether to recognize the existence of new relationships giving rise to enforceable legal rights—as, for example, the House of Lords had done in 1932 when its decision in the landmark case of *Donoghue v Stevenson* effectively created the modern law of negligence.

Lord Justice Sedley, who gave the second judgment, had no such inhibitions. As far as he was concerned, Douglas and Zeta-Jones had 'a legal right to respect for their privacy, which has been infringed'. Although the courts had done their best to protect people's privacy in the past, he explained, they had not felt able to say that they were laying down a specific principle of law.

'Nevertheless,' the judge concluded, 'we have reached a point at which it can be said with confidence that the law recognises and will appropriately protect a right of personal privacy.' The legal landscape had altered since the Gorden Kaye case a decade earlier. In any event, he hinted, that case might have been decided differently if the case had been argued on the basis that 'the tort of breach of confidence contains all that is necessary for the fair protection of personal privacy'. He concluded that the two newlyweds had 'a powerfully arguable case to advance at trial that [they] have a right of privacy which English law will today recognise and, where appropriate, protect'.

Lord Justice Sedley modestly claimed that he was simply giving a new label to something that the courts had been saying over the years. The law no longer needed to 'construct an artificial relationship of confidentiality between intruder and victim: it can recognise privacy itself as a legal principle drawn from the fundamental value of personal autonomy.' If that was proved to be wrong, and judge-made law was not strong enough to protect people's privacy, Lord Justice Sedley considered that the same result could be reached by relying on the Human Rights Act.

He went on to say there was nothing in the decisions of the European Court of Human Rights to prevent the establishment of a right to privacy in national legal systems: 'the courts of France and Germany, to take two other signatories of the convention, have both in recent years developed long-gestated laws for the qualified protection of privacy against both state and non-state invasion'.

How, though, would Lord Justice Sedley strike the balance between Article 8 and Article 10, between respect for private life and freedom of expression? It all depended on the facts of the case, he suggested. The court's aim should be 'proportionality': doing no more than was needed. The means used to impair the right to freedom of expression must be no more than is necessary to accomplish the legitimate objective of respect for private life.

Lord Justice Keene, the third judge, also remained firmly on the fence. He said that 'whether the resulting liability is described as being for breach of confidence or for breach of a right to privacy may be little more than deciding what label is attached to the cause of action, but there would seem to be merit in recognising that the original concept of breach of confidence has in this particular category of cases now developed into something different from the commercial and employ-ment relationships with which confidentiality is mainly concerned'.

The initial excitement which greeted the Court of Appeal's ruling must be tempered with the reality of what the case actually decided. A majority of the three judges did not find that the Human Rights Act had created a stand-alone right of privacy or that such a right had existed at common law independently of the new legislation. And despite being the first privacy case to reach the Court of Appeal since the Human Rights Act came into force, it remained in legal limbo for more than two years. Although the preliminary Court of Appeal ruling was delivered just before the end of December 2000, the full hearing in the High Court Chancery Division did not take place until 2003. Mr Justice Lindsay finally ruled on the facts in April of that year, before giving his decision on damages in November. Since his judgment can be best understood if events are taken in sequence, I shall sketch in the intervening events before returning to it at the end of this chapter.

T & V

Long before Mr Justice Lindsay's decision in *Douglas v Hello! Ltd*, other judges were drawing enthusiastically on what they saw as the Court of Appeal's initial reasoning. The first such ruling came only days after the appeal judges had delivered their written judgments.

Robert Thompson and Jon Venables, then both eighteen, were shortly to be released on licence from the indefinite detention to which they were sentenced for murdering 2-year-old James Bulger in 1993. Their lawyers argued that their new identities should remain private when they were released. That argument was resisted by the news media. Giving judgment in *Venables v News Group Newspapers* at the beginning of 2001, Dame Elizabeth Butler-Sloss began by quoting what the news-papers had seen as an encouraging comment by Lord Justice Brooke in

Douglas v Hello! Ltd. He had said: 'Although the right to freedom of expression is not in every case the ace of trumps, it is a powerful card to which the courts of this country must always pay appropriate respect.' Despite that, Dame Elizabeth then went on to grant indefinite injunctions preventing publication of any information that might identify the two youths. Those injunctions were granted, for the first time, against the world at large: everybody is bound by them. The judge explained that she was not making these orders out of respect for Thompson and Venables' private lives under Article 8 of the Human Rights Convention. She was, however, 'entirely satisfied that there is a real and serious risk' to them under Article 2, which protects the right to life itself, and Article 3, which says that no one shall be subjected to inhuman punishment.

The judge had heard evidence, in private, of 'solid grounds for concern that, if their identities were revealed on release, there might well be an attack or attacks on the claimants, and that such an attack or attacks might well be murderous'. Dame Elizabeth said she was not sure that she would have granted injunctions if the youths' rights under Article 8 alone were at risk. 'Serious though the breach of the claimants' right to respect for family life and privacy would be once the journalists and photographers discovered either of them, and despite the likely serious adverse effect on the efforts to rehabilitate them into society, it might not be sufficient to meet the importance of the preservation of freedom of expression in Article 10.' But these two young men were uniquely notorious: Articles 2 and 3 trumped Article 10.

As we have already seen, the judge extended the duty of confidence by ruling that 'it may arise in equity independently of a transaction or relationship between the parties'. She said: 'the court does have the jurisdiction, in exceptional cases, to extend the protection of confidentiality of information—even to impose restrictions on the press—where not to do so would be likely to lead to serious physical injury or to the death of the person seeking that confidentiality, and there is no way to protect the applicants other than by seeking relief from the court'. On the other hand, injunctions would only be granted where 'strictly necessary', she said. 'I do not see that this extension of the law of confidence, by the grant of relief in the exceptional circumstances of this case, as opening a door to the granting of general restrictions on the media in cases where anonymity would be desirable.'

Until Dame Elizabeth's ruling in this case, the courts had generally allowed injunctions to be granted only against individuals and organizations who had been made parties to a legal action. They might include a group of unnamed squatters, for example, and—under the *Spycatcher* rule, discussed in Chapter 7—a temporary injunction against one newspaper will bind others that know about it. However, commenting on the *Venables* ruling a year later in *H (A Healthcare Worker) v Associated Newspapers*, Lord Phillips, Master of the Rolls, said: 'The remarkable and novel feature of the injunction granted in that case was that it was expressly stated to be against the whole world.' He was speaking about 'the development of the law of privacy, under the stimulus of the Human Rights Act, under which the possibility of a new civil law right is being recognised as one that can be legitimately protected by the grant of an injunction'. But not all his fellow judges shared this obvious enthusiasm.

Leave it to Parliament

At the end of 2001, other judges in the Court of Appeal fired a shot across the bows of those judges who wanted to create a law of privacy. For once, the case did not involve a television personality or a newspaper, and so the usual need to balance privacy against free speech did not arise: *Wainwright v Home Secretary* was brought by a woman who was strip-searched by prison officers. Importantly, this took place before the Human Rights Act came into force in October 2000.

Mary Wainwright visited her elder son Patrick at Armley Prison, Leeds, in January 1997. She was accompanied by her younger son, Alan, then twenty-one, who had a degree of mental impairment because of cerebral palsy. Before the visit could go ahead, Mrs Wainwright and Alan were strip-searched for concealed drugs. The searches were more intrusive than was permitted by prison guidelines. Alan was told to strip naked, although he should have been asked to remove clothes from one half of his body at a time. His mother was also almost naked at one point and was searched in a room that could be viewed from outside. Both were very upset by what happened and Alan Wainwright suffered psychiatric illness as a result. A judge in Leeds decided that their privacy had been infringed but this ruling was overturned by the Court of Appeal in December 2001.

There was clearly no breach of confidence in this case. Whether people should now be allowed to sue for breach of privacy must be a decision for Parliament, concluded Lord Justice Buxton; in his view, judges were extremely ill-equipped to undertake the detailed investigations necessary before striking a balance between privacy and free speech. He was well aware of Lord Justice Sedley's now-famous remarks in *Douglas v Hello! Ltd*, that the law 'no longer needs to construct an artificial relationship of confidentiality between intruder and victim: it can recognise privacy itself as a legal principle drawn from the fundamental value of personal autonomy'. But not everything a judge says in court is law. As Lord Justice Buxton said, and as Lord Justice Sedley himself would have been the first to recognize, those comments were *obiter*—incidental observations not considered binding.

Not only was there no law of privacy, Lord Justice Buxton explained, there were also 'serious difficulties of principle' in creating one. It would protect not only individuals wanting to get on with their lives, but also companies that wanted to keep their affairs private. Lord Justice Mummery, sitting with him, saw 'serious definitional difficulties and conceptual problems in the judicial development of a "blockbuster" tort'. He added: 'I am not even sure that anybody—the public, Parliament, the press—really wants the creation of a new tort, which would give rise to as many problems as it is sought to solve.' These remarks were *obiter* too. For what it is worth, though, both judges agreed that privacy law remained as it had been in 1990, when Gorden Kaye lost his claim against the *Sunday Sport* journalists. Lord Woolf, who gave the leading judgment, remained firmly on the fence: describing Lord Justice Sedley's comments in *Douglas* as 'most instructive', the Lord Chief Justice said that the Human Rights Act could not be 'relied on to change substantive law by introducing a retrospective right to privacy which did not exist at common law'.

Commenting on the *Wainwright* ruling in his Bentham lecture, Lord Phillips noted that the cases cited by Lord Justice Buxton had been decided before the Human Rights Act had come into force. The implication of his remarks was that the courts could—or, perhaps, should—reach a different conclusion now.

Wainwright went to the House of Lords in July 2003. David Wilby, for Mrs Wainwright, asked Lord Bingham, sitting as the senior law lord, to overturn his decision in *Kaye v Robertson* and put into effect the proposals in the lecture on personal privacy he gave in 1996 (both referred to in Chapter 1). Mr Wilby asked the House of Lords to find that a law protecting personal privacy existed before the Human Rights Act took effect in 2000. He offered this definition:

An invasion of privacy occurs when the unjustified act or conduct of a person intrudes into the personal autonomy of another in his or her personal life or the privacy of his or her body or property so as to cause embarrassment or humiliation or distress or anguish of sufficient gravity to require compensation by an award of damages.

Mr Wilby maintained that he was not inviting the court to change the substantive law. Instead, it was 'an invitation to declare that the gradual absorption of Article 8 into English law . . . had been completed to such a degree by 1997' that the law lords would have protected Article 8 rights by then.

If lawmaking by osmosis was a bit too radical for the House of Lords, he offered them the alternative of extending the law laid down by *Wilkinson v Downton* more than a century earlier. That case involved an unpleasant practical joke. Thomas Wilkinson, landlord of the Albion pub in Limehouse, went by train to the races at Harlow, leaving his wife Lavinia behind the bar. Downton, a customer at the pub, deliberately told Mrs Wilkinson, the claimant, 'that her husband, while returning in a [horse-drawn] wagonette with some friends from the races, had met with an accident and had both his legs broken, that he was lying at The Elms public house at Leytonstone', and had told him to ask her 'to go at once with a cab and some pillows to fetch him home'. All this was completely false and Mr Wilkinson returned safely by train that evening. However, the story had a devastating effect on his wife. She suffered 'a violent shock to her nervous system, producing vomiting and other more serious and permanent physical consequences at one time threatening her reason, and entailing weeks of suffering and incapacity to her as well as expense to her husband for medical attendance'. Her hair turned white and for some time her life was thought to have been in danger. A jury awarded her £100 in damages for nervous shock, plus 1s 10½d (a little under 10p) for train fares to Leytonstone. Upholding the award, Mr Justice Wright said that Downton had 'wilfully done an act calculated to cause physical harm to [Mrs Wilkinson]—that is to say, to infringe her legal right to personal safety, and has in fact thereby caused physical harm to her. That proposition without more appears to me to state a good cause of action, there being no justification alleged for the act.'

Wainwright: the final ruling

Mr Wilby's arguments cut no ice with the House of Lords, where Lord Hoffmann commented scathingly that *Wilkinson v Downton* had been 'far more often discussed than applied'. After a comprehensive summary of the law, he concluded in October 2003 that the Wainwrights had no right to sue for invasion of privacy. That view was shared by Lord Bingham and the other law lords.

Lord Hoffmann took as his starting point the article by Warren and Brandeis, referred to in Chapter 1, in which they argued that the common law already recognized a right of privacy. That was in 1890. However, when Prosser had tried seventy years later to analyse and classify privacy law as it had become established in the United States, he found four separate—and entirely unrelated—torts. To Lord Hoffmann, this suggested that 'invasion of privacy' was not a general principle from which courts could deduce the rule to be applied in a particular case. That view, he explained, was supported by the decision in *Kaye v Robertson*—also discussed in Chapter 1—when the actor's privacy claim was rejected by Lord Justice Bingham and two other appeal judges:

All three judgments are flat against a judicial power to declare the existence of a high-level right to privacy and I do not think that they suggest that the courts should do so. The members of the Court of Appeal certainly thought that it would be desirable if there was legislation to confer a right to protect the privacy of a person in the position of Mr Kaye against the kind of intrusion which he suffered, but they did not advocate any wider principle. And when the Calcutt Committee reported in June 1990, they did indeed recommend that 'entering private property, without the consent of the lawful occupant, with intent to obtain personal information with a view to its publication' should be made a criminal offence: see *Report of the Committee on Privacy and Related Matters* . . . But the Calcutt Committee did not recommend, even within their terms of reference (which were confined to press intrusion) the creation of a generalised tort of infringement of privacy. This was not because they thought that the definitional problems were insuperable. They said that if one confined the tort to 'publication of personal information to the world at large' it should be possible to produce an adequate definition and they made some suggestions about how such a statutory tort might be defined and what the defences should be. But they considered that the problem could be tackled more effectively by a combination of the more sharply-focused remedies which they recommended. As for a 'general wrong of infringement of privacy', they accepted that it would, even in statutory form, give rise to 'an unacceptable degree of uncertainty'. There is nothing in the opinions of the judges in *Kaye v Robertson* which suggests that the members of the court would have held any view, one way or the other, about a general tort of privacy.

What about Lord Justice Sedley's view that the 'law no longer needs to construct an artificial relationship of confidentiality . . . it can recognize privacy itself as a legal principle'? This meant no more, according to Lord Hoffmann, than that 'in relation to the publication of personal information obtained by intrusion, the common law of breach of confidence has reached the point at which a confidential relationship has become unnecessary'. He did not understand Lord Justice Sedley to have been 'advocating the creation of a high-level principle of invasion of privacy'. On the contrary, Lord Justice Sedley's comments were no more than 'a plea for the extension and possibly renaming of the old action for breach of confidence'. There was a great difference between 'identifying privacy as a value which underlies the existence of a rule of law (and may point the direction in which the law should develop) and privacy as a principle of law in itself'.

And what did Lord Hoffmann have to say about *Peck*, the case of the would-be suicide who was seen on television after closed-circuit pictures were released for broadcast: surely the Strasbourg decision, which will be analysed more fully in Chapter 4, demonstrated the need for a general tort of invasion of privacy? No, said the law lord, it showed 'no more than the need, in English law, for a system of control of the use of film from CCTV cameras which shows greater sensitivity to the feelings of people who happen to have been caught by the lens'.

For these reasons, said Lord Hoffmann dryly, 'I would reject the invitation to declare that since at the latest 1950 there has been a previously unknown tort of invasion of privacy'.

Wilkinson v Downton was no use either. 'It does not provide a remedy for distress which does not amount to recognized psychiatric injury and, so far as there may [be] a tort of intention under which such damage is recoverable, the necessary intention was not established.'

Mr Wilby had argued during the hearing that, unless the English courts created a tort covering the Wainwrights' case, it was inevitable that the Human Rights judges would find a breach of Article 8. Lord Hoffmann was not so sure:

Although Article 8 guarantees a right of privacy, I do not think that it treats that right as having been invaded and requiring a remedy in damages, irrespective of whether the defendant acted intentionally, negligently or accidentally. It is one thing to wander carelessly into the wrong hotel bedroom and another to hide in the wardrobe to take photographs. Article 8 may justify a monetary remedy for an intentional invasion of privacy by a public authority, even if no damage is suffered other than distress for which damages are not ordinarily recoverable. It does not follow that a merely negligent act should, contrary to general principle, give rise to a claim for damages for distress because it affects privacy rather than some other interest like bodily safety.

Even if the Human Rights Court did find a breach of Article 8, that would demonstrate only that there had been a gap in the English remedies for invasion of privacy until the Human Rights Act had come into effect. But all that has now changed. Section 6 of the 1998 Act makes it unlawful for a public authority to act in a way that is incompatible with the Human Rights Convention, unless the authority could not have acted differently because of primary legislation. Section 7 of the Act allows a 'victim' of the unlawfulness to bring proceedings against the public authority and section 8 allows damages to be awarded. In *Anufrijeva v London Borough of Southwark*, decided by the Court of Appeal on the same day as the Lords' judgment in *Wainwright*, the Lord Chief Justice, sitting with the Master of the Rolls and Lord Justice Auld, laid down the principles on which these damages should be assessed: since they must be in line with Strasbourg awards, they will not be very large.

Compensation was all that was required by a breach of Article 8, Lord Hoffmann concluded: 'it does not require that the courts should provide an alternative remedy which distorts the principles of the common law'.

But what if *Wainwright* had occurred after the Human Rights Act had come into force? Would Mrs Wainwright and her son have been able to sue for breach of privacy? Lord Scott, the only other law lord who gave a reasoned judgment in *Wainwright*, said that this would have to wait until such a case arose. Though he did not say so, that could turn out to be Naomi Campbell's appeal to the House of Lords in 2004.

Scoring away from home

The unwillingness of the Court of Appeal in *Wainwright* to create a new tort of privacy in December 2001 was endorsed even more authoritatively in a high-profile decision delivered a few months later. The Lord Chief Justice, sitting in the Court of Appeal with two senior colleagues, told trial judges that they should simply not try to decide whether such a tort now existed. An action for breach of confidence would do the job just as effectively. Lord Woolf did not rule out the possibility that the Court of Appeal might go on to develop such a tort itself. However, he offered no encouragement to those who wanted to see such a tort—or who thought that privacy could already be recognized as a legal principle.

Lord Woolf was giving judgment in March 2002 on a claim brought by Garry Flitcroft, a Premier League footballer who had been cheating on his wife with two women. In the finest traditions of 'kiss and tell', they spoke to the press and he then went to court, seeking and obtaining an order that he should not be named. Flitcroft, a 29-year-old midfield player and captain of Blackburn Rovers, managed to preserve his anonymity for almost a year, raising expectations that he might turn out to be somebody more interesting. In the event, the only remarkable thing about him was that his height, according to his club's website, was '5ft 12ins'.

At first, all that the public could be told was that Mr A, 'a successful professional footballer, who is a married man with a family', had discovered that a newspaper, referred to in the judgment only as B, was planning to run stories about what it subsequently called 'his sleazy affairs with two young girls', known, inevitably, as C and D. Given that these parties were referred to only by their initials, it seemed fitting that they should have used their mobile phones to indulge in heavy sessions of textual intercourse.

After the *People* was allowed to identify itself as 'B', it ran interviews with the two women—at that stage still unnamed. Miss C, a blonde nursery school teacher and single mother, said that the footballer had met her in a bar in January 2001 and duped her into believing he was single. He proposed, showering her with champagne and bombarding her with text messages before finally texting her that he was married. That drove her to fury. In March 2001, the woman posted a transcript of the last text through the door of his parents' house. Miss C, subsequently named as Helen Hammonds, threatened to show the message to Flitcroft's wife, Karen. Not surprisingly, the relationship between Hammonds and Flitcroft came to an end. 'He is a sexual predator who used his wealth, fame and position to seduce me,' the newspaper quoted her as saying.

Miss D, a 26-year-old lap-dancer and former air stewardess (also blonde, as it happens), said she had fallen for the soccer star in November 1999, when she danced for him in a topless bar. Over the next fifteen months he met and occasionally spent the night with Miss D—whose real name was Paula James—and they frequently texted one another until Flitcroft admitted to her, too, that he was married. 'He has betrayed his wife and family and lied to me,' she said pithily.

Explaining in court how he had met these women, Flitcroft said that he used to go drinking in the evening with his fellow players in an attempt to improve 'team spirit'. He accepted that he had been seen in public with each of them at restaurants and clubs, and did not deny having affairs with them. Even so, he sought an injunction to prevent the *People* from writing about his relationship with Hammonds and James. His lawyers put forward two main grounds: breach of confidence and breach of privacy.

Mr Justice Jack granted a temporary injunction in April 2001. Three weeks later, the newspaper asked him to lift it, partly because Flitcroft had failed to disclose the fact that he had spent a night with Hammonds in February. The judge agreed, concluding that the footballer had told 'a deliberate untruth' in an attempt to mislead the Court. But before anything could be published, Flitcroft persuaded the judge to admit further evidence from his lawyer in order to explain the discrepancy. Having reconsidered his judgment in the light of this, Mr Justice Jack said he could no longer be certain that the footballer had lied and—in his third ruling on the case—reinstated the injunction.

He then had to consider the merits of Flitcroft's claim. Delivering his fourth judgment in September 2001, Mr Justice Jack concluded that, at a full hearing, the footballer was likely to be able to prove that his affairs with Hammonds and James, and the sexual acts that occurred between them privately, were covered by the law of confidence. The judge noted that *Douglas v Hello! Ltd* and *Venables v News Group Newspapers* had demonstrated that the law relating to breach of confidence was in a state of growth. The question for him to decide was whether 'sexual matters occurring between two persons are subject to a duty of confidence in the absence of any express agreement between them that they keep such matters confidential'.

He gave a positive answer. 'The law should afford the protection of confidentiality to facts concerning sexual relations within marriage (which is surely straightforward) and, in the context of modern sexual relations, it should be no different with relationships outside marriage.'

The judge seemed understandably confused about whether 'a right of privacy might now be part of English law, having emerged from the shadow of confidentiality'. In April 2001, he had concluded that it was likely that the claimant would establish such a right at trial; in September 2001, he thought it 'better to express no view'.

Giving judgment, Mr Justice Jack observed that section 12 of the Human Rights Act effectively required him to pay particular regard to the Code of Practice issued by the Press Complaints Commission (PCC). This says that everyone is entitled to respect for his or her private and family life, but adds that there may be exceptions where they can be demonstrated to be in the public interest. The public interest includes 'detecting or exposing crime or a serious misdemeanour; protecting public health and safety; and preventing the public from being misled by some statement or action of an individual or organisation'. In his view, it was not in the public interest for the articles to be published. It had been suggested that the footballer was a role model for young people. In the judge's view, however, Flitcroft was not someone who had courted publicity and thereby laid his private life open to scrutiny.

A cheating rat

Flitcroft's case then went to the Court of Appeal, which ruled in March 2002. Mr Justice Jack, whose misfortune it had been to be the duty judge on the Friday afternoon when the injunction was first sought, did not emerge unscathed from *A v B plc* (as the case was called in the law reports). 'Although the criticisms which we make of the approach of Mr Justice Jack are not individually of great significance,' said the appeal judges generously, 'collectively we do believe they resulted in his coming to a wrong decision.' Lord Woolf, sitting with Lord Justice Laws and Lord Justice Dyson, agreed that the footballer could be named unless there was to be a further appeal. The ban, they said, was 'an unjustified interference with the freedom of the press'.

Newspapers were jubilant. 'This man has spent £200,000 so far to hide the fact that he is a cheating rat,' said Neil Wallis, editor of the *People*, immediately after the hearing, showing that felicity of speech for which tabloid journalists are renowned. His remarks were echoed at the start of Flitcroft's first game after he was named by a group of home supporters chanting 'Does your missus know you're here?'

Important though the Court of Appeal judgment may have been in developing the law of confidence, it did not escape criticism. In an extraordinary leap of logic, Lord Woolf and his fellow judges turned a much-quoted aphorism on its head. 'There is a wide difference between what is interesting to the public and what is in the public interest to be made known,' Lord Wilberforce had said in *British Steel v Granada* (1980). The media 'are particularly vulnerable to the error of confusing the public interest with their own interest,' Sir John Donaldson had repeated in *Francome v MGN* (1984). But in Lord Woolf's view, 'if newspapers do not publish information which the public is interested in, there will be fewer newspapers published—which will not be in the public interest.' This ingratiating attempt to win over the media was unsuccessful. Not even a journalist would claim it was in the public interest to publish everything that interests the public. And, as we shall see, other judges, rushed to distance themselves from his remarks.

The first question considered by the Court of Appeal was whether the judge had been right, in his third ruling, to reinstate the injunction he had lifted at the second hearing. In fact, said the Court of Appeal, the case should never have got that far: his second decision had been wrong. Mr Justice Jack should never have set aside his original findings and agreed to lift the injunction because Flitcroft had lied. The number of times that the footballer had committed adultery was of marginal relevance.

Turning to the substantive appeal, Lord Woolf said there were 'important flaws' in the approach taken by Mr Justice Jack. He had not recognized that any injunction interfering with the freedom of the press—the existence of which was, itself, desirable—would need to be justified. The judge had wrongly assumed that, since the footballer had a right to privacy, an injunction should be granted unless the newspaper could show there was a public interest in what it wanted to publish.

Secondly, the judge had considered that sexual relationships outside marriage should be protected under the law of confidence in the same way as relationships within marriage. But, as the Court of Appeal said: 'This approach is objectionable because it makes no allowance for the very different nature of the relationship that A had, on his own account, with C and D from that which would exist within marriage. Quite apart from the recognition which the law gives to the status of marriage, there is a significant difference in our judgment to the confidentiality which attaches to what is intended to be a permanent relationship from that which attaches to the category of relationships which A was involved with here.'

There was also the issue of the two women's right to freedom of expression. 'Although we would not go so far as to say that there can be no confidentiality where one party to a relationship does not want confidentiality, the fact that C and D chose to disclose their relationship to B does affect A's right to protection of the information.'

Next, Mr Justice Jack had apparently found disclosure to the media more objectionable than disclosure by Hammonds and James to their friends. 'This approach ignores the importance to be attached to a free press,' said the Court of Appeal. The trial judge had apparently been influenced by the need to protect the footballer's family. But he 'should not assume that it was in the interests of A's wife to be kept in ignorance of A's relationships'.

The judge had also rejected any public-interest defence. The Court of Appeal said: 'It is not self-evident that how a Premiership football player, who has a position of responsibility within his club, chooses to spend his time off the football field does not have a modicum of public interest. Footballers are role models for young people and undesirable behaviour on their part can set an unfortunate example.' Summing up, Flitcroft's relationships with the two women were not of the kind that 'the court should be astute to protect when the other parties to the relationships do not want them to remain confidential. Any injunction granted after a trial would have to be permanent. It is most unlikely that such an injunction would ever be granted.'

The judges were not saying that relationships of this kind could never be covered by confidentiality. In their view, however, 'to grant an injunction would be an unjustified interference with the freedom of the press'. And, once it was accepted that press freedom should prevail, then the way in which the story was reported was a matter for the PCC and readers of the newspaper, not the courts.

The Court of Appeal laid down no fewer than fifteen guidelines to help judges decide urgent applications for interim injunctions. They were clearly intended to offer some help in predicting how the courts will approach privacy cases— although some of the guidelines are pretty obvious and others leave a lot to the judge's discretion. They clearly came as a disappointment to the worldly authors of *Privacy and the Media*, a Matrix Chambers publication edited by Hugh Tomlinson, QC, who concluded that the guidelines 'offer little by way of practical guidance' to journalists and are 'unlikely to be of assistance on the "back bench" and in the edit suite'.

The Woolf guidelines

Only a few of the guidelines need trouble us. After advising on when a temporary injunction should be granted, Lord Woolf, in his sixth guideline, told trial judges they should not seek to decide whether there was now a new tort involving the infringement of privacy. An action for breach of confidence could be used to protect a person's privacy instead. That, of course, would make it much harder for the higher courts to develop a privacy law: if an applicant's privacy may be protected by the law of confidence, he will have no reason to take his case to the Court of Appeal.

In his ninth guideline, Lord Woolf offered a definition of confidence. 'A duty of confidence will arise whenever the party subject to the duty is in a situation where he either knows or ought to know that the other person can reasonably expect his privacy to be protected,' he said. 'The range of situations in which protection can be provided is therefore extensive. Obviously, the necessary relationship can be expressly created. More often its existence will have to be inferred from the facts. Whether there is a duty of confidence that courts can protect, if it is right to do so, will depend on all the circumstances of the relationship between the parties at the time of the threatened or actual breach of the alleged duty of confidence'.

In his tenth guideline, Lord Woolf says: 'If there is an intrusion in a situation where a person can reasonably expect his privacy to be respected then that intrusion will be capable of giving rise to liability in an action for breach of confidence unless the intrusion can be justified.' Some examples are given, but what we are not told is when we can expect a person's privacy to be protected by the courts. It is little help for the courts to say that you are under a duty to respect someone else's privacy only if that person can reasonably expect his or her privacy to be respected—although not if the intrusion can be justified. When is it reasonable—and when is it justified?

Guideline 12 is fundamental:

Where an individual is a public figure he is entitled to have his privacy respected in the appropriate circumstances. A public figure is entitled to a private life. The individual, however, should recognise that because of his public position he must expect and accept that his actions will be more closely scrutinised by the media.

Even trivial facts relating to a public figure can be of great interest to readers and other observers of the media. Conduct which in the case of a private individual would not be the appropriate subject of comment can be the proper subject of comment in the case of a public figure. The public figure may hold a position where higher standards of conduct can be rightly expected by the public. The public figure may be a role model whose conduct could well be emulated by others. He may set the fashion. The higher the profile of the individual concerned the more likely that this will be the position.

Whether you have courted publicity or not you may be a legitimate subject of public attention. If you have courted public attention then you have less ground to object to the intrusion which follows. In many of these situations it would be overstating the position to say that there is a public interest in the information being published. It would be more accurate to say that the public have an understandable and so a legitimate interest in being told the information. If this is the situation then it can be appropriately taken into account by a court when deciding on which side of the line a case falls.

The courts must not ignore the fact that if newspapers do not publish information which the public are interested in, there will be fewer newspapers published, which will not be in the public interest. The same is true in relation to other parts of the media.

This guideline has been heavily and rightly criticized. Lord Woolf is a well-meaning judge who likes to be liked, and most news organizations were more than happy with his generous ruling in *A v B plc*. Some feared he was tilting the balance so far in the direction of the press that the Government would come under pressure to introduce statutory controls, but these concerns proved groundless.

Andrew Caldecott, the QC who had represented Naomi Campbell in her action against the *Daily Mirror*, accused the Court of Appeal of blurring the distinction 'between that which is merely of interest to the public and that which it is in the public interest to publish'. Writing in the *Guardian* in March 2002, he said: 'By this route, the publication of salacious sexual details are awarded a public interest rating, simply because a degree of prurient interest is present in most of us and indulging that interest will help sell the newspaper. While there is a clear public interest in a dynamic and diverse press, it is difficult to see why a newspaper's commercial interests could ever justify the publication of particular information otherwise deserving of protection.'

That must be right. But there is rather more sense in Lord Woolf's suggestion—in the same paragraph—that public figures have fewer rights to privacy than everyone else. It is, to some extent, the price they pay for fame. If you happen to be a sports star, a model or an entertainer, the people who pay to watch you can reasonably expect an occasional autograph or even the chance to shake your hand in a restaurant. Politicians must expect to be approached by voters just as writers should be courteous to readers who recognize them from their photographs. However, many of those who bring privacy claims will be public figures. If Lord Woolf's suggestion is followed by other judges, it will do much to reduce the effectiveness of an anti-intrusion law. We should therefore not be too surprised in the next few pages to find Lord Phillips, a keen supporter of reform, downplaying its effect.

Frisbee thrown

The first judge to apply the judgment in *A v B plc* was ruling on a dispute between Naomi Campbell and Vanessa Frisbee, who had worked as the model's personal assistant for some ten weeks. In April 2000, their relationship broke down when, according to Frisbee, Campbell violently assaulted her. Campbell denied this. At any rate,

Frisbee claimed that Campbell's behaviour had ended her contract of employment and with it the confidentiality agreement she had signed.

Frisbee then sold her story to the *News of the World* for a fee of £25,000 (plus another £5,000 for her agent, Max Clifford). She admitted telling the newspaper about an alleged sexual relationship between Campbell and Joseph Fiennes, the actor. 'Naomi was tired but ecstatic,' Frisbee gushed. 'She said they'd made love four or five times [that night].' Campbell sued for breach of confidence, and Frisbee appealed unsuccessfully against summary judgment in Campbell's favour.

Mr Justice Lightman held first that Frisbee's duty not to divulge confidential information acquired while working for Campbell remained in force even if Campbell had repudiated her contract of employment. The judge drew a distinction between an employment contract and a contract for services between an independent contractor (Frisbee) and a client (Campbell). 'In the case of contracts for services, there can be no conceivable basis for the suggestion that a repudiatory breach by the client entitles the independent contractor to a release from obligations of confidentiality.'

He then had to consider Frisbee's defence that her disclosures to the *News of the World* were justified as being in the public interest. In a ruling delivered on 14 March 2002, the judge took account of the decision delivered by Lord Woolf just three days earlier. Mr Justice Lightman acknowledged that it might sometimes be in the public interest to encroach on a contractual obligation of confidentiality. But there was a 'substantial public interest' in requiring parties who had entered into a financial arrangement, with their eyes open, to comply with their obligations not to disclose confidences. 'For the defence of public interest to override an express obligation of confidence, as a rule, the information must go beyond being interesting to the public ... there must be a pressing public need to know', he said.

Frisbee had argued that there was a public interest in correcting the false picture Campbell had painted of herself, in particular that the model enjoyed a 'close and happy sexual relationship with Mr Flavio Briatore, a sensible businessman and stabilising father-figure'. Mr Justice Lightman gave this argument short shrift. 'In my view, the information sold by the defendant to the *News of the World* was no more or less than a titillating account of one or more private sexual encounters between the claimant and Mr Fiennes and the efforts made to cover it up,' he said. He dismissed Frisbee's appeal against an order for summary judgment against her.

The judge could not see how it was 'seriously maintainable that the public had any interest in the content of the disclosures (most particularly that the claimant was cheating on her partner) or need to know; or that the defendant had any such reason or justification for making her disclosures as required that the claimant be deprived of the protection of the confidentiality obligation which the defendant willingly, solemnly and for valuable consideration provided.'

Although he was bound by the decision in *A v B plc*, Mr Justice Lightman did not feel he was required to adopt Lord Woolf's view of the public interest in paragraph 12 of his guidelines ('if newspapers do not publish information which the public are interested in, there will be fewer newspapers published, which will not be in the public interest'). Given the facts of this case, it is hard to disagree with him.

Frisbee was given one more chance to appeal against the order for summary judgment. This time, she was successful: the Court of Appeal thought it arguable that an expressly agreed duty of confidentiality carried more weight, when balanced against restrictions on freedom of expression, than one that was not supported by an express agreement. That seems a sensible approach: the law should require people to comply with legal obligations undertaken for payment. However, it was not much use to Frisbee—if anything, it put her in a weaker position than before.

If the law was unclear, said Lord Phillips, Master of the Rolls, sitting with two other appeal judges, then the case should not have been decided without full argument. 'While we do not consider that it is likely Miss Frisbee will establish that Mr Justice Lightman erred in his conclusions in a manner detrimental to her cause,' they added, 'it cannot be said she has no reasonable prospect of success on the issue.' Despite allowing her appeal with costs, Lord Phillips, the Master of the Rolls, strongly hinted that Frisbee ought to settle while she was still ahead.

Beauty and the *Daily Beast*

On the very day that the publishers of the *People* were asking the Court of Appeal to lift the ban obtained by Garry Flitcroft, they found themselves in the High Court defending an action brought by Naomi Campbell against another of their titles, the *Daily Mirror*.

The fashion model had complained about an article in February 2001 that said she was attending meetings of Narcotics Anonymous 'in a courageous bid to beat her addiction to drink and drugs'. The *Daily Mirror* carried a picture of Campbell dressed in jeans and a baseball cap, outside one of the self-help group's meetings. Readers were told she had been going to Narcotics Anonymous for the past three months, often attending twice a day. In fact, though the media did not know this, she had attended their meetings for about two years—though not nearly as frequently as twice a day. The revelations were particularly damaging as Campbell had always maintained that, unlike many other models, she did not take drugs, stimulants or tranquillizers. False explanations had been given when she visited clinics for treatment.

The model responded to the *Mirror* stories by claiming damages from the paper's publishers for 'breach of confidence and/or unlawful invasion of privacy', backed up with a claim under the Data Protection Act. The privacy claim was later dropped—perhaps wisely, in view of Lord Woolf's sixth guideline in the Flitcroft case, *A v B plc*.

In an important concession before the trial began, Campbell's lawyers accepted that the *Mirror* had been entitled to publish the fact that she 'had a drug problem' and that she was receiving treatment for addiction. By mendaciously asserting to the media that she was not a drug-taker, the model had rendered it legitimate for the media to put the record straight. However, Campbell maintained that there was no overriding public interest justifying publication of the fact that the therapy was being obtained through Narcotics Anonymous and the details of her attendance at meetings.

Campbell steps ahead

The rather tenuous distinction between the fact of Campbell's drug-taking and the details of her therapy was accepted by the judge in March 2002 when he decided the case in her favour. Giving judgment, Mr Justice Morland outlined the classic requirements of the law of confidence, finding that she had established all three. First, the details of her attendance at Narcotics Anonymous did have the necessary quality of confidence about them. It did not matter whether her therapy was obtained by professional medical input or by alternative means such as group counselling or discussion, said the judge. 'They were obtained surreptitiously, assisted by covert photography, when Miss Campbell was engaged deliberately "low key" and drably dressed in the private activity of therapy to advance her recovery from drug addiction.' Secondly, the details of her regular attendance at Narcotics Anonymous meetings for therapy must have been imparted in circumstances importing an obligation of confidence. The undisclosed source—whether a fellow sufferer or a member of Campbell's entourage—owed her an obligation of confidence. Thirdly, publication of the details was to her detriment. It was likely to have an adverse effect on her attendance at meetings.

Applying the principles laid down by Lord Woolf in *A v B plc*, Mr Justice Morland decided that there had indeed been a breach of confidentiality. He concluded, with apparent relief, that as a result of the Court of Appeal's ruling in that case it had not been necessary for him to 'address the extensive arguments on law' put to him by the two sides.

Even so, the *Daily Mirror* had argued that publication of the story was legitimate because the public interest in favour of publication outweighed any public interest in protecting Campbell's rights of confidentiality. That argument was rejected by the judge. 'Although many aspects of the private lives of celebrities and public figures will inevitably enter the public domain,' he said, 'it does not follow that even with self-publicists every aspect and detail of their private lives are legitimate quarry for the journalist. They are entitled to some space of privacy.'

How was Campbell's right to respect for her private and family life under Article 8 of the Human Rights Convention to be balanced against the newspaper's right to freedom of expression under Article 10? Mr Justice Morland said it was inevitable that 'a top fashion model of international renown' would be the subject of media interest. 'That interest and publication will be greatly increased if she has a colourful temperament and private life. This will be especially so if as in the case of Miss Naomi Campbell she exploits commercially her celebrity status by ancillary activities in connection with her enterprises in restaurants, jeans and fragrances. In such circumstances she can expect and to a degree, I would assume, welcome some media attention and intrusion when she is engaged in public promotions and appearances.'

The judge noted that Campbell had given media interviews about 'her men friends and her relationships with them', adding that it was 'greatly to her credit that they have not been kiss-and-tell revelations giving details of sexual activity.' She had admitted that she was 'notorious for tantrums'. However, she did not reveal that she was a drug addict and had been receiving therapy for some years. 'Indeed she lied about her drug addiction,' the judge concluded.

'For example, in June 1997, when she was rushed to hospital in Gran Canaria following an alleged drug overdose, she said in an exclusive interview with the *Daily Telegraph* . . . "I didn't take drugs".' She had also told a magazine that she never took stimulants. The judge said: 'I am satisfied that she lied to the interviewers when making these denials and that her assertions—persisted in by her when giving evidence before me—that her rush to hospital was caused by an allergic reaction to an antibiotic, were deliberate lies.'

Clearly, said Mr Justice Morland, people had a need to know that Campbell had been misleading the public by her denials of drug addiction. Balanced and positive journalism demanded that the public be told that she was receiving therapy. 'Clearly the *Mirror* was fully entitled to put the record straight and publish that her denials of drug addiction were deliberately misleading. She might have been thought of [as], and indeed she herself seems to be, a self-appointed role model to young black women.' However, Mr Justice Morland said the courts would protect from publication details of the 'private life which a celebrity or public figure has chosen not to put in the public domain' unless publication was justifiable. In his view, the balance came down in Campbell's favour.

The judge found that Campbell had suffered significant distress and injury to feelings caused specifically by the unjustified revelation of the details of her therapy with Narcotics Anonymous. However, she had also suffered a significant degree of distress and injury to feelings caused by publication of the fact that she was a recovering drug addict receiving therapy. The *Daily Mirror* would have been fully justified if it had confined itself to the facts: it was reporting the details of her attendance at meetings that entitled her to damages.

'In determining the extent of distress and injury to feelings for which she is entitled to compensation, I must consider her evidence with caution,' said the judge. 'She has shown herself to be over the years lacking in frankness and veracity with the media and manipulative and selective in what she has chosen to reveal about herself. I am satisfied that she lied on oath about the reasons for her rushed admission to hospital in Gran Canaria and I have doubts about the accuracy of her accounts of the assaults on her assistants and her dealings with Mr Matthew Freud, the publicist.' Nevertheless, the judge was satisfied that she genuinely suffered distress and injury to feelings caused by the unjustified publication and disclosure of details of her therapy in the two initial articles published by the *Mirror*.

Damages for the breach-of-confidence action and Data Protection Act claim (discussed below) were assessed together at £2,500. These were 'on a modest scale' because Campbell had dismissed the *Daily Mirror* article shortly after its appearance, telling an interviewer 'I saw that piece and got upset for five minutes'.

In addition, she was awarded £1,000 in aggravated damages for a subsequent article in which the newspaper compared her to a 'chocolate soldier'. The judge said he could well understand that Campbell had found the phrase hurtful and considered it racist. Desmond Brown, QC, for the *Daily Mirror*, had submitted that it was a 'commonplace simile' that originated with troops at Gallipoli or in the works of George Bernard Shaw. But the judge was 'unacquainted' with the expression. He was surprised that Piers Morgan, editor of the *Daily Mirror*, and the writer who used the phrase, 'thought it appropriate to compare Miss Campbell to a "chocolate soldier" in a highly offensive and disparaging article in 2001'. The follow-up article had not only criticized the merits of her claim in strong and colourful language but also, to use her counsel's phrase, 'trashed her as a person' in a highly offensive and hurtful manner, said the judge. 'That trashing entitles her to aggravated damages.'

Mr Justice Morland's judgment was disappointing. If it was legitimate for the newspaper to disclose that Campbell was receiving therapy for drug addiction, what additional harm did she suffer when the nature of that therapy was published? Those details would inevitably have become public once it became known that she had lied about her addiction.

Campbell takes a tumble

My view of Mr Justice Morland's ruling was shared by Lord Phillips, Master of the Rolls, sitting with Lords Justices Chadwick and Keene, when they allowed an appeal by the *Mirror* in October 2002. 'Given that it was legitimate for the [newspaper] to publish the fact that Miss Campbell was a drug addict and that she was receiving treatment, it does not seem to us that it was particularly significant to add the fact that the treatment consisted of attendance at meetings of Narcotics Anonymous,' the appeal judges said. 'What is it suggested that the *Mirror* should have published? "Naomi Campbell is a drug addict. The *Mirror* has discovered that she is receiving treatment for her addiction"? Such a story, without any background detail to support it, would have bordered on the absurd.'

With a nod to the equitable origins of the law, the judges said it was not obvious to them that 'the peripheral disclosure of Miss Campbell's attendance at Narcotics Anonymous was, in its context, of sufficient significance to shock the conscience and justify the intervention of the court. On the contrary, we have concluded it was not.' The judges added that details published by the newspaper, and a photograph of her outside the group's meeting place, 'were a legitimate, if not essential, part of the journalistic package designed to demonstrate that Miss Campbell had been deceiving the public when she said she did not take drugs'. They felt fortified by the decision in *Fressoz and Roire v France* (to be discussed in Chapter 3), in which the European Court of Human Rights said it was up to journalists to decide what details were needed to ensure credibility.

Like Mr Justice Lightman in the Frisbee case, the appeal judges seemed uncomfortable with paragraph 12 of Lord Woolf's guidelines in *A v B plc*. It had been 'misunderstood by some', they explained tactfully. 'When Lord Woolf spoke of the public having "an understandable and so a legitimate interest in being told" information, even including trivial facts, about a public figure, he was not speaking of private facts which a fair-minded person would consider it offensive to disclose.' That, they said, was clear from comments he made later in the judgment. 'For our part, we would observe that the fact that an individual has achieved prominence on the public stage does not mean that his private life can be laid bare by the media. We do not see why it should necessarily be in the public interest that an individual who has been adopted as a role model, without seeking this distinction, should be demonstrated to have feet of clay.'

As we saw in Chapter 1, the Court of Appeal said that the unjustifiable publication of information relating to an individual's private life 'would be better described as breach of privacy rather than breach of confidence'. Despite that, its reasoning was based more on the existing law of confidence than any developing notion of privacy.

Campbell was naturally disappointed with the outcome. With defamation cases in decline—only 128 claims were issued in London during 2002, compared with 241 in 2000—some lawyers had seen privacy as the new libel, an opportunity for the rich to collect large tax-free winnings while their lawyers cleaned up on costs. But there was some consolation in the fact that the law lords gave her permission to appeal, having been alerted to the recently decided *Peck* ruling in Strasbourg (discussed below). A hearing was scheduled for 2004.

Antony White, QC, Campbell's counsel, told a media law conference in September 2003 that she would challenge the Court of Appeal's finding that details of her attendance for therapy at Narcotics Anonymous and photographs of her leaving therapy sessions were not private and confidential. Relying on *Peck*, Campbell's team planned to argue that Mr Justice Morland's view was to be preferred to that of the Court of Appeal on the question of whether the developing law of privacy should protect respectable therapeutic treatment in the same way as conventional treatment. And Mr White said the law lords would be asked to 'reconsider the public-interest justification and in particular the Court of Appeal's conclusion that no sensible or credible article exposing Ms Campbell's drug addiction could have been written without including the details of her attendance at Narcotics Anonymous or the photographs'.

Earlier, in a statement issued after the Court of Appeal ruling, Campbell said: 'The idea that, because you deny something about your private life [it] automatically entitles the media to publish otherwise private information seems to me to be very harsh indeed and doesn't seem to recognise that there may be all sorts of conditions that someone could want to keep private—for the obvious reason that the matters *are* private.' Her solicitor, Keith Schilling, went on to defend his client's decision to lie about her addiction in an article for the Law Society's *Gazette*. 'In the real world, "no comment" is taken by the media as an admission. But if you decide it is morally right to deny some private fact as a means of keeping it private then—since you have falsely denied it—the [reasoning] in *Campbell* applies. The media will not only be entitled to publish it, but [also] to have regard to private and confidential material to rebut your denial.'

This cannot be a justification for lying. Schilling is skilled enough an operator to know that the normal response from lawyers and public-relations people in these circumstances is 'I'll get back to you'. With a little imagination, this response can be maintained indefinitely. It is perfectly true that reporters sometimes draw adverse inferences from non-denials. But these provide scant protection against any libel action: newspapers need to be very sure of their ground before publishing such allegations in the face of a refusal to comment.

Data Protection Act

In the High Court, Naomi Campbell won a separate claim against the *Daily Mirror* under the Data Protection Act 1998, a relatively new and fiendishly complicated piece of legislation that had been introduced to comply with a European Union Directive. Mr Justice Morland decided that information about Campbell's therapy related to her physical or mental health or condition and was therefore 'sensitive personal data' under the 1998 Act, which was not covered by the public-interest exemptions relating to journalism. The *Mirror* had breached the 'first data protection principle' because details of Campbell's therapy were not in the 'substantial public interest', viewed objectively, and she was therefore entitled to compensation.

'Personal data' is defined by the 1998 Act as any data relating to an identifiable living individual. It includes handwritten notes as well as electronic files. 'Sensitive personal data'—which includes information about an individual's racial origin, political opinions, religious belief, sex life or health—qualifies for additional protection under the Act. Its publication increases the likelihood that the Act may have been breached.

To satisfy the first data-protection principle, the personal data must be 'processed fairly and lawfully'. 'Processing' covers just about anything a journalist might do with the information, including destroying it. To be lawful under the Act, this processing must also pass through at least one of the 'gateways', as they have been called. Gateways available for personal data include the individual's consent, the public interest, and the legitimate interests of the publisher as balanced against the rights of the individual concerned. Gateways available for sensitive personal data include 'explicit' consent, 'deliberate' publication by the individual, and the 'substantial' public interest coupled with a journalistic exposure of dishonesty or malpractice.

Few people at the time realized the seriousness of Mr Justice Morland's decision to reject the newspaper's attempt to pass through this last gateway. As the Court of Appeal said, that would have meant that the Data Protection Act had created a law of privacy and achieved a fundamental enhancement of Article 8 rights at the expense of those granted by Article 10. Fortunately, the Court of Appeal overturned the judge's finding on this issue too. Crucially, it was able to find that section 32 of the Act, which provides public-interest exemptions for 'journalistic, literary or artistic material', protected journalists both before and after publication. The phrase 'with a view to publication' had persuaded Mr Justice Morland and everyone else that the protection was available only in advance. It would have been illogical, the appeal judges said, to exempt a 'data controller' (the newspaper) from having to comply with the legislation before publication while leaving it exposed to a claim for compensation immediately afterwards. Piers Morgan, the *Mirror* editor, reasonably believed that 'having regard in particular to the special importance of the public interest in freedom of expression, publication would be in the public interest'. He also reasonably believed that compliance with the data-protection principles was 'incompatible' with publication. These being the conditions set by section 32, there was no breach of the Act.

Journalists breathed a huge sigh of relief. Even so, the case established beyond doubt that the Data Protection Act does apply in cases such as this—a finding later confirmed by *Douglas v Hello! Ltd*. If a 'data subject' has not consented, publication must not go ahead unless the editor has reasonable grounds for believing that this would be in the public interest. If there has been a breach of confidence, publication will not be 'lawful' and there would have been a breach of the first data-protection principle. As the Court of Appeal found, by lying about her drug habit Campbell allowed the press to publish the details with impunity.

The Douglases come to town

More than two years after Michael Douglas and Catherine Zeta-Jones had failed to prevent *Hello!* magazine from publishing snatched photographs of their wedding, the couple came to London seeking compensation. In 2000, they had managed to split the Court of Appeal on whether 'the law recognises and will appropriately protect a right of personal privacy', to quote Lord Justice Sedley's now-famous phrase. In 2003, the couple and *OK!* magazine—to whom they had sold exclusive photographic rights—asked the High Court to award them damages, both general and aggravated, for breach of confidentiality, invasion of privacy, breaches of the Data Protection Act 1998 and interference with their respective rights and businesses.

Shortly beforehand, the claimants asked the High Court to strike out a defence lodged by *Hello!* on the ground that the magazine's publishers had made false statements to the Court of Appeal during the earlier hearing and destroyed documents. The Vice-Chancellor, Sir Andrew Morritt, ruled in January 2003 that despite 'conduct attributable to the *Hello!* defendants which leaves a very great deal to be desired with regard to the veracity of their evidence and the adequacy of their disclosure I am not persuaded that a fair trial is no longer possible or that the deficiencies in the conduct of the defence of the *Hello!* defendants justifies an order striking out the whole or any part of it'.

So the trial opened. Mr Justice Lindsay was told that the couple's wedding at the Plaza Hotel had been infiltrated by an undercover photographer. He turned out to be someone who knew more than most about invasions of privacy. Rupert Thorpe, 33, was the son of the former Liberal leader, Jeremy Thorpe. The photographer's mother, Caroline, had died in a car crash when her son was a toddler. When Rupert was 10, his father stood trial at the Old Bailey charged with conspiracy to murder Norman Scott, with whom the MP was alleged to have had a homosexual relationship. Jeremy Thorpe was acquitted, but he never returned to public life and later developed Parkinson's disease. Reckoning that Thorpe was in no position to sue for libel, newspapers and broadcasters began repeating Scott's allegations even though the former MP was still alive. That seems to have prompted Rupert Thorpe's decision to leave Britain in 1997.

His identity was not discovered until shortly before the hearing. When all the authorized pictures were examined, a man in a dinner jacket was spotted holding a small camera cupped in his hands below waist level, tilted in what he presumably hoped was the right direction.

The photographer was later identified as Rupert Thorpe. He is thought to have attended the reception with his then fiancée, Michelle Day, and both stayed at the Plaza Hotel. It was not known whether Thorpe managed to get one of the gold lapel pins that guests were given on arrival in exchange for their admission cards. Though there was no proof that he took the published pictures of the bride, the groom, the wedding dress and the cake, the trial 'proceeded on the tacit assumption that Mr Thorpe was the only paparazzo intruder and that the unauthorised photographs were taken by him', as the judge put it.

The Douglases had signed a £1m contract with *OK!* to supply wedding photographs which would be taken by photographers of their choice and, if they wished, retouched. *Hello!* had wanted to send its own photographers to the ceremony. Two days after the wedding, which had been a great success, the couple were tipped off that *Hello!* planned to publish surreptitiously taken photographs of them. Many were grainy or out of focus. When the pictures appeared, suspicion 'centred on a member of staff or, to the great distress of the Douglases, possibly one of their own friends or family members', according to their counsel, Michael Tugendhat, QC.

Amid great excitement, the couple then gave oral evidence in the Chancery Division. Douglas said it had been 'vindictive' to sneak into the party and the resulting photographs were 'lascivious' and 'voyeuristic'. The couple had ordered tight security for the wedding and 'felt comfortable to let our hair down and enjoy the wedding the way we wanted to enjoy it'. He said he felt like a Peeping Tom had been present. 'There are moments in my home or when I hire a room for my wedding when I have a total right to privacy.' The sneak photographer had been guilty of 'one of the most vindictive and mean-spirited acts you can imagine'.

Zeta-Jones told Mr Justice Lindsay that she had felt 'violated' and 'devastated' when she found out less than forty-eight hours after her wedding that the reception had been infiltrated by undercover photographers. Her distress increased when she saw Thorpe's photographs. 'The quality was what any bride would hate to have out there. It was cheap and tacky and everything I didn't want to have shown as being part of my special day,' she added, describing the pictures as 'sleazy, unflattering'.

What emerged clearly from the couple's evidence was that the case was more about control than privacy. How could it be otherwise when they had invited 350 guests to their wedding and allowed photographs of the celebrations to be published by twenty-three magazines in twenty-one countries? Their argument was that they had kept control over which pictures would be used and how they were to be retouched. Like Johnny Carson whose claim was discussed in Chapter 1, the Douglases appeared to be claiming a right of publicity—something that does not exist as a stand-alone right in English law. The case was summed up in an exchange between Douglas, and James Price, QC, who was cross-examining him on behalf of *Hello!* Privacy was not primarily in the couple's mind, suggested Price: it was control plus a little commerce. 'Control is what gives you privacy,' the actor replied.

It was not until nearly three years later that Sir Paul McCartney, the former Beatle, showed how it was possible to arrange a truly private celebrity wedding for his daughter, Stella, when she married Alasdhair Willis on the Scottish island of Bute in August 2003. No magazine was offered the rights.

OK! OK

Mr Justice Lindsay delivered a long and careful ruling in April 2003, finding for Douglas, Zeta-Jones and the publishers of *OK!* His conclusion could not have been clearer: 'I hold the *Hello!* defendants to be liable to all three claimants under the law as to confidence,' he said. The level of compensation would be decided at a later hearing if not agreed—though, as the Court of Appeal had said two years earlier, the damages were 'likely to be enormous'. The judge also found in the claimants' favour under the data-protection laws and held that they were entitled to an injunction preventing further publication of the unauthorized pictures. Mr Justice Lindsay's ruling appears in the law reports as *Douglas v Hello! Ltd (No 6)*.

While Lord Justice Sedley's famous remarks, quoted at the beginning of this chapter, provided 'a powerful case for the existence, already, of a law of privacy,' said Mr Justice Lindsay, 'that another view is tenable can be seen from the judgments in *Wainwright v Home Secretary*'. That, you will remember, was the case brought by the woman who was strip-searched for drugs when she went to visit her son in prison—the case in which Lord Justice Buxton explained that there would be serious difficulties in creating a law of privacy and in which Lord Justice Mummery said it would give rise to as many problems as it sought to solve. That was in the Court of Appeal: the House of Lords had not yet ruled.

Mr Justice Lindsay's second reason for declining to create a privacy law was entirely pragmatic. Lord Justice Sedley's case for a general tort depended on the existing law being inadequate to protect the right to private and family life under the Human Rights Convention. But that was not the case here. 'As I have already held Mr and Mrs Douglas to have been protected by the law of confidence, no relevant hole exists in English law such as, on the facts of the case before me, a due respect for the convention requires should be filled.'

The judge's third reason was equally shrewd, and is worth quoting in full:

So broad is the subject of privacy and such are the ramifications of any free-standing law in the area that the subject is better left to Parliament which can, of course, consult interests far more widely than can be taken into account in the course of ordinary *inter partes* litigation. A judge should therefore be chary of doing that which is better done by Parliament. That Parliament has failed so far to grasp the nettle does not prove that it will not have to be grasped in the future. The recent judgment in *Peck v UK*, in the European Court of Human Rights, shows that in circumstances where the law of confidence did not operate our domestic law has already been held to be inadequate. That inadequacy will have to be made good and if Parliament does not step in then the courts will be obliged to.

Peck was the would-be suicide whose privacy was invaded when he was recorded, holding a knife, on CCTV; the case was mentioned briefly in Chapter 1 and is discussed more fully in Chapter 4. The judge continued:

Further development by the courts may merely be awaiting the first post-Human Rights Act case where neither the law of confidence nor any other domestic law protects an individual who deserves protection. A glance at a crystal ball of, so to speak, only a low wattage suggests that, if Parliament does not act soon, the less satisfactory course—of the courts creating the law bit by bit at the expense of litigants and with inevitable delays and uncertainty—will be thrust upon the judiciary. But that will only happen when a case arises in which the existing law of confidence gives no or inadequate protection; this case now before me is not such a case and there is therefore no need for me to attempt to construct a law of privacy and, that being so, it would be wrong of me to attempt to do so.

Moving to his next reason for declining to create a law of privacy, Mr Justice Lindsay quoted the sixth guideline given by Lord Woolf in *A v B plc* (discussed above): instead of trying to decide whether there was a law of privacy, trial judges should use the existing law of confidence. His fifth and final point was that even if there had already been a law of privacy it was not suggested that the Douglases would have received any more in damages.

The couple also won their claim under the Data Protection Act 1998. Unlike the Naomi Campbell case, in which a public-interest exemption was allowed by the Court of Appeal, there was no evidence on which the judge could apply section 32 of the Act: as he explained, 'that the public would be interested is not to be confused with there being a public interest.' However, since it would not have been fair for the Douglases to have received higher overall damages simply because a second law had been breached by the same wrongdoing, the judge awarded them only a 'nominal' sum under this heading.

Douglas and Zeta-Jones were also entitled to a perpetual injunction to prevent any further publication of the unauthorized photographs. Even though the pictures had already been published, their confidentiality had not been irretrievably lost.

The nine subsidiary arguments on which the Douglases were defeated are of little significance. The judge found there was no attempt by *Hello!* to injure the claimants by publishing the pictures of them in breach of their duty of confidence or under the Data Protection Act. *Hello!* had not achieved the lifting of the original injunction against it by deploying a false case in the Court of Appeal. There was no conspiracy by some of the individual defendants or by the publishers to injure the claimants by unlawful means. There was no evidence that *Hello!* had avoided disclosure of documents. The Marquesa de Varela, *Hello!*'s celebrity fixer, was not liable personally in damages. A higher award of exemplary damages would not be appropriate when neither magazine was 'wholly without blemish'. Nor had the *Hello!* defendants' behaviour been so 'flagrant or offensive as to justify an award of aggravated damages': newspaper headlines such as 'Catherine Eater Jones'—showing the bride eating her wedding cake—'conduce more to a groan than to offence'.

Despite this crushingly expensive defeat, *Hello!*'s much-parodied soft-focus view of the world allowed it to maintain in a press release that it was 'enormously pleased'. It dismissed the issues on which the judge had found against it as 'frankly, commercial ones'—which was legally correct in the sense that the judge treated the claim as one of commercial confidence. Sally Cartwright, *Hello!*'s publishing director, explained that the contract between the Douglases and *OK!* was 'similar to a trade secret', adding that this was 'completely new in English law'. In fact, most confidence cases that had come before the courts until fairly recently dealt with commercial matters such as business information. Not only did *Coco v Clark*, the leading case we considered in Chapter 1, involve an industrial design, but Mr Justice Lindsay went on to cite a 'trade secret' case from as far back as 1894.

In its attempt to put a brave face on the result, *Hello!* was loyally supported by its solicitors, the firm of Charles Russell, which issued a press release pointing out that nine out of the thirteen claims brought by *OK!* had been dismissed. Though this was also true, depending on how one counted the individual claims, it was irrelevant to the question of damages—a good test of which side has come out on top. Charles Russell acknowledged as much by saying that *Hello!* was considering an appeal. But that did not prevent two leading newspapers from swallowing the *Hello!* line and reporting that the magazine had won. The *Evening Standard* headline read: 'ZETA-JONES LOSES HER CLAIM FOR PRIVACY'.

That was accurate only in the narrow sense that Mr Justice Lindsay declined to hold that there was an existing law of privacy under which Douglas and Zeta-Jones could claim compensation. His ruling on that point—for which he gave five reasons—will come as little surprise to readers of this book: as a trial judge, sitting 'at first instance', he could hardly have decided otherwise.

The owners of *OK!*, Express Newspapers, even complained to the PCC about coverage in the *Standard*, published by its rivals at Associated Newspapers. *OK!* argued that the coverage had been inaccurate because the magazine had won its confidentiality complaint against *Hello!* and the court had not ruled on breach-of-privacy claims. The Commission refused to adjudicate, explaining that it never entertained complaints by one newspaper group against another; to do otherwise, it believed, would put it in an invidious position.

NY Confidential

How, then, did Mr Justice Lindsay justify his finding that what he called the '*Hello!* defendants'—*Hello!* Ltd, its parent company Hola SA and the magazine's editor-in-chief Eduardo Sanchez Junco—were liable to pay unspecified damages to Douglas, Zeta-Jones and *OK!* for breach of confidence?

He stressed at the outset that the case had not initially been about money. The claimants had originally sought and obtained an injunction to restrain publication of the unauthorized photographs and it was the Court of Appeal that had lifted the order and told them that they would have to be satisfied with damages if they won. As we saw at the beginning of this chapter, the 'balance of convenience' favoured *Hello!*

It was clear from the facts as outlined by the judge that since *Hello!* and *OK!* were 'keen rivals in the same market', it clearly helped to get in first: *OK!* had made its £1m offer for the photographic rights to the couple's wedding (and, somewhat optimistically, their honeymoon) not just before Douglas and Zeta-Jones had decided to marry but even before she had become pregnant with his child. The rival offer from *Hello!* came some months later. It was, eventually, higher—£1.5m—but unsuccessful, partly because of the personalities involved. *Hello!* then started discussions through intermediaries with Phil Ramey, the paparazzo who might be able to obtain snatched shots of the wedding—although there was insufficient evidence to show that it had actually commissioned the unauthorized pictures.

The couple said they thought that selling the rights to a single publication was the best way to control the media and protect their privacy. Somewhat naively, perhaps, their publicist believed that 'if other publications knew that one magazine was going to have an exclusive story with beautiful photographs and access to Michael and Catherine they would think there was no point in publishing poor-quality photographs with no quotes from the bride and groom or the family'.

Though it was put to the Douglases in cross-examination that they were more interested in money than privacy, the judge held that 'the notion of an exclusive contract as a means of reducing the risk of intrusion by unauthorised members of the media and hence of preserving the privacy of a celebrity occasion is a notion that can reasonably be believed in as a potentially workable strategy to achieve such ends and was honestly believed in by Miss Zeta-Jones, Mr Douglas and their advisers'. He continued: 'Whilst I would not hold the £1m on offer to be other than a real blandishment even to a couple as rich as Mr Douglas and Miss Zeta-Jones, I see their expectation that an exclusive contract to one selected publisher offered the best strategy for obtaining a wedding of the kind they both wanted and offered also the certainty of fair coverage of it as their chief reasons for making such a contract.'

Holding, on the evidence, that it was a 'private wedding' rather than a celebrity event, the judge said that Eduardo Sanchez Junco, *Hello!*'s editor-in-chief, must have known, as he selected the unauthorized photographs for publication, that taking them must have involved some deceit or misrepresentation on the part of the photographer.

Word reached *OK!* a day after the wedding that unauthorized pictures were circulating and the magazine contacted the Douglases through a member of their staff. The newlyweds had already heard. 'It was an appalling and very upsetting shock to discover that our wedding had been invaded in that way,' said Zeta-Jones in evidence. 'Our peace and happiness evaporated. I felt violated and that something precious had been stolen from me. Our distress and anger at what *Hello!* did to us continues to this day.' Her husband confirmed that the couple were 'devastated and shocked' by the news. 'We felt as if our home had been ransacked and everything taken out of it and spread in the street. It was a truly gut-wrenching and very disturbing experience which left both of us deeply upset.'

Mr Justice Lindsay accepted their evidence at face value. 'It is easy to regard such language as exaggerated but it has to be remembered that the Douglases were speaking of a time when their joy at how success-ful their wedding plans had proved to be was at its height. They crashed down from a relatively euphoric height,' he said. 'I have no doubt but that Mr Douglas and Miss Zeta-Jones both suffered real distress, though it is no present task of mine to attempt to put some compensatory cash value upon it. An aspect of their distress, which led Miss Zeta-Jones to tears, was their wondering, if it was a guest, which of their guests it was that had betrayed them.'

After referring to many of the cases on confidence that have already been mentioned in this book, Mr Justice Lindsay set out his own under-standing of the law as it stood in April 2003. The following is my summary of that assessment:

(1) Breach of confidence is an established cause of action but its scope now needs to be evaluated in the light of the Human Rights Act. That can be achieved by regarding the rights conferred by Articles 8 and 10 of the European Convention as absorbed into the action for breach of confidence and as thereby to some extent giving it new strength and breadth. The Human Rights Convention thus comes into play even in private-law cases (as well as actions against the state). It will be necessary for the courts to identify, on a case-by-case basis, the principles by which the law of confidentiality must accommodate Articles 8 and 10. The weaker the claim for privacy, the more likely it will be outweighed by a claim based on freedom of expression. A balance between the conflicting interests has to be struck.

(2) The right to freedom of expression in Article 10(1) of the Convention is subject not only to the Article 8 right for respect to private and family life but also to rights of confidence. In consequence, privacy rights under Article 8 may not, as such, be required to be considered in a particular case but nonetheless there can be an internal conflict within Article 10 between the rights in Article 10(1) and the exceptions in Article 10(2).

(3) Even a public figure is entitled to a private life although he or she may expect and accept that his or her circumstances will be more carefully scrutinized by the media. But the fact that an individual has achieved prominence on the public stage does not mean his private life can be laid bare by the media.

(4) If public attention has been courted by a claimant then that may lead that claimant to have less ground upon which to object to intrusion.

(5) Freedom of expression on the media's part, as a counter-force to, for example, privacy is not invariably the ace of trumps but it is a powerful card to which the court must always pay appropriate respect. Put another way, there is no 'presumptive priority' given to such freedom of expression when it is in conflict with another Convention right. Nor is there any such presumptive priority where the conflict is with rights under the law of confidence; it would be pointless of Article 10(2) to make freedom of expression subject to such rights if it invariably overrode them.

(6) Where the court is considering whether to grant any relief that might affect the exercise of the right to freedom of expression then, if the proceedings relate to journalistic material, the court must have particular regard to any relevant privacy code.

(7) The PCC has such a code, with provisions on privacy. It says: 'The use of long lens photography to take pictures of people in private places without their consent is unacceptable.' Under the heading 'Misrepresentation' it adds: 'Journalists must not generally obtain or seek to obtain information or pictures through misrepresentation or subterfuge . . . Subterfuge can be justified only in the public interest and only when material cannot be obtained by any other means.' The Code provides that there may be exceptions to these provisions where they can be demonstrated to be in the public interest. *Hello!* had not claimed any material public interest in publication of the unauthorized pictures. In the absence of any public interest, the court is especially bound to pay particular regard to the Code; and a newspaper that flouts the Code may have its claim to freedom of expression trumped by Article 10(2) considerations of privacy.

(8) The fact that someone else is about to publish is not to be taken as necessarily justifying publication by the defendant. On the contrary, that may make it harder for the unauthorized publisher to justify his breach.

(9) If there is an intrusion in a situation in which a person can reasonably expect his privacy to be respected then that will be capable of giving rise to liability in an action for breach of confidence unless it can be justified.

(10) It is still the case that a duty of confidence arises whenever the party subject to the duty is in a situation where he either knows or ought to know that the other person can reasonably expect his privacy to be protected.

(11) The existence of a relationship that may create a duty of confidence may, and in personal confidence cases commonly will, have to be inferred from the facts.

(12) The fact that the information at issue is obtained by unlawful activity does not mean that its publication will necessarily be restrained but it may be a compelling factor when the court's discretion comes to be exercised.

(13) Unauthorized photographs can be regarded as 'information' for the purposes of the law of confidence. In this case, they conveyed information about what the wedding and the happy couple looked like.

(14) It is a familiar course for Chancery judges to grant injunctions to restrain the publication of photographs taken surreptitiously on private occasions.

(15) It is well settled that the law of equity may intervene to prevent a publication of photographic images taken in breach of confidence. If, on some private occasion, the prospective claimant makes it clear, expressly or impliedly, that no photographic images are to be taken of him, then all those present will be bound by the obligation of confidence created by their knowledge (or imputed knowledge) of that restriction.

These principles relate mainly to cases of personal or individual confidence. Turning specifically to commercial confidence, the judges added that a trade secret could be shared with others and still retain its confidentiality. He cited a case from 1894 in which someone involved in the production of W S Gilbert's new comic opera *His Excellency* had leaked the plot to a newspaper before it had opened; an injunction was granted by Mr Justice Chitty in favour of Gilbert and the theatre manager. The opera (it can now be revealed) involves the Governor of Elsinore, a notorious practical joker, and the Prince Regent of Denmark, who appears disguised as a vagabond; the music by Frank Osmond Carr was not particularly popular and the opera had a relatively short run.

Possums

Though citing nineteenth-century cases fits the popular stereotype of the Chancery judge—especially one who preferred *innuendi* as the plural of *innuendo*; who quarantined the North American import *tuxedo* in quotation marks and who still used the archaic spellings of *shewn* and *shewing*—Mr Justice Lindsay did not display the leisurely approach demonstrated by Sir Jeremiah Harman, the senior Chancery Division judge who resigned in 1998 after the Court of Appeal criticized him for taking twenty months to deliver a reserved judgment.

He proved to be astute and up-to-date, referring in his ruling to a twenty-first century judgment from the High Court of Australia that had already received much attention in the English courts. It had been brought against the Australian Broadcasting Corporation by Lenah Game Meats, a company that killed, processed and sold game. Animal-liberation campaigners had installed hidden cameras in the meat producer's abattoir and filmed the way in which Tasmanian brush-tail possums were slaughtered. The film was passed to the ABC, which wanted to televise it. Lenah argued unsuccessfully that this would be a breach of its privacy. Explaining the difficulties in constructing a law of privacy, Chief Justice Gleeson said:

There is no bright line which can be drawn between what is private and what is not. Use of the term 'public' is often a convenient method of contrast, but there is a large area in between what is necessarily public and what is necessarily private. An activity is not private simply because it is not done in public. It does not suffice to make an act private that, because it occurs on private property, it has such measure of protection from the public gaze as the characteristics of the property, the nature of the activity, the locality, and the disposition of the property owner combine to afford. Certain kinds of information about a person, such as information relating to health, personal relationships or finances, may be easy to identify as private; as may certain kinds of activity, which a reasonable person, applying contemporary standards of morals and behaviour, would understand to be meant to be unobserved. The requirement that disclosure or observation of information or conduct would be highly offensive to a reasonable person of ordinary sensibility is in many circumstances a useful practical test of what is private.

That was not the definition of what was confidential under English law, Mr Justice Lindsay pointed out, adding for completeness that, although he would not have held the unauthorized wedding photographs to have been offensive at all, 'that their taking and their publication, in all the surrounding circumstances, was likely to offend the Douglases'.

The judge then applied Mr Justice Megarry's three-part test for breach of confidence, set out in *Coco v Clark* and discussed in Chapter 1. First, he regarded 'photographic representation of the wedding reception as having had the *quality* of confidence about it'. Of course, the couple's appearance was well known to the public. 'But that does not deny the quality of commercial confidentiality to what they looked like on the exceptional occasion of their wedding.' The very fact that the two magazines were ready to pay so much for exclusive access pointed to the commercial confidentiality of the event.

Next, there was an *obligation* of confidence. The judge seemed untroubled by Lord Justice Sedley's earlier concern that the photographer might turn out to have been 'an intruder with whom no relationship of trust had been established':

As for the *Hello!* defendants, their consciences were, in my view, tainted; they were not acting in good faith nor by way of fair dealing. Whilst their position might have been worse had I held that the taking of unauthorised pictures for use by them had been truly commissioned in advance, even without that there is in my view enough to afflict their conscience. They knew that *OK!* had an exclusive contract; as persons long engaged in the relevant trade, they knew what sort of provisions any such contract would include and that it would include provisions intended to preclude intrusion and unauthorised photography. Particularly would that be so where, as they knew, a very considerable sum would have had to have been paid for the exclusive rights which had been obtained. As to their knowledge of steps taken to protect the secrecy of the event, their own written text in their Issue 639 spoke of 'elaborate security procedures'. The surrounding facts were such that a duty of confidence should be inferred from them. The *Hello!* defendants had indicated to paparazzi in advance that they would pay well for photographs and they knew the reputation of the paparazzi for being able to intrude. The unauthorised pictures themselves plainly indicated they were taken surreptitiously. Yet these defendants firmly kept their eyes shut lest they might see what they undeniably knew would have become apparent to them. Breach of confidence apart, had the *Hello!* defendants opened their eyes they would have seen that the taking of the photographs which they bought had involved at least a trespass. The fact, as I have held it to be, that they did not in advance and in terms require or authorise on their behalf trespass and surreptitious photography by Thorpe or by any other paparazzo does not disprove the unconscionability, as I hold it to be, under English law, of their publication of the unauthorised photographs in England and Wales.

The third requirement for a confidence claim is an unauthorized use to the *detriment* of the claimant: that too had been made out. The Douglases had been forced to rearrange their plans for approving the authorized photographs and *OK!* might have sold fewer copies of their magazine than would otherwise have been the case.

It was at this point that the judge was required to strike a balance between confidentiality and freedom of expression. He turned to the PCC Code of Practice, with its insistence that 'the use of long-lens photography to take pictures of people in private places without their consent is unacceptable'. Clearly, Thorpe had not used a telephoto. But that made no difference to the judge: 'long' could mean 'short'. 'The very same principle in the code that provides that the use of long lenses to take pictures of people in private places without their consent was unacceptable must, as I read it, inescapably also make the surreptitious use of short lenses to take pictures of people in private places without their consent at least equally unacceptable,' he said. And given that Thorpe had dressed as if he was a guest at the wedding, the unauthorized pictures had also been obtained by misrepresentation and subterfuge, another breach of the Code in the absence of any public-interest defence.

Hello! put up a number of arguments, all of which were dismissed. Of these, perhaps the most interesting was the claim that what the Douglases had been seeking was neither privacy nor confidentiality but control. No problem, said the judge: 'control is not an improper objective of the law of confidence'.

Finally, the judge found 'the *Hello!* defendants to have acted unconscionably and that, by reason of breach of confidence, they are liable to all three claimants to the extent of the detriment which was thereby caused'.

For these reasons, he concluded, the *Hello!* defendants were liable to Douglas, Zeta-Jones and *OK!* under the law of confidence. 'It will have been noted,' the judge added, 'that an important step in my coming to that conclusion has been that, on balancing rights to confidence against freedom of expression for the purpose of granting or withholding relief, I have been required by statute to pay, and have paid, regard to the code of the Press Complaints Commission. The *Hello!* defendants broke their own industry's code.'

In a statement, the couple said: 'We deeply appreciate that the court has recognized the principle that every individual has the right to be protected from excessive and unwanted media intrusion into their private lives.'

Confidence after *Douglas*

Mr Justice Lindsay demonstrated that the nineteenth-century, judge-made, law of confidence was in good heart, well able to manage anything that a newly minted statutory tort of privacy could do. His use of the PCC's Code to indicate a breach of confidence was also a salutary warning to those journalists who saw it as no more than a vague set of aspirations. The practice of 'spoiling' exclusives is one that now carries a clear commercial risk and *Hello!* must have wondered whether its real problem had been its success in having the injunction against it lifted in December 2000.

The judge did not decide immediately how much compensation the Douglases and *OK!* should receive: a further hearing proved necessary. This lasted for an extraordinary twelve days and judgment was delivered in November 2003. Despite the Court of Appeal's optimistic prediction, Mr Justice Lindsay found it far from easy to work out the magazine's loss of revenue. After detailed calculations, he ordered *Hello!* to pay *OK!* £1,033,156.

In addition, Michael Douglas and Catherine Zeta-Jones had claimed compensation for their distress in seeing unauthorized wedding pictures published in *Hello!*, although the magazine was not considered responsible for the relatively marginal additional upset the couple must have suffered when they heard there had been an intruder present. Following precedent as best he could, the judge decided to award the couple compensation of £3,750 each for this distress, plus £7,000 for the inconvenience of having to choose the approved pictures for publication in *OK!* earlier than intended. In addition, they received a nominal award of £50 each under the Data Protection Act. Their total award of £14,600 was a fraction of the £600,000 they had apparently been seeking. Even so, the Douglases put a brave face on it, saying they had taken the legal action as a matter of principle and were delighted that Mr Justice Lindsay's ruling had vindicated their position and that of *OK!*

So *Hello!* was left facing an overall damages bill of £1,047,756, which the judge thought was in line with Lord Justice Brooke's prediction that it would have to pay 'very substantial sums of money'. The magazine's publishers said they would appeal. Damages of just over £1m were not large enough to 'stifle free expression', Mr Justice Lindsay thought, while still being 'such as may make *Hello!* alive to the unwisdom of its acting as it did'. Sally Cartwright, the magazine's publishing director, said the damages bill, plus any future court costs, would not threaten its future. The media, she thought, should be alarmed at the heavy financial consequences to *Hello!* of having run a 'spoiler'.

Putting it in a subtly different way, Martin Kramer, the solicitor for *OK!*, said the record damages 'should serve as a warning to the media that it cannot spoil opponents' exclusives with impunity and that it must adhere to its own code of practice as regards rights of privacy and intrusive conduct'. He also regarded it as 'a landmark decision' establishing that people in the public eye have the right to a private life.

That may have been so, but the damages awarded to the Douglases personally will not act as much of a disincentive to newspapers that may be tempted to invade people's privacy in the future. Unless they are causing commercial damage by spoiling a rival's exclusive, it seems they will not have much to lose.

Zeta-Jones seemed to have developed a taste for litigation, if not for low-carbohydrate diets. On the very day that she was awarded damages in London, her Los Angeles attorney, John H Lavely, Jr, was writing to the Courtroom Television Network in New York, a company that specializes in broadcasting court hearings. Despite its aggressive tone, his letter appeared to be a circular sent to a number of media organizations. It was marked 'confidential legal notice, not for publication or other use'—which was probably why it appeared on the Internet within a couple of days.

'It has come to Ms Zeta-Jones's attention,' Lavely said, 'that her valuable name, likeness and persona have been improperly linked by the media to the world-renowned Atkins diet, and certain publications have falsely stated that my client has used and/or endorsed the Atkins diet.' She had never used it or endorsed it, he explained. It had been derided for decades. 'Given the negative reports regarding the Atkins diet,' he continued, 'whether they are true or not, any such false media report would cause significant damage to my client's reputation and undoubtedly would adversely affect her ability to attract endorsement deals, particularly with regard to health-related products.'

Everyone responsible for disseminating or republishing these 'false and damaging stories' would be sued, Lavely promised. He then pleaded with the media to contact him if they knew who was circulating them, before ending with a pithy threat that could usefully be lifted by any lawyer writing a letter before action: 'Govern yourself accordingly and proceed at your peril'.

Although Zeta-Jones's attorney did not explain further, he must have been referring to the American right of publicity referred to in *Carson v Here's Johnny Portable Toilets Inc* and identified in Dean Prosser's four categories of US privacy torts. Lavely himself specializes in right-of-publicity and privacy law. His firm, Lavely & Singer, which describes itself modestly as 'one of the world's premiere [*sic*] talent-side entertainment litigation firms', represents 'clients against the tabloids and other media and internet outlets in disputes which arise prior to, as well as after, the publication of articles which defame the clients or invade their privacy', adding: 'we also police the manner in which the names and likenesses of our clients are commercially exploited throughout the world.' As we saw in Chapter 1, the nearest we come to that in English law is passing off. But that would not have applied here: neither Atkins nor Zeta-Jones had claimed that they had been endorsed by the other. Nor can it yet be defamatory to say that somebody has been on the Atkins diet. Fortunately, it is hard to see how Zeta-Jones could have threatened the British media in quite the same way.

CHAPTER 3

Free Speech

Freedom of expression is one of the essential foundations of a democratic society. That was said by the European Court of Human Rights as long ago as 1976; although the judges who put their name to this resounding principle went on to find that limitations on free speech were justified in the particular case they were hearing. Their message, though, was perfectly clear: although free speech can never be an absolute right, any restrictions must be as limited as possible.

A handy side to take

The case in which the Strasbourg judges saluted free speech without actually upholding it was brought against the British Government by a publisher named Richard Handyside. After making his reputation with editions of Che Guevara, Fidel Castro and a work by the Women's Liberation Movement, he acquired the English rights to a handbook aimed at children aged twelve and upwards. Its title, redolent of Chairman Mao, was *The Little Red Schoolbook* and, tellingly, it was to appear on 1 April 1971.

In the idiom of the age, it carried an introduction headed 'All grown-ups are paper tigers' along with a number of passages on sex and drugs (if not rock and roll). This was a typical extract:

Maybe you smoke pot or go to bed with your boyfriend or girlfriend—and don't tell your parents or teachers, either because you don't dare to or just because you want to keep it secret. Don't feel ashamed or guilty about doing things you really want to do and think are right just because your parents or teachers might disapprove. A lot of these things will be more important to you later in life than the things that are 'approved of'.

Handyside sent out review copies to newspapers, which responded with predictable outrage; indeed, their reaction would have been much the same today. What differed though was how the authorities reacted. Prompted by the protests, the Director of Public Prosecutions, Sir Norman Skelhorn, decided to call in the police. They raided the publisher's office and seized around 1,000 copies of the book (though they missed another 19,000 copies which were later sold). Handyside was convicted under the Obscene Publications Acts and fined £50 with costs of £110 (substantial sums, given that the book sold for 30p). An appeal was dismissed (this time the publisher was ordered to pay costs of £854) and the books were destroyed. Handyside then brought out a bowdlerized version without further complaint.

What had upset the courts so much? There was a certain amount of practical advice, ranging from crude to shrewd: 'When a boy puts his stiff prick into a girl's vagina and moves it around, it is called intercourse, or making love, or sleeping together (even if they don't sleep at all).' But what the court found objectionable in the paragraph quoted above was that there was no reference—at that point in the book—to the illegality of smoking pot. Similarly, there was no specific mention at all in the book that it was illegal for a boy aged fourteen or over to have sexual intercourse with a girl under sixteen. This, and much else, 'had a tendency to deprave and corrupt'.

Freedom of expression

In Strasbourg, Handyside's appeal turned on Article 10 of the European Convention on Human Rights. Like the rest of the Convention, this provision is drafted in resoundingly clear prose. 'Everyone has the right to freedom of expression,' booms Article 10(1). 'This right shall include freedom to hold opinions and to receive and impart information and ideas without interference by public authority and regardless of frontiers,' it adds generously. Then come the caveats.

Plummeting from principle to bathos, the draftsman begins with a specific exception: 'This Article shall not prevent States from requiring the licensing of broadcasting, television or cinema enterprises.' Nothing wrong with that, we imagine, until we find ourselves swamped with a host of generic get-out clauses in Article 10(2):

The exercise of these freedoms, since it carries with it duties and responsibilities, may be subject to such formalities, conditions, restrictions or penalties as
are prescribed by law and are necessary in a democratic society, in the interests of national security, territorial integrity or public safety, for the prevention of disorder or crime, for the protection of health or morals, for the
protection of the reputation or rights of others, for preventing the disclosure
of information received in confidence, or for maintaining the authority and
impartiality of the judiciary.

In the *Handyside* case, the British Government was represented by
Gordon Slynn, QC (later Lord Slynn, who retired as a law lord in 2002)
and Nicolas Bratza (who became a judge at Strasbourg in 1998). They
persuaded the Court, on instructions, that burning books was necessary
to protect morals. As liberal-minded individuals, though, they must
have been pleased to see this classic and far-sighted paean to free speech
in the judges' ruling:

The court's supervisory functions oblige it to pay the utmost attention to the
principles characterising a 'democratic society'. Freedom of expression constitutes one of the essential foundations of such a society, one of the basic conditions for its progress and for the development of every man. Subject to
paragraph 2 of Article 10, it is applicable not only to 'information' or 'ideas'
that are favourably received or regarded as inoffensive or as a matter of indifference, but also to those that offend, shock or disturb the state or any sector
of the population. Such are the demands of that pluralism, tolerance and
broadmindedness without which there is no 'democratic society'. This means,
amongst other things, that every 'formality', 'condition', 'restriction' or
'penalty' imposed in this sphere must be proportionate to the legitimate aim
pursued.

While accepting that *The Little Red Schoolbook* contained 'factual information that was generally correct and often useful', the Strasbourg
judges said it also included material 'that young people at a critical stage
of their development could have interpreted as an encouragement to
indulge in precocious activities harmful for them or even to commit
certain criminal offences'. In these circumstances, said the Human
Rights Court, the competent English judges were entitled to think that
the book would have 'pernicious effects on the morals of many of the
children and adolescents who would read it'.

Too many exceptions?

As we saw earlier, Article 10(2) is full of exceptions to freedom of expression. Article 8, with its protection for people's private lives, amounts to a further restriction on freedom of expression—as we shall discover in the next chapter. What, then, is left of free speech?

According to the European Court of Human Rights, the answer is a great deal. If we imagine the individual words of Article 10 as a series of barges or pontoons floating lazily down the Rhine, we can only marvel at the way in which the Strasbourg judges have pulled them into the tributary that flows past their court, tied them firmly to the bank and then constructed a rigid superstructure of case law on their unpromising foundations. This structure is now well advanced, though building work still continues and there are occasional modifications.

Before ruling on an individual claim, the Human Rights judges invariably sum up the case law as it currently stands. These summaries are drafted by officials (unlike the judges' dissenting opinions) and therefore follow a standard format. The following assessment of Article 10 is taken verbatim from a case decided in 1997. Although the floor plan is still much as we remember it from *Handyside* in 1975, the building has now grown two stories higher.

(1) Freedom of expression constitutes one of the essential foundations of a democratic society and one of the basic conditions for its progress and for each individual's self-fulfilment. Subject to Article 10(2), it is applicable not only to 'information' or 'ideas' that are favourably received or regarded as inoffensive or as a matter of indifference, but also to those that offend, shock or disturb. Such are the demands of that pluralism, tolerance and broadmindedness without which there is no 'democratic society'. As set out in Article 10, this freedom is subject to exceptions, which must, however, be construed strictly, and the need for any restrictions must be established convincingly.

(2) The adjective 'necessary' in Article 10(2) implies the existence of a 'pressing social need'. States have a certain margin of appreciation [or latitude] in assessing whether such a need exists, but it goes hand in hand with European supervision, embracing both the legislation and the decisions applying it, even those given by

an independent court. The court is therefore empowered to give the final ruling on whether a 'restriction' is reconcilable with freedom of expression as protected by Article 10.

(3) In exercising its supervisory jurisdiction, the court must look at the impugned interference in the light of the case as a whole, including the content of the remarks held against the applicant and the context in which he made them. In particular, it must determine whether the interference in issue was 'proportionate to the legitimate aims pursued' and whether the reasons adduced by the national authorities to justify it are 'relevant and sufficient'. In doing so, the court has to satisfy itself that the national authorities applied standards which were in conformity with the principles embodied in Article 10 and, moreover, that they based themselves on an acceptable assessment of the relevant facts.

Expressions of the Court

That summary of the law comes from a case brought against Turkey by a Kurdish separatist and local mayor, Mehdi Zana. He had been convicted by a military court of supporting the activities of the PKK, described by the Court as an armed organization whose aim was to break up Turkey's national territory. While in a military prison, Zana had told a newspaper reporter: 'I support the PKK national liberation movement; on the other hand, I am not in favour of massacres. Anyone can make mistakes, and the PKK kill women and children by mistake . . .'

Had the additional penalty he received for making those comments amounted to a violation of his right to free speech? No, said twelve of the twenty members of the European Court who heard the case (including the British judge Sir John Freeland, a former Foreign Office legal adviser who had been appointed to what was then the traditional retirement job). Zana's comments had coincided with murderous attacks carried out by the PKK on civilians in south-east Turkey. Support for the PKK by a former mayor in a major national newspaper had had to be regarded as likely to exacerbate an already explosive situation in that region. Since the penalty imposed on him could reasonably have been regarded as answering a pressing social need, the interference with his freedom of speech was proportionate to legitimate aims pursued. It was a depressingly cautious judgment—if not downright political.

The Court delivered an equally disappointing majority judgment two years later. Józef Janowski, a Polish journalist, was walking through a square in his local town of Zduńska Wola when he noticed two municipal guards ordering street vendors to move their makeshift stands to a nearby marketplace. The guards claimed that selling was not authorized in that square although, as Janowski correctly pointed out, the local authority had not imposed any ban. This he made clear to the guards in no uncertain terms, calling them 'oafs' and 'dumb' (*ćwoki* and *głupki*). For this, he was convicted of insulting the guards in the course of their duties.

No problem at all, said seven of the twelve European judges who ruled on the case in January 1999. 'Civil servants must enjoy public confidence in conditions free of undue perturbation if they are to be successful in performing their tasks and it may therefore prove necessary to protect them from offensive and abusive verbal attacks when on duty . . . It is true that the applicant resorted to abusive language out of genuine concern for the well-being of fellow citizens in the course of a heated discussion. This language was directed at law-enforcement officers who were trained how to respond to it. However, he insulted the guards in a public place, in front of a group of bystanders, while they were carrying out their duties. The actions of the guards, even though they were not based on the explicit regulations of the municipal council but on sanitary and traffic considerations, did not warrant resort to offensive and abusive verbal attacks.'

This time there was fortunately a powerful dissenting judgment from Sir Nicolas Bratza (by now the British judge on the Court after his promotion from the recently abolished Human Rights Commission). The Polish law under which Janowski had been convicted was far too broad, he said. The domestic courts could not examine the circumstances in which insulting words were used, whether there was justification or provocation, or whether the use of the words in any way hindered the guard in the performance of his official duties. 'I am quite unable to accept that the application of this provision in the present case was necessary in a democratic society to achieve any legitimate aim,' he said. 'The use of the Article to prosecute, convict and fine the applicant was in my view neither a response to a pressing social need, nor proportionate to any legitimate aim served.'

A free press

Remember that Article 10 includes the right to receive *and impart* information and ideas. Janowski might have had more success if he had been
writing about the guards in a newspaper rather than 'insulting' them in
the street: on the very same day that he was losing his case, the Court
held that Article 10 protects the rights of journalists to 'divulge information on issues of general interest provided that they are acting in
good faith and on an accurate factual basis and provide reliable and
precise information in accordance with the ethics of journalism'.

That was in a case brought by Roger Fressoz, publisher of the satiri-
cal weekly *Le Canard enchaîné*, and Claude Roire, one of his journalists.
At a time of industrial unrest, their newspaper reported that Jacques
Calvet, chairman of the car manufacturer Peugeot, had received a 45.9
per cent pay rise over a two-year period during which his workers had
received an increase of just 6.7 per cent. The information was based on
stolen tax returns, sent to the paper anonymously.

Fressoz and Roire were charged with handling photocopies of the
chairman's tax returns obtained through a breach of professional confidence by an unidentified tax official. They were acquitted by the trial
court but convicted on appeal. The Human Rights Court had to
consider whether these restrictions on the journalists' freedom of
expression were 'necessary in a democratic society'. In particular, the
judges had to decide whether the reasons put forward by the French
Government for interference with that right were 'relevant and sufficient'.

In the Court's view, they were not. 'The article was published during
an industrial dispute—widely reported in the press—at one of the major
French car manufacturers. Workers were seeking a pay rise which the
management were refusing. The article showed that the company chairman had received large pay increases during the period under consideration while at the same time opposing his employees' claims for a rise.
By making such a comparison against that background, the article
contributed to a public debate on a matter of general interest. It was not
intended to damage Calvet's reputation but to contribute to the more
general debate on a topic that interested the public.'

Although it was a breach of French law to publish copies of tax
returns, the Government admitted that disclosure of the chairman's

income was permitted. In that case, said the Court, the journalists' conviction for merely having published the tax assessments could not be justified under Article 10. 'In essence, that Article leaves it for journalists to decide whether or not it is necessary to reproduce such documents to ensure credibility. It protects journalists' right to divulge information on issues of general interest provided that they are acting in good faith and on an accurate factual basis and provide "reliable and precise" information in accordance with the ethics of journalism.' The journalists had indeed acted in good faith. The French Government was ordered to reimburse them for the damages of one franc (plus the 10,000 francs in costs—about £1,000) that they had been ordered to pay Calvet.

Bust surgeon

A similar approach was taken the following year in a case brought against Norway by *Bergens Tidende*, the largest regional newspaper on the Norwegian west coast. In 1986 it had published interviews with three women about 'calamitous' breast-enhancement operations they had suffered at the hands of a cosmetic surgeon in Bergen. The women, who were required to pay cash for the operations, suffered great pain, scarring and disfigurement.

The surgeon's practice suffered from the adverse publicity: perhaps inevitably, he went bust. Even so, he was cleared of incompetence by the local health authorities and sued the newspaper for defamation. The unnamed surgeon eventually won his claim in Norway's Supreme Court and was awarded nearly £400,000 in compensation and costs, the largest financial penalty ever imposed by a Norwegian court in a defamation case. Although the newspaper accounts had been factually accurate, the Supreme Court held that their 'natural and ordinary' meaning was that the surgeon had performed his activities in a reckless way—which was false.

Bergens Tidende and its staff claimed there had been a breach of Article 10. Again, the Human Rights Court had to decide whether the interference with their freedom of expression was necessary in a democratic society.

It was not, said the 'chamber' of judges assigned to the case, Sir Nicolas Bratza presiding. The Court did not consider that the surgeon's

undoubted interest in protecting his professional reputation 'was sufficient to outweigh the important public interest in the freedom of the
press to impart information on matters of legitimate public concern'. In
the Court's view, 'there was no reasonable relationship of proportionality between the restrictions placed by the measures applied by the
Supreme Court on the applicants' right to freedom of expression and
the legitimate aim pursued'.

Seal of approval

That encouraging judgment echoed another Norwegian case, decided
in May 1999. Pål Stensaas was the editor of the local newspaper in
Tromsø, centre of the Norwegian seal-hunting industry. He published
an interview which was critical of the methods used by seal hunters and
was sued, successfully, for defamation. The newspaper and its editor
claimed that this finding amounted to a breach of Article 10.

After recalling that the test of 'necessity in a democratic society'
required it to decide whether the interference corresponded to a 'pressing social need', the Court said:

One factor of particular importance for the court's determination in the
present case is the essential function the press fulfils in a democratic society.
Although the press must not overstep certain bounds, in particular in respect
of the reputation and rights of others and the need to prevent the disclosure of
confidential information, its duty is nevertheless to impart—in a manner
consistent with its obligations and responsibilities—information and ideas on
all matters of public interest. In addition, the court is mindful of the fact that
journalistic freedom also covers possible recourse to a degree of exaggeration,
or even provocation. In cases such as the present one the national margin of
appreciation is circumscribed by the interest of democratic society in enabling
the press to exercise its vital role of 'public watchdog' in imparting information
of serious public concern.

On the facts of *Bladet Tromsø and Stensaas v Norway*, the judges found for
the journalists. 'The court cannot find that the crew members'
undoubted interest in protecting their reputation was sufficient to
outweigh the vital public interest in ensuring an informed public debate
over a matter of local and national as well as international interest,' they
said. The Government's reasons were 'not sufficient to show that the

interference complained of was necessary in a democratic society'. Despite Norway's margin of appreciation, the Court decided 'that there was no reasonable relationship of proportionality between the restrictions placed on the applicants' right to freedom of expression and the legitimate aim pursued'.

In simple terms, the restrictions on free speech were out of all proportion to the protection of the seal hunters' reputation: the words 'sledgehammer' and 'nut' come immediately to mind. Plain and obvious though this may appear, it is not a concept native to the English common law.

Proportionality, appreciation and respect

Since the Human Rights Act requires English courts to 'take into account' Strasbourg decisions, our judges are now grappling with what is, to them, the novel concept of proportionality. This principle—derived, originally, from nineteenth-century Prussian law and developed subsequently by the Human Rights Court—requires there to be a reasonable relationship between a particular objective to be achieved and the means used to achieve that objective.

As we have seen, the question for the judges is whether an interference with someone's rights is proportionate to the legitimate aims pursued. The question commonly arises when the Court considers whether interference with a qualified right can be justified as being 'necessary in a democratic society'. In Article 10 cases, the Court may also consider whether the reasons given by the national authority were 'relevant and sufficient'. How have the English courts coped with this concept?

Proportionality was mentioned as long ago as 1984 by Lord Diplock in the influential GCHQ case (*Council of the Civil Service Unions v Minister for the Civil Service*). Delivering his classification of judicial review into 'illegality', 'irrationality' and 'procedural impropriety', the distinguished law lord predicted that development on a case-by-case basis might add further grounds: 'I have in mind particularly the possible adoption in the future of the principle of "proportionality" which is recognised in the administrative law of several of our fellow members of the European Economic Community,' he said.

Judicial review is the process by which a claimant can challenge the way in which a public body has exercised its powers and 'irrationality' was Lord Diplock's term for what lawyers still refer to as '*Wednesbury* unreasonableness', after the famous post-war case of *Associated Provincial Picture Houses Ltd v Wednesbury Corporation*. 'It applies to a decision which is so outrageous in its defiance of logic or of accepted moral standards that no sensible person who had applied his mind to the question to be decided could have arrived at it,' Lord Diplock explained.

On the face of it, the burden of establishing that a decision-maker has 'taken leave of his senses' and reached such an unreasonable decision seems difficult to satisfy. As a result, decision-makers were left with a fairly broad area of discretion. Indeed, the *Wednesbury* margin was far too wide to accommodate the demands of the Convention: a decision might not be considered unreasonable and yet still amount to a breach of human rights.

Although proportionality did not become a free-standing ground for judicial review before the Human Rights Act took effect in 2000, the courts often nodded towards its underlying principles. In 1995, Lord Bingham, then Master of the Rolls, gratefully adopted the approach to the issue of irrationality put forward by a leading barrister in the case of *R v Ministry of Defence, ex p Smith, Grady, Beckett and Lustig-Prean* (discussed later in this chapter). David Pannick, QC, for the Government, argued that in judging whether a decision-maker had acted unreasonably, the human-rights context was important. 'The more substantial the interference with human rights, the more the court will require by way of justification before it is satisfied that the decision is reasonable,' he said.

But this modified *Wednesbury* test was not strong enough to satisfy the Human Rights Court. It was clear, the Strasbourg judges said, that 'the threshold at which the High Court and the Court of Appeal could find the Ministry of Defence policy irrational was placed so high that it effectively excluded any consideration by the domestic courts of the question of whether the interference with the applicants' rights answered a pressing social need or was proportionate to the national security and public order aims pursued, principles which lie at the heart of the court's analysis of complaints under Article 8 of the convention'.

Now, however, the English courts must take into account the Strasbourg approach to proportionality when dealing with human

rights. In May 2001, little more than six months after the Human Rights
Act came into effect, Lord Slynn said in the House of Lords that the
time had come to recognize proportionality as part of English administrative law. 'Trying to keep the *Wednesbury* principle and proportionality in separate compartments seems to me to be unnecessary and
confusing,' he explained. However, his comments in the *Alconbury* case
were *obiter* and therefore not binding.

In May 2001, the law lords allowed an appeal by George Daly, a prisoner who claimed that searches of legally privileged correspondence in
his cell, carried out in his absence, violated his rights under Article 8.
The House of Lords recognized the need for these searches to take place
and—on occasion—to take place in the prisoner's absence. But it held
that the policy of routinely excluding all prisoners during these searches
could not be justified. The infringement of the prisoner's rights represented by the policy was greater than the legitimate public objectives
behind it. In short, it went further than necessary.

Lord Steyn said that the proportionality approach required a somewhat greater 'intensity of review' than before:

First, the doctrine of proportionality may require the reviewing court to assess
the balance which the decision maker has struck, not merely whether it is
within the range of rational or reasonable decisions. Secondly, the proportionality test may go further than the traditional grounds of review inasmuch as it
may require attention to be directed to the relative weight accorded to interests and considerations. Thirdly, even the heightened scrutiny test developed in
R v Ministry of Defence, Ex p Smith, Grady, Beckett and Lustig-Prean is not necessarily appropriate to the protection of human rights.

'In applying that doctrine,' added the Master of the Rolls, Lord Phillips,
in 2002, 'the width of the margin of appreciation that must be accorded
to the decision-maker will vary, depending upon the right that is in play
and the facts of the particular case.' However, there are limits to judicial
interference. 'When applying a test of proportionality, the margin of
appreciation or discretion accorded to the decision-maker is all important, for it is only by recognising the margin of discretion that the court
avoids substituting its own decision for that of the decision-maker,' Lord
Phillips explained.

The Master of the Rolls, sitting in the Court of Appeal with Lord
Justice Potter and Lady Justice Arden, was giving judgment in a case

brought by Louis Farrakhan, the American spiritual head of the Nation of Islam movement who had been excluded from Britain since 1986. That ban was maintained on public-order grounds by successive Home Secretaries but challenged by Farrakhan's followers, who wanted to hear him preach in Britain. Their challenge was rejected.

In *Farrakhan*, the Court of Appeal acknowledged that even a foreign national seeking permission to enter the country could claim the right to freedom of expression. As we have seen, though, Article 10(2) allows free speech to be restricted 'for the prevention of disorder'. The judges decided that this exception applied. While accepting that any restriction on free speech had to be proportionate, they allowed the Home Secretary a wide margin of discretion in reaching his conclusion. He had given detailed consideration to his decision, consulting widely, and the judges said he was 'far better placed to reach an informed decision as to the likely consequences of admitting Farrakhan to this country than is the court'.

During the half-century in which *Wednesbury* ruled supreme, the judges had rightly been reluctant to interfere with ministerial discretion unless they felt something had gone badly wrong. If *Farrakhan* is anything to go by, it seems that the judges are taking a similar approach towards the new test of proportionality. Provided that the Home Secretary has gone through the motions, the courts will still be reluctant to interfere.

This, too, must be a disappointing conclusion. Lord Phillips referred several times to Blunkett's 'margin of appreciation'. That doctrine, so named, does not apply in these circumstances. Clayton and Tomlinson, in *The Law of Human Rights*, point out that 'margin of appreciation' is a poor translation of the concept of French administrative law known as '*marge d'appréciation*': a better phrase would be 'margin of judgment'. It was devised to take account of the natural reluctance of an international court to substitute its judgment for that of the domestic authorities, which are seen as better placed to evaluate local needs and conditions. The doctrine has therefore been defined as the line at which international supervision should give way to the state's discretion in enacting or enforcing its laws. It is therefore wrong or, at least, confusing to talk in terms of a decision-maker being allowed a margin of appreciation by a national court. Commentators and judges alike have provided what Clayton and Tomlinson call 'overwhelming support' for the view that

the doctrine of margin of appreciation has no role to play when considering the doctrine of proportionality under the Human Rights Act.

That is not to say that ministers and other public authorities should
be denied the discretion to choose between competing considerations.
However, proportionality requires the courts to go much further than
the test of 'Wednesbury unreasonableness' in assessing the actions of a
decision-maker. The two tests should not be assimilated to the point
where proportionality is as weak a check on the executive as Wednesbury
has sometimes proved to be.

Lord Woolf took up this theme at a speech delivered to judges at the
European Court of Human Rights in January 2003. That court's practice of allowing states a 'margin of appreciation as to how they give
effect to the convention rights' was 'not directly transposable to the
domestic situation', he confirmed, 'because domestic courts do not have
to determine the relationship between an international body and a
national body'. Instead, the British courts had developed a parallel
doctrine; 'the doctrine of deference, or as I prefer to say the doctrine of
respect'. This required the United Kingdom courts to recognize that
there were situations where Parliament and executive were better placed
than the courts to make the difficult choices between competing
considerations.

Our courts, he said, 'should respect an area of judgment "within
which the judiciary defer on democratic grounds to the considered
opinion of the elected body or person whose actual decision is said to
be incompatible with the convention". Such an area of judgment is
more readily found where the convention requires a balance to be
struck, or where the case raises issues of social and economic policy. It
is less likely to be applied in situations where the convention right is
unqualified or where the rights are of a nature which the domestic
courts are well placed to assess.'

Lord Woolf warned his fellow judges not to slip back to the old
Wednesbury approach. 'Our courts are not approaching the issue of
respect by merely asking whether a decision reached was one to which
the decision maker could reasonably come. The court instead applies the
doctrine of respect in the context of considering the proportionality of
the balance struck by the decision maker. As Lord Steyn pointed out in
Daly, this requires the reviewing national court to assess the balance
struck by the decision maker from the point of view of proportionality,

to assess the relative weight accorded to the relevant interests and to enquire whether a limitation on a convention right was necessary in a democratic society.'

In other words, said Lord Woolf, 'the court has to ask itself whether there is a pressing social need justifying the decision and whether the response was proportionate to the legitimate aim being pursued. The doctrine of deference can only come into play by extending a degree of respect, and no more, to the national authorities when considering the issue of proportionality.'

Lord Hoffmann went even further in May 2003, disapproving of the word 'deference' with 'overtones of servility, or perhaps gracious concession.' He was one of the law lords who gave judgment in *R (ProLife Alliance) v BBC*, a case in which a campaign group failed to establish a right to show images of aborted foetuses as part of an election broadcast to which it was entitled under rules agreed with the broadcasters. As Lord Hoffmann explained:

In a society based upon the rule of law and the separation of powers, it is necessary to decide which branch of government has in any particular instance the decision-making power and what the legal limits of that power are. That is a question of law and must therefore be decided by the courts. This means that the courts themselves often have to decide the limits of their own decision-making power. That is inevitable. But it does not mean that their allocation of decision-making power to the other branches of government is a matter of courtesy or deference. The principles upon which decision-making powers are allocated are principles of law.

Does proportionality exist as a free-standing ground of review in cases that do not involve the Human Rights Act? That question arose in *R (ABCIFER) v Defence Secretary*, decided by the Court of Appeal in April 2003. The Association of British Civilian Internees, Far Eastern Region unsuccessfully challenged a voluntary Government compensation scheme on the grounds that British claimants were not entitled to payments of £10,000 unless they could prove that they, a parent or a grandparent had been born in the United Kingdom. Their counsel argued that this requirement was disproportionate to the aims of the policy.

Lord Justice Dyson, speaking for a court that included Lord Phillips, said: 'We have difficulty in seeing what justification there is now for retaining the *Wednesbury* test. But we consider that it is not for this court to perform its burial rites.' The law lords had upheld the test in a recent case and only they could lay it to rest. Since the Government's policy was not irrational, judged on these traditional grounds, the challenge failed. So, the narrow *Wednesbury* test still reigned supreme in cases that did not involve human rights or European Community law.

Incorporating the Convention

The Human Rights Act 1998 is often said to 'incorporate' the European Convention on Human Rights into the domestic legal systems of the United Kingdom. Its true effect is more subtle.

Since 2000, courts in the United Kingdom have been required, as far as possible, to give effect to all other legislation in a way that is compatible with the Convention. To do so, courts must take into account decisions of the Human Rights Court and of the now-defunct Human Rights Commission. If a domestic court cannot stretch the language of an Act of Parliament so that it can be interpreted in a way that is compatible with the Convention, the most the judges can do is to say so: they cannot overturn it. Such a declaration of incompatibility does not affect the validity of the provisions in respect of which it is given and is not even binding on the parties to the proceedings in which it is made.

Under section 7 of the Act, people who claim that a public authority has acted incompatibly with the Convention may take proceedings against that authority to enforce their Convention rights. The term 'public authority' is deliberately given a vague, circular definition: 'any person certain of whose functions are functions of a public nature'. It probably includes the BBC, for example, but not the *Daily Telegraph*: the courts will have to decide in individual cases. But what happens if the person who is said to have acted incompatibly with the Convention is clearly *not* a public authority? Can you enforce your rights against an individual or a commercial organization?

At first sight, the answer should be 'no'. All cases at the European Court of Human Rights are brought against states: although the government may not itself have caused the alleged breach of human rights, it will be held responsible by the Human Rights Court if it has failed to provide for individuals to enjoy the rights guaranteed by the Convention.

So, how can individuals and companies be sued for breaching the Convention? The answer is to be found in section 6(3) of the Act, which says that 'public authority' includes a court or tribunal. So if I sue you, the court that hears our case must decide it in a manner compatible with the Convention.

This effect of the Human Rights Act is described as 'horizontal' because it governs relations between individuals at the same level rather than the 'vertical' relationship between a state and its citizens that is the main focus of the legislation. It is one of the great mysteries of the Act, mysterious because the courts have been left to work out how far to go in allowing the legislation to be used in resolving private disputes. Indeed, Clayton and Tomlinson, writing before the Act took effect, said that the 'extent of the horizontal application of convention rights is fundamental to the whole operation of the Human Rights Act'.

On the whole, the judges have shied away from trying to resolve what Lord Justice Buxton (in *Wainwright*) called 'such a large question'. Tugendhat and Christie, writing in 2002, thought that the Act would indeed have horizontal effect. They said: 'The prevailing view of the Human Rights Act is of constitutional significance and that the schedule of convention rights should indeed be considered to be a set of principles or values which should be applied generally throughout English law.'

Article 10 and the English courts

The English courts swallowed the entire European Convention with hardly a burp when the Human Rights Act took effect in October 2000. That came as no surprise to those who had observed their creativity in applying the new law even before it came into effect. In May 1999, for example, Lord Steyn was eager to rely on Article 10 in an appeal before the House of Lords. The Act had already been passed by Parliament in 1998, but the Home Secretary delayed implementation for two years so that the judiciary could be trained.

How could the law lords apply a law that was not yet in force? Simple: they just treated it as part of English common law, an approach they had followed more than once in the past. In 1988, for example, Lord Goff had been giving judgment in the House of Lords on *Attorney*

General v Guardian Newspapers (No 2), one of the many cases involving *Spycatcher*, the memoirs of the former MI5 officer Peter Wright. Talking of the rule that the public interest in the protection of confidences may be outweighed by a countervailing public interest in favour of disclosure, the law lord said, somewhat smugly:

I can see no inconsistency between English law on this subject and Article 10 of the European Convention on Human Rights. This is scarcely surprising, since we may pride ourselves on the fact that freedom of speech has existed in this country perhaps as long as, if not longer than, it has existed in any other country in the world. The only difference is that, whereas Article 10 of the convention, in accordance with its avowed purpose, proceeds to state a fundamental right and then to qualify it, we in this country (where everybody is free to do anything, subject only to the provisions of the law) proceed rather upon an assumption of freedom of speech, and turn to our law to discover the established exceptions to it. In any event I conceive it to be my duty, when I am free to do so, to interpret the law in accordance with the obligations of the Crown under this treaty.

As we shall see in Chapter 6, the House of Lords decided in 1993 that local authorities and government departments could not sue for libel, because it was 'of the highest public importance that a democratically elected governmental body, or indeed any governmental body, should be open to uninhibited public criticism'. Giving judgment in *Derbyshire County Council v Times Newspapers*, Lord Keith noted that the Court of Appeal had reached that conclusion after considering Article 10. He continued, equally smugly:

I have reached my conclusion upon the common law of England without finding any need to rely upon the European Convention. Lord Goff, in *Attorney-General v Guardian Newspapers Ltd (No 2)*, expressed the opinion that in the field of freedom of speech there was no difference in principle between English law on the subject and Article 10 of the convention. I agree, and can only add that I find it satisfactory to be able to conclude that the common law of England is consistent with the obligations assumed by the Crown under the treaty in this particular field.

So, in 1999, Lord Steyn was able to cite these passages and 'respectfully follow the guidance of Lord Goff of Chieveley and Lord Keith of Kinkel'. He then delivered this resounding defence of free speech:

Freedom of expression is, of course, intrinsically important: it is valued for its own sake. But it is well recognised that it is also instrumentally important. It serves a number of broad objectives. First, it promotes the self-fulfilment of individuals in society. Secondly, in the famous words of Justice Holmes (echoing John Stuart Mill), 'the best test of truth is the power of the thought to get itself accepted in the competition of the market.' Thirdly, freedom of speech is the lifeblood of democracy. The free flow of information and ideas informs political debate. It is a safety valve: people are more ready to accept decisions that go against them if they can in principle seek to influence them. It acts as a brake on the abuse of power by public officials. It facilitates the exposure of errors in the governance and administration of justice of the country.

Lord Steyn was giving judgment in *R v Home Secretary, ex p Simms*, a case brought by two prisoners who maintained they had been wrongly convicted. They wanted to talk about their cases to visiting journalists, including the experienced campaigner Bob Woffinden, but this was no longer permitted by the prison authorities. Lord Steyn continued:

Until the Home Secretary imposed a blanket ban on oral interviews between prisoners and journalists in or about 1995, such interviews had taken place from time to time and had served to identify and undo a substantial number of miscarriages of justice. There is no evidence that any of these interviews had resulted in any adverse impact on prison discipline. Secondly, the evidence establishes clearly that without oral interviews it is now virtually impossible under the Home Secretary's blanket ban for a journalist to take up the case of a prisoner who alleges a miscarriage of justice. In the process a means of correcting errors in the functioning of the criminal justice system has been lost.

As Lord Steyn explained, it was by turning off the 'safety valve' of free speech that Jack Straw had acted unlawfully:

Not all types of speech have an equal value. For example, no prisoner would ever be permitted to have interviews with a journalist to publish pornographic material or to give vent to so-called hate speech. Given the purpose of a sentence of imprisonment, a prisoner can also not claim to join in a debate on the economy or on political issues by way of interviews with journalists. In these respects the prisoner's right to free speech is outweighed by deprivation of liberty by the sentence of a court, and the need for discipline and control in prisons. But the free speech at stake in the present cases is qualitatively of a very different order. The prisoners are in prison because they are presumed to have been properly convicted. They wish to challenge the safety of their convictions. In principle it is not easy to conceive of a more important function which free speech might fulfil.

In April 2001, Lord Steyn's ruling allowed me to visit and interview Sally Clark, the solicitor who had been wrongly convicted of murdering two of her children. She was cleared on appeal in January 2003.

The *Simms* judgment was also cited with approval by Mr Justice Gray when he allowed an anti-war protester to maintain a vigil opposite the Houses of Parliament in October 2002. Brian Haw had begun his 24-hour protest a year earlier, maintaining that children were dying because of sanctions against Iraq. Westminster City Council claimed that he was acting unreasonably in obstructing the highway. However, the judge ruled that the obstruction caused by Haw's placards and his 2-foot-wide bed were not unreasonable and so not unlawful. The judge took Article 10 into account in deciding whether Haw's actions were reasonable. He also acknowledged the fact that the 11-foot-wide pavement around the centre of Parliament Square is little used by pedestrians.

After seeing off the Council, Haw first thanked two Buddhist supporters who had spent the hearing kneeling in prayer outside the High Court, themselves obstructing the footpath as they prostrated themselves before photographs of sick Iraqi children. Then responding in doggerel to reporters' questions, Haw said: 'All God's children, all the same; wherever born, and naught to blame. Oh what pain; tortured, murdered, in peace name.' Throwing scansion to the winds, he concluded: 'We blame these children for this crime. They are born in the wrong country, at the wrong time.'

Mr Justice Gray's judgment included a rare if not unique citation from a judgment given by Lord Irvine, the last serving Cabinet minister to sit as a judge in the House of Lords. In *DPP v Jones*, the Lord Chancellor had said 'the public highway is a public place which the public may enjoy for any reasonable purpose, provided the activity in question does not amount to a public or private nuisance and does not obstruct the highway by unreasonably impeding the primary right of the public to pass and repass: within these qualifications there is a public right of peaceful assembly on the highway'.

When it became clear in the summer of 2003 that Haw was not going to let a little thing like the overthrow of Saddam Hussein and the end of sanctions against Iraq deflect him from his aspiration to turn the whole frontage of the Square into a permanent eyesore, MPs starting talking about passing legislation to restrict protests outside Parliament.

Hot news from Strasbourg

The latest ruling from the European Court of Human Rights in support of free speech is *Ernst v Belgium*, decided in July 2003. Martine Ernst, a television journalist, and three newspaper reporters complained about extensive police raids on their homes and offices in 1995. All four had reported on investigations into the murder of a socialist politician, using leaked information. The raids were aimed at discovering the identity of their sources, believed to have been officials within the state legal system.

Ruling on their complaints against the Belgian Government, the Human Rights judges found that there had been an interference with their right to freedom of expression under Article 10. The Strasbourg Court was struck by the large scale of the searches, apparently involving some 160 police officers in eight almost simultaneous operations. Other means could have been used to identify those responsible for the leaks, it thought. The Court found that the Belgian Government had not shown that a fair balance had been struck between the competing interests of the state and the journalists. Reasons put forward by Belgium were not 'sufficient' to justify searches and seizures on such a large scale: the means employed had not been 'reasonably proportionate to the legitimate aims pursued'.

There had also been a breach of Article 8, the judges held. The searches of the applicants' places of work, homes and, in some instances, their cars amounted to an interference with their right to respect for their homes. None of the journalists had been accused of any offence, and the search warrants were drafted in wide terms. They allowed police to search for and seize 'any document or object that might assist the investigation', without limitation, and gave no information about the investigation concerned, the premises to be searched or the objects to be seized. Again, the searches had not been proportionate to the legitimate aims pursued. It was encouraging to see this support for the principles of open journalism and protection of sources.

The reach of Article 10

The far-reaching effect of Article 10 is well demonstrated by an entertaining case decided by the law lords in June 2003. It concerns the

Treason Felony Act 1848, passed to make prosecutions for constructive treason easier by providing the lower 'felony' punishment of life imprisonment at a time when juries were reluctant to convict defendants of a crime carrying the death penalty. The Act ostensibly makes it an offence to call for the abolition of the British monarchy. Section 3 says, in part:

And be it enacted, That if any Person whatsoever after the passing of this Act shall, within the United Kingdom or without, compass, imagine, invent, devise, or intend to deprive or depose our most Gracious Lady the Queen, Her Heirs or Successors, from the Style, Honour, or Royal Name of the Imperial Crown of the United Kingdom, or of any other of Her Majesty's Dominions and Countries, or to levy War against Her Majesty, Her Heirs or Successors, within any Part of the United Kingdom, in order by Force or Constraint to compel Her or Them to change Her or Their Measures or Counsels, or in order to put any Force or Constraint upon or in order to intimidate or overawe both Houses or either House of Parliament, or to move or stir any Foreigner or Stranger with Force to invade the United Kingdom or any other Her Majesty's Dominions or Countries under the Obeisance of Her Majesty, Her Heirs or Successors, and such Compassings, Imaginations, Inventions, Devices, or Intentions, or any of them, shall express, utter, or declare, by publishing any Printing or Writing, or by open and advised Speaking, or by any overt Act or Deed, every Person so offending shall be guilty of Felony, and being convicted thereof shall be liable, at the Discretion of the Court, to be transported beyond the Seas for the Term of his or her natural Life, or for any Term not less than Seven Years, or to be imprisoned for any Term not exceeding Two Years, with or without hard Labour, as the Court shall direct.

On the advice of Geoffrey Robertson, QC, who himself came from 'beyond the seas' in Australia, the *Guardian* decided in December 2000 to challenge this legislation as being incompatible with Article 10. Alan Rusbridger, the editor, and Polly Toynbee, a columnist, invited the Attorney General, the late and much lamented Lord Williams of Mostyn, to promise that they would not face prosecution if they published an article calling for a republic. When Lord Williams did not rise to the bait, the *Guardian* went ahead and published anyway. Naturally, there was still no prosecution.

Undaunted, the newspaper launched an expensive legal action, seeking a declaration that it was no longer an offence in the light of the Human Rights Act to support a republican form of government. Its case was thrown out by the High Court but reinstated by the Court of Appeal. The Attorney General appealed to the House of Lords.

Lord Scott, who gave the liveliest speech, noted that Rusbridger and Toynbee feared they might be prosecuted for treason. They believed that the 1848 Act had a chilling effect on their Article 10 rights to free speech. 'I do not believe a word of it,' said Lord Scott. 'It is plain as a pike staff to the [*Guardian* journalists] and everyone else that no one who advocates the peaceful abolition of the monarchy and its replacement by a republican form of government is at any risk of prosecution.' Robertson was 'a very good lawyer', Lord Scott noted. 'But you do not have to be a very good lawyer to know that to advocate the abolition of the monarchy and its replacement by a republic by peaceful and constitutional means will lead neither to prosecution nor to conviction. All you need to be is a lawyer with commonsense.'

Since the newspaper had taken 'unnecessary' legal action to obtain obvious results, while 'the valuable time of the courts should be spent on real issues', the *Guardian* was ordered to pay the costs of the Attorney's appeal to the Lords. Why, though, was the result obvious? Simply because the 1848 Act could not stand up to scrutiny under Article 10 of the Human Rights Convention. 'Any suggestion that a total legislative ban on republican discourse in print could be compatible with article 10 would stretch judicial gullibility to breaking point,' said Lord Steyn. 'It, therefore, appears inevitable that any resultant incompatibility would have to be read down under the strong interpretative obligation' under section 3(1) of the Human Rights Act.

Section 3(1), you will remember, says legislation must, so far as possible, be given effect in a way that is compatible with the Human Rights Convention. Lord Steyn's reference to a 'strong interpretative obligation' reminds judges that they should strive to find a way of reinterpreting existing legislation in a way that is compatible with the Convention. In other words, freedom of expression would triumph. As Lord Steyn concluded, 'The part of section 3 of the 1848 Act which appears to criminalise the advocacy of republicanism is a relic of a bygone age and does not fit into the fabric of our modern legal system. The idea that section 3 could survive scrutiny under the Human Rights Act is unreal.'

That was enough for the *Guardian* to claim that it had been vindicated when the House of Lords said that nobody could be prosecuted for advocating abolition of the monarchy. In reality, the law remained entirely unchanged as the result of its expensive legal action.

German bastards wanted

Another of Geoffrey Robertson's wheezes, announced at the same time as his challenge to the Treason Felony Act, was a human-rights challenge to the Act of Settlement 1701. That legislation, passed at a time of widespread fear of Catholics, restricts the succession to descendants of Princess Sophia, Electress of Hanover and the granddaughter of James I of England, but excludes anyone who is a Roman Catholic or has married a Catholic or who is not the natural child of married parents. Many of those excluded were thought to be minor German princelings who had fallen on hard times. So the *Guardian* placed a classified advertisement in the *Süddeutsche Zeitung* among those offering washing machines and cameras for sale: 'British newspaper seeks German descendants of Queen Victoria. Have you been cheated of the chance to become King or Queen because you are Catholic, the child of unmarried parents or because you are adopted?' But nobody came forward: the case was abandoned when it turned out to be a cause without a rebel.

Inquiries on TV

How public is a public inquiry? If you are a broadcaster, an inquiry is truly public only if you are permitted to broadcast its proceedings. Current practice, however, is not to allow the evidence of witnesses to be broadcast. This is not because television cameras would be unlawful: a public inquiry is not a 'court'—even if the proceedings are conducted by a judge and take place in a courtroom—and so the restrictions on photographing witnesses and others in court under the Criminal Justice Act 1925 do not apply. However, judges and lawyers appointed to conduct public inquiries generally take the view that television cameras would make giving evidence even more stressful than it is already. Since many public inquiries are not set up under statutory powers, anybody can decline to give evidence. Those chairing them do not want to give witnesses any excuse for withdrawing their co-operation. Even when an inquiry has been established under the Tribunals of Inquiry (Evidence) Act 1921, which gives the inquiry powers to compel witnesses to attend, there is every reason for limiting the stress many witnesses must feel.

But does Article 10 give broadcasters a right to televise public inquiries? Would a refusal to allow in the cameras breach their rights to freedom of expression? On the face of it, apparently not—since they are still able to 'impart information and ideas without interference by public authority'. However, Geoffrey Robertson, QC, has twice attempted to run this argument on behalf of broadcasters—on both occasions, without success.

The first attempt was at the Shipman Inquiry, which concluded in July 2002 that Harold Shipman, a doctor from Hyde in Greater Manchester, murdered 215 of his patients over a 23-year period. In October 2001, Dame Janet Smith, the appeal judge chairing the Inquiry, ruled on an application by CNN, the US-based television network, to televise the proceedings. Dame Janet had taken advice from David Pannick, QC. He (and his junior counsel, Jane Mulcahy) said:

In the present case, we consider that a court would accept that the inquiry is not simply denying access to information in the form of television pictures, but is preventing the receipt of information by a particular means when the public has access to the information by other means. That is an interference with freedom of expression. We consider that the court would apply the basic principle, stated for example in *Thorgeirson v Iceland*, that it is incumbent on the press 'to impart information and ideas on matters of public interest. Not only does it have the task of imparting such information and ideas; the public also has the right to receive them'.

Counsel advised Dame Janet that Article 10 did indeed apply to her inquiry and that if she were to prevent broadcasting of the Inquiry there would be an interference with freedom of expression. The important issue, they added, was whether any restrictions she might impose were justified under Article 10(2). However, Dame Janet disagreed. 'My conclusion', she said, 'is that Article 10 does not provide a right to film a public event if the person with lawful control of the event is not willing to allow it.' Pannick and Mulcahy seemed to be suggesting that if the people were entitled to walk into the Inquiry chamber and listen to the evidence, they must also be equally entitled to receive the information in the form of television pictures.

I cannot accept that argument. It seems to me to confuse knowledge and information. The public is entitled to come into the chamber and see and hear the proceedings. They can use and disseminate the knowledge they have gained in any way they like. But this does not entitle them to receive different information, namely a permanent sound and visual record, just because that different information would contain the same knowledge as they can receive by coming into the chamber.

Then Dame Janet came up with the killer argument. If Article 10 gave broadcasters the right to film judicial inquiries, you would have thought it would have given them the right to film the proceedings of the European Court of Human Rights, a body not unfamiliar with the Human Rights Convention.

It appears no formal claim to film and broadcast its proceedings has ever been advanced. But it appears that the Court has given some thought to the question. I have been told that the Court allows broadcasters limited rights to film its proceedings. Permission covers the first few minutes of each party's submission and the whole of the judgement. It appears that this practice has never been challenged as a breach of the broadcasters' Article 10 right. Mr Robertson suggested that perhaps the Court's proceedings were not sufficiently newsworthy. I do not think that could be the explanation. Mr Joshua Rozenberg, the well-known legal journalist and broadcaster, whose evidence in support of CNN is before me, says that in practice the Court's press office exercises discretion as to what permission is granted for filming. It would be remarkable, if broadcasters have a presumptive right to film the proceedings of the Court pursuant to Article 10, that the Judges should allow their discretion (which would have to be exercised so as to satisfy Article 10(2)) to be exercised by a press officer. I conclude that Article 10 of the Convention does not apply and does not give CNN a presumptive right to film or broadcast the proceedings of the Inquiry.

In August 2003, Robertson tried again. This time, he was representing ITN, BSkyB, Channel 4, Channel 5 and ITV, who wanted to televise Lord Hutton's Inquiry into the death of the Government scientist, Dr David Kelly. The BBC also wanted to broadcast the proceedings, of course, but felt inhibited about supporting the application since it was one of the organizations whose actions might have helped precipitate Kelly's apparent suicide. However, Lord Hutton agreed with Dame Janet:

Mr Robertson relied in his written submissions on the decision of the

European Court of Human Rights in *Jersild v Denmark*, and *Castells v Spain*. I consider that these decisions do not assist his argument. It is clear that *Jersild* related to the dissemination by a journalist of statements made by another person in an interview with him, and *Castells* related to the publication in a magazine of an article criticising the government written by a politician. Therefore I rule that the applicants have no right under Article 10 and the Human Rights Act 1998 to film the proceedings although, as I have stated, I have given permission before the commencement of the inquiry for filming of my opening statement and the filming of statements which will be made by counsel.

Though disappointing, these decisions are in accordance with authority and common sense. It would have made gripping television to watch the Prime Minister and his closest advisers being questioned by counsel. But even the most accomplished witnesses may feel under pressure in unfamiliar surroundings. As Dame Janet said:

Until now, it has been the expectation of any citizen who has to give evidence in a court of law that they will do so in public but not on television. I do not think it has ever been the general expectation that more will be required of one called to give evidence at a public inquiry. If and when Parliament decides, as it could, that the hearings of a public inquiry will normally be televised . . . then the expectation of witnesses will be that they will have to submit to being filmed. But we are not in that situation now.

Instead of televising the proceedings, Lord Hutton arranged for a running verbatim transcript to appear on his website, together with copies of documents submitted in evidence. This was an extraordinarily valuable resource, allowing people anywhere in the world to follow the proceedings in detail whenever they wished. It contributed a great deal to press freedom and should become standard practice for all future public inquiries.

Laws against free speech

From time to time, Parliament passes laws restricting free speech. One such law is the Protection from Harassment Act 1997. This legislation makes it a criminal offence for a person to pursue a course of conduct amounting to harassment and which he or she ought to know is harassment. It also provides a civil remedy for an actual or apprehended breach, including damages, an injunction and a power of arrest. The person accused of harassment has a defence if he can show that his course of conduct was 'reasonable'. The Act does not define harassment—beyond saying that a person ought to know his course of conduct amounts to harassment if a reasonable person would think that it did—but the Conservative Government of the day assured us that it was aimed at stalking, anti-social behaviour by neighbours and racial harassment.

Maybe it was—but the drafting was far too loose. In 2000, Esther Thomas, a former civilian clerk with the City of London Police, launched a claim under the Act against the publishers of the *Sun*, seeking damages of up to £50,000. She sued over a report that said that two police sergeants had been demoted because of a supposedly 'private' remark about an asylum seeker. The newspaper said this had occurred after a 'black clerk at their station complained about the way they treated a Somali woman trying to reach an asylum centre in Croydon, south London'. It named Thomas. The newspaper published a follow-up article and a series of letters under the headline 'Don't punish cops over a joke made in private'. Race-hate mail addressed to Thomas began to arrive at her police station. In fear, and believing she was being targeted, she left her job.

The Court of Appeal refused a request by the newspaper to strike out the action ahead of a full hearing. Lord Phillips, Master of the Rolls, said it was arguable that publication of the newspaper articles would lead some readers to send Thomas hostile mail, causing her distress. It was also at least arguable that the articles contained racist criticism of her. The test was 'whether a proposed series of articles, which is likely to cause distress to an individual, will constitute an abuse of the freedom of the press which the pressing social needs of a democratic society require should be curbed'.

Another recent piece of legislation can be used to prevent the venerable practice of 'doorstepping', in which reporters gather outside someone's home or place of work in the hope of photographing their quarry and, usually, of persuading him to make a comment on some topic of the hour. Section 42 of the Criminal Justice and Police Act 2001 says that where a police officer reasonably believes that a person is outside someone's home in order to persuade an individual not to do something he is entitled to do, or to do something he is not obliged to do—and the officer believes the person inside is likely to suffer harassment, alarm or distress—he can order the person outside to move on or face arrest and imprisonment.

A trump card?

As I said at the beginning of this chapter, free speech is not a trump card; nor should it be. I shall have more to say in Chapter 5 about how freedom of the press operates in practice. First, though, we must consider the restrictions on free speech to be found in Article 8 of the European Convention.

CHAPTER 4

Respecting Private Life

'Everyone has the right to respect for his private and family life, his home and his correspondence,' says Article 8(1) of the Human Rights Convention. But, as with Article 10, what the Convention giveth with one hand it taketh away with the other. So in Article 8(2) we read: 'There shall be no interference by a public authority with the exercise of this right except such as is in accordance with the law and is necessary in a democratic society in the interests of national security, public safety or the economic well-being of the country, for the prevention of disorder or crime, for the protection of health or morals, or for the protection of the rights and freedoms of others.'

That's privacy?

We can see immediately that Article 8 provides no right to privacy, as such: respect for a person's 'private and family life' is a subtly different concept. But that did not seem to deter Sir David and Sir Frederick Barclay, the reclusive twin newspaper proprietors who own the island of Brecqhou, near Sark in the Channel Islands. They objected when an enterprising television reporter named John Sweeney landed on their island from a small boat in 1995, carrying recording equipment. The brothers had previously declined his request for an interview and refused him permission to land.

Their first complaint was to the BBC, for which Sweeney was making a programme. That was rejected, so they approached the Broadcasting Complaints Commission (which preceded the Broadcasting Standards Commission and Ofcom). The Commission said it could do nothing before a programme was transmitted, so they went next to the High Court. Dismissing the brothers' application for judicial review in 1996, Mr Justice Sedley confirmed that the Commission's statutory powers were limited to broadcast programmes. 'It cannot therefore entertain an anticipatory complaint even where, once the programme is broadcast, the complaint is bound to succeed,' he said. 'It follows that in this field and to this extent, as elsewhere in English law, the individual is without an effective remedy before a national authority if the right to respect for his or her private and family life is violated.' As we saw from the initial proceedings in *Douglas v Hello! Ltd*, Lord Justice Sedley (as he became) strongly supported the introduction of a privacy law: he appeared here to be clearing the ground for what he must have hoped would be a successful application to the European Court of Human Rights.

After the programme had been broadcast, with Sweeney's covert audio recording illustrated by shots of a building site, the brothers' objections were duly upheld by the Complaints Commission. That was not enough for them and so they went to Strasbourg. But, in 1999, the Human Rights Court declared their application inadmissible. It accepted that an interference with an applicant's private life could result from an unauthorized entry into and filming on premises where the applicant had established his home life. However, it explained, 'the mere ownership of property is not sufficient to render it a "home" for the purposes of Article 8; nor does unauthorised entry onto property owned by another, without more, necessarily entail any interference with respect for private life.'

Even though the Broadcasting Complaints Commission considered this to have been a breach of privacy, Article 8 provided no protection. Still less did the Human Rights Court require the authorities to create a law of privacy in Britain.

That's privacy!

If it is not necessarily a breach of the right to respect for private life to invade someone's property, we should not be surprised to discover that a person may have the right to privacy while walking down the street. That emerged from a curious case decided in January 2003.

Geoffrey Peck, then 40, was suffering from depression in 1995 and decided to cut his wrists. At 11.30 one night he walked alone down

Brentwood High Street in Essex with a kitchen knife in his hand. He stopped, unknown to him, in front of a newly installed CCTV camera. A sharp-eyed operator monitoring the cameras for the borough council spotted the knife and called the police. Peck received medical treatment at the police station and was then taken home.

CCTV cameras in public places were relatively new in 1995. No doubt proud of their success in preventing a suicide, Brentwood Council decided to release recordings of the incident. Video footage, in which Peck could be seen holding the knife but not cutting his wrists, was shown on the BBC's *Crime Beat* programme; still pictures appeared in local newspapers. Peck's face was obscured in the programme but not in advance trailers and he was recognized by a large number of family members, friends and colleagues.

While accepting that Brentwood Council may have saved his life, Peck complained to Strasbourg about the decision to release identifiable pictures of him to large audiences without his knowledge or consent. Finding in his favour, the Human Rights Court said that Article 8 'protects a right to identity and personal development, and the right to establish and develop relationships with other human beings and the outside world . . . There is, therefore, a zone of interaction of a person with others, even in a public context, which may fall within the scope of "private life".'

The judges explained that it was not the monitoring of someone in a public place that interfered with his privacy. 'On the other hand, the recording of the data and the systematic or permanent nature of the record may give rise to such considerations.' The Court concluded that disclosure by Brentwood Council 'constituted a serious interference with the applicant's right to respect for his private life'. But was there a defence? Was it proportionate to the legitimate aim of preventing crime and protecting others? No, said the Court. Brentwood Council could have tracked Peck down or made sure his face was properly masked.

The next question for the Human Rights judges was whether Peck had been denied an 'effective remedy' by the English courts. Judicial review had proved ineffective and damages could not be awarded by the Press Complaints Commission (PCC) or the Broadcasting Standards Commission. It was not suggested by the British Government that Peck could have won an action for breach of confidence. Accordingly, Britain was also in breach of Article 13—the right to an effective remedy.

Peck was awarded £7,820 damages, plus costs. But the ramifications of his success may go further. Countries that sign the Human Rights Convention 'undertake to abide by the final judgment of the Court in any case to which they are parties'. The body responsible for ensuring that they do so is the Committee of Ministers of the Council of Europe, which in practice means the Strasbourg-based diplomats from the member states. These officials would have been satisfied with a narrow interpretation of the judgment; it would have been possible for Britain to 'abide by' it if anyone photographed on CCTV in a public place, but in 'private' circumstances, was given a way of preventing his image from being circulated widely. But some English judges saw this ruling as providing an opportunity to go much further. In his Bentham lecture, delivered two months after the *Peck* decision, Lord Phillips, Master of the Rolls, said the judgment suggested 'that either the courts or the legislature are going to have to establish a tort of invasion of privacy if this country is to comply with its convention obligations'.

The Commons Media Committee, whose report calling for a privacy law is discussed in Chapter 8, found the effect of *Peck* 'confusing' because the Human Rights Act had come into effect after the facts complained of but before the Court's ruling. As we have seen, the Strasbourg judges found English law deficient in providing a remedy for Peck. 'The deficiency was highlighted by the fact that Mr Peck's cause of action did not engage the breach of confidence law that has long stood as proxy for a privacy law,' the Committee added. Some witnesses, notably Michael Tugendhat, QC, (now Mr Justice Tugendhat) told the Committee that the Human Rights Act had 'rectified this deficiency'. Other lawyers, including Professor Eric Barendt, told the Committee that 'relying on the courts and cases to develop the law sufficiently in reasonable time is not enough'.

The Government's view was that changes in the law since the time of Peck's nocturnal stroll in 1995 were sufficient to avoid the need for further changes in the law. 'As the council is a public body, Peck could [now] sue for damages under the Human Rights Act 1998 which you could not have done prior to the introduction of the 1998 Act,' Lady Scotland, QC, who was then a minister in the Lord Chancellor's Department, told the committee in oral evidence. 'He may also have an action against the council as a data controller under the Data Protection Act 1988. As breach of confidence has also developed, he could bring an action for breach of confidence against the council and any print or broadcast media which used the images,' she added.

We can see already that respect for a person's private and family life is rather different from what we would understand as pure privacy. So, before discussing the exceptions in Article 8(2)—which are rather fewer than those in Article 10(2)—we should look more closely at the unexpected breadth of the rights protected by Article 8(1).

The breadth of privacy

An unusual case from 1992 provides a good illustration of this. Gottfried Niemietz, a lawyer and local councillor from Freiburg im Breisgau, Germany, was a member of the Anti-Clerical Working Group, which sought to curtail the influence of the Church in Germany. As such, he was strongly suspected of having sent a fax in 1985 complaining about privileges that the Church had apparently enjoyed since Hitler's concordat with the Vatican in 1933.

Whoever did write the fax was objecting to the fact that the state still collected taxes on behalf of the Church—requiring employers, whether they were Christians or not, 'to pay over Church tax for their Christian employees and thus relieve the Church of financial administrative work'. One employer who complained about this law had recently been charged with 'insulting behaviour', an offence with a maximum penalty of one year in prison. The judge who was due to try this defendant—and who was said to have ordered a 'compulsory psychiatric examination' on him—was the very person to whom the offending fax had been addressed.

According to the local prosecutor, sending the fax also amounted to 'insulting behaviour' and a search warrant was issued for Niemietz's office. In the event, nothing was found and no charges were brought over the fax. Niemietz then challenged the search warrant, first in the German courts and then at the European Court of Human Rights.

The first question for the Strasbourg judges was whether the search warrant amounted to an interference with the applicant's private life and home, given that it had been executed at his business premises rather than his residence. In their view, 'home' need not be confined to the place where a person lived:

The court does not consider it possible or necessary to attempt an exhaustive definition of the notion of 'private life'. However, it would be too restrictive to limit the notion to an 'inner circle' in which the individual may live his own personal life as he chooses and to exclude [from it] entirely the outside world not encompassed within that circle. Respect for private life must also comprise, to a certain degree, the right to establish and develop relationships with other human beings.

There appears, furthermore, to be no reason of principle why this understanding of the notion of 'private life' should be taken to exclude activities of a professional or business nature since it is, after all, in the course of their working lives that the majority of people have a significant, if not the greatest, opportunity of developing relationships with the outside world . . .

To deny the protection of Article 8 on the ground that the measure complained of related only to professional activities—as the Government suggested should be done in the present case—could moreover lead to an inequality of treatment, in that such protection would remain available to a person whose professional and non-professional activities were so intermingled that there was no means of distinguishing between them . . .

As regards the word 'home', appearing in the English text of Article 8, the court observes that in certain contracting states, notably Germany, it has been accepted as extending to business premises. Such an interpretation is, moreover, fully consonant with the French text, since the word *domicile* has a broader connotation than the word 'home' and may extend, for example, to a professional person's office.

In this context also, it may not always be possible to draw precise distinctions, since activities which are related to a profession or business may well be conducted from a person's private residence and activities which are not so related may well be carried on in an office or commercial premises. A narrow interpretation of the words 'home' and *domicile* could therefore give rise to the same risk of inequality of treatment as a narrow interpretation of the notion of 'private life'.

More generally, to interpret the words 'private life' and 'home' as including certain professional or business activities or premises would be consonant with the essential object and purpose of Article 8, namely to protect the individual against arbitrary interference by the public authorities.

Having concluded that the search was an interference with Niemietz's rights under Article 8, the Court concluded that it could not be justified as necessary in a democratic society because it went too far: 'the search impinged on professional secrecy to an extent that appears disproportionate in the circumstances'.

At first sight, it seems strange that an office was more worthy of protection than the building where the Barclay brothers were to establish their home. However, the concept of private life includes a person's physical and psychological integrity; Article 8 is intended to ensure the development, without outside interference, of the personality of each individual in his relations with other human beings.

Private conversations and private lives

Other cases decided by the Strasbourg Court have been closer to the concept of privacy as we would understand it. Alison Halford was Britain's highest-ranking woman police officer when she became Assistant Chief Constable at Merseyside in 1983. However, she was subsequently passed over for promotion on eight occasions. Halford took her Chief Constable to an industrial tribunal, accusing him of discriminating against her on the grounds of her sex. The case was settled in 1992 and Halford retired from the police.

During the tribunal proceedings, Halford claimed that her office telephone had been tapped by her employers. The Human Rights Court agreed. 'The evidence justifies the conclusion that there was a reasonable likelihood that calls made by Ms Halford from her office were intercepted by the Merseyside police with the primary aim of gathering material to assist in the defence of the sex-discrimination proceedings brought against them,' it said.

To make private calls to her lawyers, Halford had used a telephone provided by her employers especially for the purpose. That phone was connected to the public exchange through the police switchboard, and there was nothing in law to prevent the police using their own telephone equipment to monitor her calls: internal systems were not covered by the Interception of Communications Act 1985 (now replaced by the Regulation of Investigatory Powers Act 2000). On that basis, the Strasbourg judges concluded that the interference with her right to respect for her private life and correspondence had not been in accordance with the law and she was awarded £10,000 compensation, plus costs. The Court said: 'There is no evidence of any warning having been given to Ms Halford, as a user of the internal telecommunications system operated at the Merseyside police headquarters, that calls made on that system would be liable to interception. She would, the Court considers, have had a reasonable expectation of privacy for such calls.'

The judgment was a useful example of how the Convention could be used to protect personal and professional privacy and will, no doubt, be followed when the Court is asked to consider the interception of personal e-mails.

But there are limits. In 1988, Margaret Murray was arrested by the Army in Northern Ireland on suspicion of involvement in collecting money to buy arms for the IRA in the USA. She was taken to the Army screening centre at Springfield Road in Belfast and photographed without her knowledge or permission. In *Murray v UK* the Court accepted that taking someone's photograph without her consent interfered with the exercise of her right to respect for her private and family life and her home. However, it was not contrary to English common law and, in the particular circumstances of the case, it was necessary in a democratic society.

Gay rights

Many of the most influential decisions from Strasbourg in Article 8 cases brought against the United Kingdom have been concerned with the individual's personal or sexual identity rather than his or her privacy. The Government's initial reluctance to change domestic law over homosexuality and transsexuality led to recent and entirely predictable defeats at the European Court, followed inevitably by legislation at home.

Homosexual acts between consenting adults in private were decriminalized in 1967. However, for the next three decades they remained grounds for discharge from the armed forces. In 1995, four former members of the military challenged decisions that they should be sacked because of their homosexuality. Jeanette Smith was an RAF nurse, Graeme Grady was an RAF sergeant leading the support staff team of the British Defence Intelligence Staff in Washington, John Beckett was a Royal Navy weapons engineering mechanic in the Royal Navy and Duncan Lustig-Prean was a Naval Lieutenant Commander. All four had exemplary service records: it was never suggested that their sexual orientation had in any way affected their ability to carry out their work

or had led to any ill effect on discipline. But Ministry of Defence practice was to sack homosexuals once their sexuality was discovered: the
US approach was 'don't ask, don't tell' while the British policy was 'once
you're "out", you're out'.

Refusing an application for judicial review brought in the High
Court by the four former service personnel, Lord Justice Simon Brown
remarked that 'Lawrence of Arabia would not be welcome in today's
armed forces'. In his view, the four homosexuals had won the argument.
'The tide of history is against the ministry,' he added. 'Prejudices are
breaking down; old barriers are being removed. It seems to me improb-
able, whatever this court may say, that the existing policy can survive for
much longer.'

However, Labour had not yet come to power and implementation of
the Human Rights Act was still five years off. Lord Justice Simon Brown
therefore had to approach the case on conventional *Wednesbury* principles (explained in Chapter 3). The Defence Secretary had argued that
his policy was justified by the need to deliver an operationally efficient
and effective fighting force. Did the judge think it reasonable for the
minister to take the view that allowing homosexuals into the forces
would imperil that interest?

I have already said enough to indicate my own opinion that it is a wrong view,
a view that rests too firmly upon the supposition of prejudice in others and
which insufficiently recognises the damage to human rights inflicted. But can
it properly be stigmatised as irrational?

Only if it were plain beyond sensible argument that no conceivable damage
could be done to the armed services as a fighting unit would it be appropriate
for this court now to remove the issue entirely from the hands both of the
military and of the government. If the [Human Rights] convention were part
of our law and we were accordingly entitled to ask whether the policy answers
a pressing social need and whether the restriction on human rights involved
can be shown proportionate to its benefits, then clearly the primary judgment
(subject only to a limited 'margin of appreciation') would be for us and not
others: the constitutional balance would shift. But that is not the position . . .

With all these considerations in mind, I have come finally to the conclusion
that, my own view of the evidence notwithstanding, the minister's stance
cannot properly be held unlawful. His suggested justification for the ban may,
to many, seem unconvincing; to say, however, that it is outrageous in its defiance of logic is another thing . . .

What I have just said, of course, relates only to the domestic position.

Overhanging this lies Strasbourg . . . I for my part strongly suspect that so far as this country's international obligations are concerned, the days of this policy are numbered.

He was right, although Lord Justice Simon Brown's reasoning on the pre-Human Rights Act law was upheld later in 1995 by Lord Bingham, sitting as Master of the Rolls in the Court of Appeal. 'The existing policy cannot in my judgment be stigmatised as irrational at the time when these applicants were discharged,' said Lord Bingham. 'The threshold of irrationality is a high one. It was not crossed in this case'.

So the four took their claims to the European Court of Human Rights. In 1999, the Court concluded that 'investigations by the military police into the applicants' homosexuality, which included detailed interviews with each of them and with third parties on matters relating to their sexual orientation and practices . . . constituted a direct interference with the applicants' right to respect for their private lives'. But was it necessary in a democratic society?

An interference will be considered 'necessary in a democratic society' for a legitimate aim if it answers a pressing social need and, in particular, is proportionate to the legitimate aim pursued . . . [The hallmarks of a democratic society include] pluralism, tolerance and broadmindedness . . .

The court recognises that it is for the national authorities to make the initial assessment of necessity, though the final evaluation as to whether the reasons cited for the interference are relevant and sufficient is one for this court. A margin of appreciation is left open to contracting states in the context of this assessment, which varies according to the nature of the activities restricted and of the aims pursued by the restrictions.

Accordingly, when the relevant restrictions concern 'a most intimate part of an individual's private life', there must exist 'particularly serious reasons' before such interferences can satisfy the requirements of Article 8(2).

When the core of the national security aim pursued is the operational effectiveness of the armed forces, it is accepted that each State is competent to organise its own system of military discipline and enjoys a certain margin of appreciation in this respect . . . However, the national authorities cannot rely on such rules to frustrate the exercise by individual members of the armed forces of their right to respect for their private lives, which right applies to service personnel as it does to others within the jurisdiction of the State.

After a detailed assessment of Britain's arguments, the Court concluded that 'convincing and weighty reasons have not been offered by the

Government to justify the policy against homosexuals in the armed forces or, therefore, the consequent discharge of the applicants from those forces'. To the surprise of nobody, least of all Lord Justice Simon Brown, the judges held that 'neither the investigations conducted into the applicants' sexual orientation, nor their discharge on the grounds of their homosexuality in pursuance of the Ministry of Defence policy, were justified under Article 8(2)'.

A year later, the Government was ordered to pay the applicants £19,000 each as compensation for the way they had been treated—a very substantial sum by the less than generous standards of the Strasbourg Court. In addition, there were full awards for loss of past and future earnings and pension rights: £59,000 to Smith, £40,000 to Grady, £55,000 to Beckett and £94,875 to Lustig-Prean. Their legal costs were also paid.

It was an expensive defeat, and one for which the authorities were fully prepared. At the beginning of 2000, the Defence Secretary, Geoff Hoon, lifted the ban on gay troops. The 600 men and women sacked over the previous ten years were invited to re-enlist. Compensation was paid to some who chose not to do so. A new code of conduct was introduced, simply banning all sexual behaviour that could undermine the trust, cohesion and morale of a unit. No adverse consequence appeared to follow from the change of policy and one might ask why the Government had not acted sooner. The answer appears to have been a misplaced fear of criticism from senior military officers or armchair generals. As it turned out, though, the Government could say it had done everything possible to prevent an outcome that probably suited it perfectly well.

Trans people

Another entirely predictable defeat at the Strasbourg Court on an issue of political sensitivity came in 2002, when Britain defended claims by two individuals who wanted their gender reassignment operations to be recognized by law. One of them was Christine Goodwin, a former bus driver who had been registered as male, married a woman and fathered four children before having sex-change surgery on the National Health Service in 1990. Goodwin dressed as a girl from childhood and underwent aversion therapy in 1963. She was later diagnosed as a transsexual and began hormone treatment on the National Health Service in 1985, coupled with an operation on her vocal cords. In proceedings before the Strasbourg Court, Goodwin accused the Government of failing to ensure the right to respect for her private life.

A year earlier, a majority of the Court of Appeal dismissed a case brought by Elizabeth Bellinger, a male-to-female transsexual who wanted her twenty-year 'marriage' recognized. The English judges, headed by Dame Elizabeth Butler-Sloss, were dismayed to hear that the Home Office had no plans to act on the findings of an interdepartmental working group on the subject that had reported in April 2000. 'The problems will not go away and may well come again before the European Court sooner rather than later,' said Dame Elizabeth in 2001. It did not take long for her to be proved right.

Goodwin's claim was the fifth successive challenge brought against the United Kingdom by a transsexual seeking recognition of an assumed gender. The Court overruled its earlier decisions on the same broad issue in *Rees* (1986), *Cossey* (1990), *X, Y and Z* (1997) and *Sheffield and Horsham* (1998).

In the latter case, the Court had held by a narrow majority that the refusal of the United Kingdom Government to issue transsexuals with new birth certificates was not an interference with the right to respect for private life. Even Sir John Freeland, the soon-to-retire British judge and former Foreign Office legal adviser, was moved to say that he had decided against a violation of Article 8 'with much hesitation and even with some reluctance'. He warned the Government that 'continued inaction on the part of [the United Kingdom], taken together with further developments elsewhere, could well tilt the balance in the other direction'. But none of his former colleagues in Whitehall appeared to be listening.

While the Human Rights Court is not formally bound to follow its previous judgments, it does not depart from precedent without good reason. However, the judges will take account of changing conditions within member states. Privately, they were influenced by the fact that even the majority of the Court of Appeal in *Bellinger* was calling on the Government to take action. Giving their ruling in *Christine Goodwin v UK*, the Court said it was 'of crucial importance that the convention is interpreted and applied in a manner which renders its rights practical and effective, not theoretical and illusory'. A 'dynamic and evolutive approach' was needed. 'In the present context the court has, on several occasions since 1986, signalled its consciousness of the serious problems facing transsexuals and stressed the importance of keeping the need for appropriate legal measures in this area under review,' it recalled.

The very essence of the convention is respect for human dignity and human freedom. Under Article 8 of the convention in particular, where the notion of personal autonomy is an important principle underlying the interpretation of its guarantees, protection is given to the personal sphere of each individual, including the right to establish details of their identity as individual human beings. In the twenty-first century, the right of transsexuals to personal development and to physical and moral security in the full sense enjoyed by others in society cannot be regarded as a matter of controversy requiring the lapse of time to cast clearer light on the issues involved. In short, the unsatisfactory situation in which post-operative transsexuals live in an intermediate zone as not quite one gender or the other is no longer sustainable . . .

The Court does not underestimate the difficulties posed or the important repercussions which any major change in the system will inevitably have, not only in the field of birth registration, but also in the areas of access to records, family law, affiliation, inheritance, criminal justice, employment, social security and insurance. However, as is made clear by the report of the interdepartmental working group, these problems are far from insuperable, to the extent that the working group felt able to propose as one of the options full legal recognition of the new gender, subject to certain criteria and procedures. As Lord Justice Thorpe observed in the *Bellinger* case, any 'spectral difficulties', particularly in the field of family law, are both manageable and acceptable if confined to the case of fully achieved and post-operative transsexuals . . .

No concrete or substantial hardship or detriment to the public interest has indeed been demonstrated as likely to flow from any change to the status of transsexuals and, as regards other possible consequences, the Court considers that society may reasonably be expected to tolerate a certain inconvenience to enable individuals to live in dignity and worth in accordance with the sexual identity chosen by them at great personal cost . . .

The Court finds that the respondent Government can no longer claim that the matter falls within their margin of appreciation, save as regards the appropriate means of achieving recognition of the right protected under the Convention. Since there are no significant factors of public interest to weigh against the interest of this individual applicant in obtaining legal recognition of her gender re-assignment, it reaches the conclusion that the fair balance that is inherent in the Convention now tilts decisively in favour of the applicant.

There has, accordingly, been a failure to respect her right to private life in breach of Article 8 of the Convention.

The Court also found a breach of Article 12, which guarantees the right of men and women to marry. 'The Court is not persuaded that at the date of this case it can still be assumed that these terms must refer to a determination of gender by purely biological criteria,' it said. Goodwin's legal costs were paid, though the Court did not see why she should receive compensation when others had been turned down.

In December 2002, the Government accepted the judgment and announced that transsexuals would be allowed to marry in an assumed gender. They would also be able to obtain new birth certificates showing only their new name and sex rather than the identity registered shortly after birth. There would be no way of telling by looking at the document that the holder had changed sex. Asked whether such a certificate would amount to 'a lie', Rosie Winterton, a minister at the Lord Chancellor's Department, said that original birth records would remain unamended and that a link from the new certificate could be traced by bodies such as the Criminal Records Bureau. 'This is what happens in most other countries,' she added. A birth certificate giving no indication of any amendment was needed to protect the holder's privacy.

Six months later, the Government published a draft Gender Recognition Bill, which it said would give legal recognition to the acquired gender of transsexual people who could demonstrate that they had taken decisive steps towards living fully and permanently in that gender. Surgery would not be necessary. A transsexual seeking recognition would apply to a panel of lawyers and doctors. The panel would assess the medical evidence and decide whether the applicant now had or had previously had the medical condition known as gender dysphoria. In addition, applicants would have to show that they had lived in the acquired gender throughout the preceding two years and intended to continue to live in that gender. If satisfied, the Gender Recognition Panel would issue a certificate allowing an applicant to obtain a new birth certificate which, in turn, would entitle him or her to marry a person of the opposite gender. Original birth records would remain unchanged, and could still be made available in limited circumstances— though the link between the original and revised record would remain confidential within the Registrar General's office.

Law students often used to be told that Parliament could do anything except turn a man into a woman and a woman into a man. As we can see from the Gender Recognition Bill, expected to come before Parliament in 2004 after a period of pre-legislative scrutiny, this was always a misconception: the effect of the legislation, once enacted, is that a male-to-female transsexual will be legally recognized as a woman by the authorities in Britain, and a female-to-male transsexual will become a man in the eyes of the law.

In the meantime, Elizabeth Bellinger lost her final appeal to the House of Lords in April 2003. She took little consolation from the fact that the law lords declared that English law was incompatible with the Human Rights Convention and ordered Lord Irvine, the Lord Chancellor, to pay half the legal costs of her appeal.

Lord Nicholls, who gave the leading judgment, was 'profoundly conscious of the humanitarian considerations underlying Bellinger's claim'. In his view, 'much suffering is involved for those afflicted with gender identity disorder'. However, he added, allowing someone to become regarded as a person of the opposite sex would represent a major change in the law with far-reaching ramifications. Such decisions required wide public consultation and, in his view, should be taken by Parliament rather than the courts.

There were questions of definition, he explained. What form of surgery, if any, should be required? The law lords were not in a position to say what conditions were necessary before there could be recognition of a person's acquired gender, a matter on which there was no agreement in other jurisdictions. Still less could the judges make a 'fundamental change in the traditional concept of marriage' and allow same-sex couples to marry, one of the solutions suggested to help people such as Bellinger.

Despite this sympathetic approach by the law lords, Bellinger seemed disgusted at the outcome, maintaining that the House of Lords had declared her to be a 'bloke' and that the law lords were regarding Michael Bellinger—the man with whom she had gone through a ceremony of marriage in 1981—as a homosexual. 'The man I have been married to all these years and been his wife, his dishwasher, cleaner and cook . . . it means he has never existed,' she said bitterly. 'Everything was taken away from me today.'

Section 12

Shortly before Lord Wakeham stepped down as chairman of the PCC in 2002, he made a speech praising section 12 of the Human Rights Act, a provision added at the last moment in response to political pressure. It appears to limit restrictions on freedom of expression.

This section, he believed, set a 'very high threshold' which would need to be satisfied before an objector could prevent publication of a newspaper article. He added: 'Very importantly, the Act in effect reverses the burden of proof: any applicant seeking an injunction will have to prove why an article should not be published, rather than the newspaper defending the reasons for publication.'

It is not quite as simple as that. Courts often speak about the parliamentary draftsman and what he or she must have meant by phrasing legislation in a particular way. Although the Government maintained that section 12 was 'specifically designed to safeguard press freedom', I have it on good authority that the parliamentary draftsman intended that it should make as little difference as possible to the overall scheme of the Act.

The clause that became section 12 was introduced in response to concern—from Wakeham, among others—that the new legislation might impede freedom of expression by giving too much protection to privacy. This followed advice from David Pannick which persuaded the Lord Chancellor that the PCC would be a 'public authority' within the meaning of the Human Rights Act, and therefore required to act in a manner compatible with the legislation.

Section 12 applies if 'a court is considering whether to grant any relief which, if granted, might affect the exercise of the Convention right to freedom of expression'. The person against whom the application for relief is made (the 'respondent') will generally be a publisher or a journalist.

If the respondent is neither present in court nor represented when an application is made, no such relief is to be granted unless the court is satisfied either that the applicant has taken all practicable steps to notify that person or there are compelling reasons why he should not be told. Jack Straw, the Home Secretary responsible for the Human Rights Bill, told Parliament in 1998 that 'compelling reasons' might arise in a case raising issues of national security where the mere knowledge that an injunction was being sought might cause the respondent to publish the material immediately. But this provision, in section 12(2), simply puts into statutory form what had previously been a rule of court procedure. Indeed, no judge would act otherwise.

Section 12(3) says that no such relief is to be granted so as to restrain publication before trial unless the court is satisfied that the applicant is likely to establish that publication should not be allowed. Straw said that this subsection was designed to deal with 'Friday-night injunctions'— interim injunctions granted to preserve the status quo but which newspapers suspected were always intended to prevent publication until the story was no longer newsworthy. His junior minister explained that it was designed to tighten the law so that applicants would have to establish a stronger case than the normal test for interim injunctions.

It is true that someone seeking an interim injunction normally need show only that there is a 'serious question to be tried'. But this 'balance of convenience' rule, named after the *American Cyanamid* case, has never applied in libel cases, where the courts have been more cautious about stopping the presses. This must now be the approach in all cases where freedom of expression is at stake. However, the change in emphasis hardly 'reverses the burden of proof', in Wakeham's phrase.

Section 12(4) is more interesting. It says that 'the court must have particular regard to the importance of the Convention right to freedom of expression'. What does 'particular' mean?

It cannot alter the Human Rights Convention itself, under which freedom of expression is not an absolute right. Courts are not being told that they must have any less regard to competing interests, such as respect for private and family life. So does it mean anything at all? The leading textbook writers disagree.

Clayton and Tomlinson say 'it appears that this sub-section is intended to "tip the balance" in favour of expression in applications for injunctions to restrain breaches of privacy'. Grosz, Beatson and Duffy believe the subsection 'is a direction to the court to lean in favour of freedom of expression, in particular in cases concerning the freedom of the press to publish material on matters of public interest'.

But Lester and Pannick insist that section 12 'serves no sensible purpose'. Any satisfaction that journalists may have with section 12 is 'misguided', they explain. First, it does not affect the breach-of-confidence claims that may already be brought to protect privacy. Secondly,

Article 8 still guarantees the right to respect for private life (though it is not absolute). Thirdly, the Government did not intend the judges to do anything other than to apply the Human Rights Convention. As Straw explained, 'so far as we are able in a manner consistent with the convention and its jurisprudence, we are saying to the courts that whenever there is a clash between Article 8 rights and Article 10 rights, they must pay particular attention to the Article 10 rights'. The initial part of his sentence is crucial. Fourthly, it would be pointless for the Act to create special principles not found in the Convention. Those who felt their right to private life had been violated by section 12 could still take the Government to Strasbourg.

Section 12(4) goes on to say that, where the proceedings relate to journalistic, literary or artistic material, the court must have particular regard to the extent to which the material has, or is about to, become available to the public or the extent to which it is, or would be, in the public interest for the material to be published.

'If the court and the parties to the proceedings know that a story will shortly be published anyway, for example, in another country or on the internet, that must affect the decision whether it is appropriate to restrain publication by the print or broadcast media in this country,' Straw told MPs. This was an obvious reference to the memoirs of former MI5 and MI6 officers, which were published abroad before being released in Britain. However, the courts are now much more realistic about their powers to stop banned material reaching the public. They will not grant injunctions only to see them frustrated.

Where the proceedings relate to journalistic, literary or artistic material, section 12(4) says the court must also have particular regard to any relevant privacy code. 'Depending on the circumstances, that could be the newspaper industry code of practice operated by the Press Complaints Commission, the Broadcasting Standards Commission code, the Independent Television Commission code, or a broadcaster's internal code such as that operated by the BBC,' said Straw. 'The fact that a newspaper has complied with the terms of the code operated by the PCC—or, conversely, that it has breached the code—is one of the factors that we believe the courts should take into account in considering whether to grant relief.'

The Government's wish—if not the law's requirement—is that judges should leave decisions on invasion of privacy to self-regulation by the industry. Those who blame the newspaper industry itself for invading their privacy may not feel the same way. In any case, the industry codes of conduct were never drafted with the intention that they should be subjected to detailed analysis by the courts.

The definition of 'journalistic, literary or artistic material' is extended to cover 'conduct connected with such material'. This is intended for cases where journalistic inquiries suggest the presence of a story, but no actual material yet exists, perhaps because the story has not yet been written.

At first blush, section 12 must look attractive to journalists. As we are about to see, though, it has proved no match for a determined judge.

Mary Bell

Mary Bell and her 18-year-old daughter achieved the ultimate respect for their private and family lives in May 2003 when the High Court issued an injunction to protect their anonymity. The orders were granted *contra mundum*—against the world.

In 1968, Bell killed two small children, aged 3 and 4, when she herself was only 11 years old. She was convicted of manslaughter on the grounds of diminished responsibility and spent twelve years in detention before being released in 1980 and given a new identity—the first of three changes. Though these killings did not capture the public imagination in the same way as the murder of James Bulger, they remained notorious. Interest was revived in Bell's case by the trial of Robert Thompson and Jon Venables, who murdered the Liverpool toddler when they themselves were aged only 10; considerably more interest was aroused in 1998 when the author Gitta Sereny published a book about her, for which Bell was paid a 'substantial' sum.

Bell's daughter was made a ward of court shortly after birth in 1984. That allowed the child's identity to be protected, along with that of her mother—though Bell and her daughter were forced to move home five times as a result of press intrusion and harassment. The question for the High Court nearly two decades later was whether the anonymity order should continue when the child reached 18 and ceased to be a ward. There was evidence that Bell was a 'vulnerable personality with mental health problems' and that the absence of an injunction would have a serious effect on her health and well-being.

Giving judgment, Dame Elizabeth Butler-Sloss accepted that Bell's life was not at risk from vigilantes. Unlike Thompson and Venables, Bell could not bring her claim within Article 2 of the Human Rights Convention, which protects the right to life. But that did not matter, because the judge concluded that the privacy provisions of Article 8 applied. She cited *Botta v Italy*, a case from 1998 brought by a wheel-chair user who complained that the Italian authorities had not complied with their obligations to provide access at private beaches for disabled people who wanted to swim in the sea. Rejecting his claim, the European Court of Human Rights said that Mr Botta's 'right to gain access to the beach and the sea, at a place distant from his normal place of residence during his holidays, concerns interpersonal relations of such broad and indeterminate scope that there can be no conceivable direct link between the measures the state was urged to take in order to make good the omissions of the private bathing establishments and the appli-cant's private life'. However, the Court went on to say, 'private life includes a person's physical and psychological integrity'—and this was the aspect of the case on which Dame Elizabeth relied.

The judge also relied on *Bensaid v UK*, decided by the Human Rights Court in 2001, a case in which an Algerian who had used a 'marriage of convenience' to deceive the authorities into allowing him to stay in Britain claimed that his removal from the country would lead to a relapse in his schizophrenia. Again, the case was thrown out. The Court said: 'Even assuming that the dislocation caused to the applicant by removal from the United Kingdom where he has lived for the last 11 years was to be considered by itself as affecting his private life, in the context of the relationships and support framework which he enjoyed there, the court considers that such interference may be regarded as complying with the requirements of the second paragraph of Article 8, namely as a measure "in accordance with the law", pursuing the aims of the protection of the economic well-being of the country and the prevention of disorder and crime, as well as being "necessary in a demo-cratic society" for those aims.' Again, though, it laid down general prin-ciples that Dame Elizabeth found helpful:

Not every act or measure which adversely affects moral or physical integrity will interfere with the right to respect to private life guaranteed by Article 8. However . . . treatment which does not reach the severity of Article 3 [inhuman or degrading] treatment may nonetheless breach Article 8 in its private-life aspect where there are sufficiently adverse effects on physical and moral integrity . . . Article 8 protects a right to identity and personal development, and the right to establish and develop relationships with other human beings and the outside world. The preservation of mental stability is in that context an indispensable precondition to effective enjoyment of the right to respect for private life.

There was a powerful case for granting Bell's application for anonymity, the judge said, based on her 'young age at the time she committed the offences, the length of time which has elapsed since the offences were committed, the limited nature of the information to be protected and, in particular, [Bell's] medical condition . . . together with the absence of any objection by the media'. This last point was telling: news organizations had no particular wish to reveal Bell's new name—or, at least, they were unwilling to pay counsel to argue the point—and there was no opposition in court to the orders sought.

It turned out that Bell was suffering from a 'chronic affective disorder manifested by anxiety and depression'. This had been precipitated, according to evidence from Professor John Gunn, the distinguished forensic psychiatrist, by 'appalling early childhood experiences . . . [and] . . . the acting out of childhood fantasies which led to her incarceration, to intense guilt, to stigma and to public opprobrium'. Later, he added, 'she experienced further abuse, including some damage at the hands of a prison official, physical and emotional damage from her first male partner and the very stressful experience of a journalist researching and writing her story'.

If anonymity was to be granted to Bell, said the judge, it would also have to be granted to her daughter, who would be living with her for the foreseeable future: their lives were so inextricably linked that it would not be possible to treat them separately.

While acknowledging that respect for private life had to be balanced against the right to freedom of expression in Article 10, the judge concluded that the scales came down firmly in favour of an injunction. There were four main reasons:

- Only a limited amount of information needed protection.
- Enough was known about Bell to allow the media to comment on her case, although only limited information was available about her attempts at rehabilitation.

- There were exceptional reasons for granting anonymity, including the important fact that her mental illness would be exacerbated if she were to be identified and pursued by press and public.
- Her semi-iconic status, demonstrated by continuing media interest thirty-five years after she committed her crimes, made the risk of publicity a very real one.

The judge faithfully followed Lord Woolf's guidelines in *A v B plc*, taking section 12 of the Human Rights Act into account and paying regard to the PCC and its Code of Practice. She stressed that notoriety did not, of itself, entitle an offender to anonymity. 'That would open the floodgates to widespread injunctions for criminals and would be contrary to the protection rightly afforded to freedom of expression.'

But her decision in *X (formerly Mary Bell) v S O* is still a matter for great concern. The judge went to great lengths to stress how exceptional this case was. Her decision to grant an injunction was not intended to increase 'the pool of those who might in the future be granted protection against potential breaches of confidence'. As far as she was aware, there were at that time no other child killers who had been released from prison or detention.

In fact, there was probably at least one more. Dame Elizabeth did not mention the case of Sharona Joseph, a 2-year-old girl from Borehamwood, to the north of London, who was assaulted and murdered there in 1988 by a deeply disturbed boy of 12. Her body, like that of James Bulger, was found on a railway line. Partly because the victim's grief-stricken middle-class family shunned publicity, and partly because the killer was allowed to keep his anonymity, the case attracted relatively little press coverage. Interviewed by newspapers in the summer of 2001, Sharona's parents said they had not been told whether the murderer had yet been released from his sentence of indefinite detention. In fact, there must be every chance that he is now out on licence. Geoffrey and Ora Joseph recalled that the judge who presided at the trial of their daughter's killer said afterwards that he was not to be named. But it seems unlikely that this order is still in force: Dame Elizabeth said, in terms, that James Bulger's killers were the only people to have been granted lifetime anonymity before Bell and her daughter.

No responsible newspaper would want to stop Sharona's killer living a good and useful life. It may be that he has recovered from a childhood of neglect and abuse, deprived of the love that Sharona was so visibly enjoying at the moment he abducted her from a family party. Or it may be that he is still a threat to others and that his past should not be kept from those closest to him now. Either way, there is a legitimate public interest in writing about him—though any moves to identify him would require careful thought.

What, then, if he were now to seek a lifelong injunction preserving his anonymity? Would he not have what lawyers call a 'legitimate expectation' of being treated in the same way as Mary Bell? Why should he be any less deserving, especially if he turns out to have a child of his own by now? That's the trouble with one-off decisions: they tend to become precedents. In the case of Thompson and Venables, Dame Elizabeth granted injunctions under Article 2 of the Human Rights Convention on the basis that their lives would otherwise be at risk. Giving judgment in *Venables v News Group Newspapers*, she said she was not sure 'whether it would be appropriate to grant injunctions to restrict the press in this case if only article 8 were likely to be breached'. As she explained, 'serious though the breach of the claimants' right to respect for family life and privacy would be, once the journalists and photographers discovered either of them, and despite the likely serious adverse effect on the efforts to rehabilitate them into society, it might not be sufficient to meet the importance of the preservation of the freedom of expression in article 10(1).' But the Mary Bell case, just two years later, was just such an example. Only Article 8 was in play. Ah well, said the judge, she had not intended 'to preclude a much closer examination of the competing rights under Articles 8 and 10 in an appropriate case, such as the present one'.

Dame Elizabeth's decision in *Venables* must be correct, so long as you accept her assessment of the evidence: if identifying Thompson and Venables would pose a real risk to their lives then it must be right to protect their privacy, however much one favours free speech. But, on the judge's own assessment, that risk does not apply to Bell and her daughter. I have little doubt that if Bell were tracked down once more her fragile mental state would suffer further. But she has only herself to blame: Bell's privacy would probably not have been disturbed by the press in 1998 if she had not sold her story, through Gitta Sereny, to a newspaper. No doubt there are many former criminals who would welcome any chance to keep their names out of the papers. The

Rehabilitation of Offenders Act 1974 to some extent allows offenders to wipe the slate clean once their offences are considered 'spent'. A court order protects the identity of two brothers who were *cleared* of murdering Damilola Taylor in 2001, even though they are now adults. Anonymity for defendants is a seductively slippery slope. Once we start to slide, it will be hard to avoid granting widespread anonymity to all who have been convicted of serious crimes, child and adult alike.

Which should prevail?

Like many of the cases discussed so far in this book, Bell's claim for anonymity involved what Lord Woolf called the 'tension' between privacy and freedom of expression 'which requires the court to hold the balance between the conflicting interests they are designed to protect'. In *Campbell v MGN*, Mr Justice Morland struck that balance by finding that it was 'entirely legitimate' for the *Mirror* to write about the fact that Naomi Campbell was receiving therapy for her drug addiction while at the same time deciding that it was 'unjustified' for the newspaper to print details of that therapy. That ruling was overturned by the Court of Appeal; Mr Justice Morland's nice distinction might have been upheld if the model had not lied about her addiction. Taking a similar approach, Mr Justice Ouseley allowed the press to report Jamie Theakston's visit to a brothel but not publish photographs of it.

But can these crude compromises ever be justified? Either a person's privacy is to be protected, or it is not. If freedom of expression is in the public interest, why limit it in this way? It would be easy to argue that the prerequisite for a free press is self-regulation, unfettered by legislation or judge-made law. One might ask why people should ever have grounds for complaint when newspapers publish the truth about them, however intrusive those publications may be. Those who court publicity must surely accept its consequences, the argument goes, and the judges should never interfere.

Attractive though that black-and-white approach may be, it is not the view of the Human Rights Convention, the judges of England and Wales, the PCC or the author of this book. Freedom of expression should generally prevail, but there must be some protection for personal privacy. That protection should be strictly limited: only in the most exceptional cases should public figures be entitled to prevent newspapers writing about them.

The refusal of the Court of Appeal to uphold the injunctions obtained by Garry Flitcroft is to be admired. We are, after all, talking about respect for a person's private and family life. What can be private about a series of affairs, played out in public clubs, hotels and restaurants? Why should a law designed to protect a person's family life cover adulterous affairs? Should a privacy law really be used to protect commercial interests, such as which weekly magazine should be able to cover a show-business wedding, or issues of personal vanity, such as whether the media can publish pictures of the claimant in a bad light? The answer must surely be no. Our judges should think carefully before restricting press freedom.

CHAPTER 5

Regulating the Press

As a journalist, I make my living by writing about other people and the legal disputes in which they become involved. That frequently requires some intrusion into what they may regard as their personal privacy. Sometimes, they are happy for me to publicize their victories in the courts. On occasions when the outcome is unfavourable they must wish they had followed the old saw and avoided litigation 'like the plague'. Even so, there is nothing they can or should do to prevent me from reporting a newsworthy court case. I try to keep within the bounds of good taste, avoiding prurience and sometimes sparing my readers the most offensive language and intimate details. I do, of course, aim to follow the Code of Practice issued by the Press Complaints Commission (PCC). And I take care not to publish people's full addresses unless I need to distinguish between different people with similar names. That said, if a case is important enough I have little hesitation in writing about matters that the parties might prefer to have kept private. I could not have written this book otherwise.

I'm right

The message of this chapter—if not of the entire book—is that conflicts between privacy and the press in Britain should generally be resolved in favour of the media. I do not seek to defend every excess of the tabloid press or, indeed, the broadsheets. I do not seek to argue that personal privacy should *never* merit the law's protection. But the justification for legal intervention has to be of a very high order indeed. Personally, I am not convinced that the lives of Robert Thompson and Jon Venables are still at risk from vigilantes more than ten years after they murdered James Bulger, though I am relieved that the task of assessing the level of risk fell to someone else. If Dame Elizabeth Butler-Sloss was correct in concluding that their lives would otherwise be in danger, then it is right that the press should be prevented from discovering and publishing their new identities. The same arguments would apply to 'supergrasses'— former criminals who give evidence against their associates. The police may be justified in using the blanket powers in the Terrorism Act 2000 to stop and search individuals and vehicles in appropriate cases. I can also see that the law should protect legitimate commercial agreements. But that is about as far as it should go.

If left to regulate themselves, journalists do not always seek to publish everything they know. A leading barrister contacted me in 2001 on the day he learned that, once again, he had been turned down by the Lord Chancellor for appointment to the rank of Queen's Counsel. Well aware—because others had told him—that he was good enough for promotion, he wanted people to know he had been treated unfairly. He was willing to be named and photographed. It was an excellent story and one I was keen to run. However, it could also have been professionally damaging, alerting his clients to the fact that had been turned down for promotion several times. Perhaps lacking the ruthlessness that other correspondents might have shown, I was reluctant to risk ruining his career for the sake of a story.

I therefore gave this barrister the advice he must often have given to others: sleep on it and let me know in a day or so whether you still want your story in print. Having discussed it with his family, he decided to go ahead. In this, he showed excellent judgment; some months later, it emerged that—contrary to all the publicly declared rules—his promotion been held back by a single unsubstantiated comment from one of the judges and QCs who used to be consulted about candidates. My article was published and did him no harm at all: two years later, he became a QC—just getting under the wire on the day that Lord Irvine, the soon-to-retire Lord Chancellor, indicated that he was proposing to abolish the system. The institutional failings identified by the investigation into this case rightly helped to seal the fate of a system under which the leaders of an independent profession were selected by a government minister.

More frequently, I suppose, we reporters go further than our sources might have wanted. I once interviewed a rather new member of the Government for my newspaper column. Just as I was coming to the end—but before I had switched off the audio-recorder I use to check quotes—I suggested that the Government would eventually have to make certain concessions on a controversial area of policy. Instead of dismissing my predictions, he smiled in a way that I took as confirmation of my hypothesis. I reported this as part of the interview, much to his irritation as I subsequently discovered. He thought I had broken the unwritten rules by publishing something that had taken place outside the confines of our interview. I explained to him later that, while I would always respect a confidence, I considered anything that took place during an on-the-record conversation with a professional politician was fair game.

He became much more wary of me for the next few months. And therein lies the reporter's dilemma. If we try to protect our sources from themselves, we will end up with no stories. But if we publish regardless of the consequences, we will end up with no sources.

Responsible journalism

It is well known that journalists, especially newspaper reporters, come pretty low in the public's estimation. A survey conducted by the market-research company MORI in February 2003 rated them even lower than government ministers, finding that 75 per cent of adults would not trust a journalist to tell them the truth. Little wonder that the press is thus excoriated if people hold it responsible for one of the most traumatic events in recent public life, the death of Diana, Princess of Wales, following a traffic accident in 1997. Describing it as a 'defining moment in British journalism', the journalist Ian Hargreaves, in his recent book *Journalism: Truth or Dare?*, notes that her car had been chased through a Paris underpass by freelance photographers working for British and other newspapers, leading the Princess's brother, at her funeral, to accuse publishers of having 'blood on their hands'.

Hargreaves finds 'some force' in the following observations by the writer Janet Malcolm:

Every journalist who is not too stupid or full of himself to notice what is going on knows that what he does is morally indefensible. He is a kind of confidence man, preying upon people's vanity, ignorance and loneliness, gaining their trust and betraying them without remorse . . . Journalists justify their treachery in various ways according to their temperaments. The more pompous talk about freedom of speech and 'the public's right to know'; the least talented talk about Art; the seemliest murmur about earning a living.

Since I am perfectly happy to defend my job on moral grounds, I suppose that makes me either stupid or pompous: perhaps both. Call me arrogant, but I think that we do a worthwhile job. More than that: I believe we fulfil an important role in the democratic process, sometimes holding ministers and judges to account more effectively than the Parliamentary Opposition. Certainly, they are likely to be questioned far more rigorously by legal correspondents at press briefings than when they appear before MPs in select committees or elsewhere in Parliament.

The more traditional defence of the legal reporter was put very well by Lord Denning, the most famous judge of his day, in *The Road to Justice*, a book he wrote in 1955:

A newspaper reporter is in every court. He sits through the dullest cases in the Court of Appeal and the most trivial cases before the magistrates. He says nothing but writes a lot. He notes all that goes on and makes a fair and accurate report of it. He supplies it for use either in the national press or in the local press according to the public interest it commands. He is, I verily believe, the watchdog of justice. If he is to do his work properly and effectively we must hold fast to the principle that every case must be heard and determined in open court. It must not take place behind locked doors. Every member of the public must be entitled to report in the public press all that he has seen and heard. The reason for this rule is the very salutary influence which publicity has for those who work in the light of it. The judge will be careful to see that the trial is fairly and properly conducted if he realises that any unfairness or impropriety on his part will be noted by those in court and may be reported in the press. He will be more anxious to give a correct decision if he knows that his reasons must justify themselves at the bar of public opinion.

Times have changed, of course, and there is no longer a reporter in every court, not even in every division of the Court of Appeal. But the principle holds good. Citing Lord Denning's remarks in 1986, Lord Justice Watkins said they emphasized the 'vital significance of the work of the journalist in reporting court proceedings and, within the bounds of impartiality and fairness, commenting upon the decisions of judges and justices and their behaviour in and conduct of the proceedings'. Lord Justice Watkins was giving judgment in *R v Felixstowe Justices, ex p Leigh*, a case in which the *Observer* journalist David Leigh, backed by his

REGULATING THE PRESS 143

newspaper and the National Union of Journalists, established that it was normally unlawful for sitting magistrates to withhold their names (as they had in Felixstowe). 'There is, in my view, no such person known to the law as the anonymous JP,' said the judge, whose courage as the holder of a wartime VC was belied by his diminutive stature. As Lord Taylor, the Lord Chief Justice, observed when Lord Justice Watkins retired as his deputy in 1993, he was thus an exception to the rule *de minimis non curat lex*—'the law does not concern itself with trifles'.

Protecting journalists' sources

The English courts have not always shown such respect for the press, particularly when the issue has been one of journalists' sources. That was demonstrated very clearly in the *Interbrew* case, which threatened to test the capacity of accountants to run a paper in a brewery.

Interbrew is an international beer producer, based in Belgium. In November 2001, it sought written advice from merchant banks on a possible takeover bid for another company. Someone else got hold of that advice, apparently 'doctored' it by inserting false market-sensitive information, and sent it to several newspapers with the aim of creating a false market in the shares of both companies. In an attempt to find out who was responsible, Interbrew asked for the return of its documents. Reuters news agency provided a copy—but not the original document. The *Financial Times*, the *Independent*, the *Guardian* and *The Times* were not prepared to hand over the documents either. The *Daily Telegraph* did not have a copy.

The five news organizations which had the documents were sued by the brewers. Mr Justice Lightman was in no doubt that the unknown source was acting in breach of a duty of confidence he owed to Interbrew. 'A document containing confidential information reached his hands, a duty of confidence thereupon attached to him and in breach of that duty he sent the document on,' the judge said. However, the brewery could not point to anything in the document that remained confidential at the time of publication and so its claim for breach of confidence was dismissed.

Interbrew had another card up its sleeve. A long-standing rule of equity provides that, where a person—through no fault of his own—

gets 'mixed up' in the wrongful acts of others so as to facilitate their wrongdoing, he comes under a duty to assist the person who has been wronged by giving him full information and disclosing the identity of the wrongdoer. Equity requires that he should co-operate in righting the wrong if he unwillingly facilitated its perpetration.

There are two exceptions. First, the obligation does not extend to mere witnesses or people who simply happen to have relevant evidence in their possession: it extends only to those who are involved in or who facilitated the wrongdoing. Secondly, there may be a rule of public policy that precludes application of the principle in a particular case. This is known as the *Norwich Pharmacal* principle, after Lord Reid's authoritative restatement of the law in the 1973 case of *Norwich Pharmacal v Customs and Excise Commissioners*.

The principle was followed and extended in 1980 when the House of Lords, led by Lord Wilberforce, ruled in a case brought by the British Steel Corporation against Granada Television. A *World in Action* programme about the national steel strike included confidential documents Granada had received from an informer at a senior level in British Steel. These disclosed that the Corporation's attempts to settle the strike had been blocked by the Conservative Government. British Steel wanted its documents back in order to identify the mole. Granada complied, but not before removing all identifying marks in the hope of protecting its source.

Despite retaining Patrick Neill, QC, later to become Lord Neill of Bladen and Vice-Chancellor of Oxford University, along with Alexander Irvine, QC, later to become Lord Irvine of Lairg and Lord Chancellor, Granada lost its appeal to the House of Lords by a majority of four to one. The news media had no immunity from the obligation to disclose their sources of information when disclosure was necessary in the interests of justice, according to the majority; in certain circumstances there might be a public interest in non-disclosure, but this was not such a case. There was a brave dissent from Lord Salmon, of Sandwich, who thought it wrong to sweep away the immunity of the press to reveal its sources of information. 'The freedom of the press depends upon this immunity,' he said. 'Were it to disappear, so would the sources from which its information is obtained, and the public be deprived of much of the information to which the public of a free nation is entitled.'

Contempt of court

The majority decision proved highly controversial, and Lord Scarman, another distinguished law lord, proposed legislation that was to become section 10 of the Contempt of Court Act 1981. That says:

No court may require a person to disclose, nor is any person guilty of contempt of court for refusing to disclose, the source of information contained in a publication for which he is responsible, unless it be established to the satisfaction of the court that disclosure is necessary in the interests of justice or national security or for the prevention of disorder or crime.

It was the next best thing to incorporating Article 10 of the Human Rights Convention. Lord Scarman campaigned for many years to have the Convention made part of domestic law; he feared, wrongly as it turned out, that it would not happen during what turned out to be his long lifetime. Article 10 of the Convention permits the right to freedom of expression to be circumscribed only if 'necessary in a democratic society' to achieve a number of specified legitimate aims. Similarly, section 10 of the 1981 Act provides that the freedom of the press may be circumscribed only if a judge says disclosure is necessary for a number of specified purposes.

And that necessity was just what Mr Justice Lightman found in *Interbrew*. 'The circumstances of this case are exceptional,' he said. 'Vital public as well as individual interests are at stake in securing the integrity of the share market. There is an overriding need for the disclosure sought in the interests of justice and for the prevention of crime.' In these exceptional circumstances, the judge added, there would be no real damage to the public perception that the press would normally protect its sources. 'No fair-minded observer could reasonably take the view that a person acting as the source has in this case would be protected from identification by press privilege,' he believed. Indeed it might bring the privilege into disrepute if it could prevent enquiries aimed at preventing further frauds on the public.

This proved to be a little naive, if not oversubtle. The news organizations took the view that sources should never be identified, however fraudulent their motives. If a would-be mole was considering whether to post a document to the press, he or she would not stop to consider the careful balancing exercise that had persuaded Mr Justice Lightman to order disclosure in this case. All that would be remembered was that on this occasion journalists had been unable to protect an unknown source. The whole incident brought back particularly painful memories at the *Guardian*, which received a secret document in 1983 indicating when the first cruise missiles would be arriving at US airbases in Britain. Peter Preston, the editor, returned the document to the Government on legal advice and, as a result, the unknown source was identified as Sarah Tisdall, a young Foreign Office clerk who in 1984 was sentenced to six months' imprisonment for breaching the Official Secrets Act 1911. The newspaper's unsuccessful appeals are reported as *Secretary of State for Defence v Guardian Newspapers Ltd.*

So the news organizations felt they had to go to the Court of Appeal. Mr Justice Lightman's ruling did not emerge entirely unscathed—in particular, the appeal judges were not convinced that the Interbrew documents were false, explaining that they had no way of knowing whether the source, if cornered, would demonstrate that he had simply assembled authentic documents from different places within Interbrew and the merchant banks. However, Lord Justice Sedley said Interbrew's entitlement to the documents was established 'because—and solely because—it may enable them to ascertain the identity of the proper defendant to a breach of confidence action relating to the relatively anodyne, though not the explosive, parts of the document'.

Turning to section 10 of the Contempt of Court Act, Lord Justice Sedley said that Interbrew could argue that 'disclosure is necessary in the interests of justice'. The critical issue was the source's evident purpose. 'It was on any view a maleficent one, calculated to do harm whether for profit or for spite, and whether to the investing public or Interbrew or both.' He, too, thought that such a source was less worthy of protection: newspapers had to accept that 'the public interest in protecting the identity of the source of what they have been told is disinformation may not be great'.

Elegant though this argument might have been, it too would have cut no ice with potential whistleblowers—or, indeed, with newspaper lawyers who might have to decide whether their accounts might be safely published. Alan Rusbridger, editor of the *Guardian*, said afterwards that the two *Interbrew* judgments would have a chilling effect—not so much on the media but on potential sources.

'Anything that chills the willingness of sources to come forward is not just a concern for the press', he added, 'it is of fundamental concern to democracy itself.' In his view, judges should only compel disclosure if it is a 'matter of grave and pressing social need'. Speaking at a conference organized by his newspaper in November 2002, he took the hypothetical example of a reporter who had interviewed a bomber and who knew that the bomber might strike again. In his view, such a journalist might be under an obligation to reveal a source; though he acknowledged that others might disagree. It was a pragmatic solution to the universal dilemma: an honest whistleblower should not be deterred from coming forward on some future occasion by the knowledge that a newspaper had once helped capture a terrorist. Other terrorists, on the other hand, might not feel so charitably disposed.

Rusbridger acknowledged that *Interbrew* was not a case of great iniquity, although he said there was no proof that it was an attempt at market manipulation and therefore unworthy of protection. 'But nobody should be blasé about it and then protest that the Press did a lousy job in exposing Maxwell, Enron, WorldCom or the next corporate scandal'.

The news organizations' attempts to appeal to the House of Lords against the Court of Appeal decision in *Interbrew* were unsuccessful. Permission was refused because the law lords had only recently given judgment in the *Ashworth* case (discussed in the following section) and this was thought to cover broadly the same ground. But the newspapers still refused to hand over their documents. Interbrew was left to enforce its injunction, if negotiations failed, by taking contempt-of-court proceedings against the news organizations.

Their discussions with the Stella Artois brewer's 'reassuringly expensive' lawyers were going reasonably well until the *Guardian* infuriated them by pointing out that its copy of the document was not in the hands of the newspaper itself: it was still in the reporter's possession. Faced with the prospect of having to start fresh legal proceedings against the reporter, Interbrew's lawyers warned the *Guardian* that it might send in sequestrators—court-appointed accountants who would run the newspaper. Perhaps they imagined that the sequestrators would then find the offending documents filed in the editor's safe under 'S' for 'secret'. However, even as prudent *Guardian* reporters were ensuring that their expenses claims were up-to-date, wiser counsels prevailed. Interbrew realized that taking over the *Guardian* would do little for its public image. The company agreed to withdraw from the legal action on the understanding that inquiries would be made by the Financial Services Authority—which has a statutory responsibility to investigate market manipulation and bring prosecutions where appropriate. The Authority asked for the documents to be handed over but did not seem too bothered when its request was refused. In the meantime, the journalists sought to take their case to the European Court of Human Rights, while acknowledging that this would not protect them against contempt proceedings for non-compliance with the court order.

The case demonstrated, once again, that there is a natural reluctance to turn journalists into martyrs. A few days before Interbrew backed off, the Attorney General, Lord Goldsmith, had announced that he would not, after all, be bringing contempt-of-court proceedings against Steve Panter, a journalist on the *Manchester Evening News* who had refused six months earlier to name the source of a story identifying the prime suspect for the IRA bomb attack on the city in 1996. Lord Goldsmith said he had decided not to take action because it was 'not appropriate' and 'not in the public interest' to do so. This was a wise move.

Ashworth and *Ackroyd*

The leading case on disclosure of journalists' sources is now *Ashworth Hospital Authority v MGN Ltd*, decided by the House of Lords in June 2002. Ashworth, the secure mental hospital on Merseyside, had sued the publishers of the *Daily Mirror* over an article it published in December 1999 about Ian Brady, the Moors murderer who was detained there indefinitely. The article said that Brady had started a hunger strike seven weeks earlier in protest against what he alleged was an unprovoked attack by prison officers in riot gear during which his arms were wrenched violently up his back, fracturing a bone in his wrist. It contained verbatim extracts from Brady's clinical notes and reported that a hospital manager had mocked Brady while he was being forcibly fed. The hospital wanted to find out whether a member of staff had leaked the information. If that proved to be the case, the employee would be sacked. Having lost in the High Court and the Court of Appeal, the newspaper appealed once again.

Sitting, unusually, in the House of Lords, Lord Woolf held that the *Norwich Pharmacal* jurisdiction (discussed above) applied on these facts.

Lord Justice Sedley, in *Interbrew*, had decided that detection of crime was not a proper object of the jurisdiction. On that point, however, he was overruled by the law lords. 'If the law has developed so as to enable, in the appropriate circumstances, the wrongdoer to be identified if he has committed a civil wrong, I can find no justification for not requiring the wrongdoer to be identified if he has committed a criminal wrong,' Lord Woolf explained. The more restrictive interpretation of *Norwich Pharmacal* attached 'excessive significance' to the historic origins of the jurisdiction. 'The limits which applied to its use in its infancy should not be allowed to stultify its use now that it has become a valuable and mature remedy,' Lord Woolf insisted. You could almost hear the journalists groan.

Turning next to the relationship between Article 10 of the Human Rights Convention and section 10 of the Contempt of Court Act, Lord Woolf said that judicial opinions differed on whether section 10 was passed in order that domestic law might reflect Article 10. 'However, whatever was the objective of those promoting section 10, there can be no doubt now that both section 10 and Article 10 have a common purpose in seeking to enhance the freedom of the press by protecting journalistic sources,' he explained.

'The important protection which both section 10 and Article 10 provide for freedom of expression is that they require the court stringently to scrutinise any request for relief which will result in the court interfering with freedom of expression, including ordering the disclosure of journalists' sources,' said Lord Woolf. 'Both section 10 and Article 10 are one in making it clear that the court has to be sure that a sufficiently strong positive case has been made out in favour of disclosure before disclosure will be ordered.'

Was that the case here? 'Any disclosure of a journalist's sources does have a chilling effect on the freedom of the press,' Lord Woolf acknowledged. 'It is for this reason that it is well established now that the courts will normally protect journalists' sources from identification. However, the protection is not unqualified. Both section 10 and Article 10 recognise this.'

In Lord Woolf's view, the disclosure was necessary and not disproportionate. 'The care of patients at Ashworth is fraught with difficulty and danger,' he said. The disclosure of the patients' records increases that difficulty and danger and to deter the same or similar wrongdoing in the future—particularly as the wrongdoer had received a cash payment—it was essential that the source should be identified and punished.

Really? There is no doubt that Ashworth had to tighten its security procedures after the leak, restricting access to its computer system. This must be an inconvenience to employees who require access to patient records. But there is little evidence that patients and staff had been put at risk. True it is that potential leakers would have been encouraged if the case had gone the other way. But these people, unless they are 'whistleblowers' protected by the Public Interest Disclosure Act 1998, know that they face dismissal if identified. Employers should not expect the media to help them track down untrustworthy staff.

Section 10 of the Contempt of Court Act and Article 10 of the Human Rights Convention are fine in principle. Nobody could expect sources to enjoy totally unrestricted protection. Although freedom of expression should generally prevail, it cannot be a trump card. But these decisions in *Interbrew* and *Ashworth* both demonstrate an alarming tendency for the courts to order disclosure where there is no real need for it. Look what happened when the court's orders were ignored. The stock market continued to trade, despite the apparent attempt to manipulate it. Ashworth continued to hold patients securely. As Lord Woolf himself said, *any* disclosure of a journalist's sources has a chilling effect on the freedom of the press. Judges should remember that remark and draw the line much more narrowly than he had been prepared to. As we shall see, some of them did.

A source disclosed

The *Daily Mirror* neatly sidestepped the House of Lords decision in *Ashworth* by naming its source as Robin Ackroyd, a freelance journalist who had sold it the story. 'As part of a public company we cannot expose ourselves to the risk of being held in contempt of court,' the paper explained to the sound of bucks being passed.

That was not what the hospital had been expecting: it knew that Gary Jones, the *Mirror* reporter who wrote the original story, had obtained his information from an intermediary but Jones had told the High Court he believed that that 'knowledge of the identity of the intermediary would in all probability lead to the identity of the source

of the leak'. This suggested that the intermediary was a friend or relative of the source, rather than another journalist. So the hospital then
sought a disclosure order against Ackroyd himself.

Mersey Care NHS Trust, which had by then taken responsibility for
Ashworth, argued that Ackroyd was in the same position as the *Daily
Mirror* and therefore had no real prospect of defending the claim for
disclosure. In October 2002, Mr Justice Gray agreed that the hospital
authority was entitled to summary judgment, without the need to argue
its case in detail. While acknowledging that a public-interest defence
was available in breach-of-confidence cases—and that this applied
equally to claims based on a contractual duty of confidence—he considered that Ackroyd would not be able to win on the basis of a public-
interest defence in this case. That was because he believed the journalist
could still have disclosed the fact that Brady was being force-fed without access to his medical records. 'As the newspaper itself argued in the
MGN case, the content of those records was essentially trivial,' the judge
said. 'There is nothing in them to warrant the conclusion that their
disclosure to the media was in the public interest.'

In an important victory for the press, Mr Justice Gray's ruling was
overturned by the Court of Appeal in May 2003. Ackroyd was awarded
his costs against the hospital—he had been funded by the National
Union of Journalists—and he was told he would be allowed to defend
Ashworth's claim at a full hearing if Ashworth pursued the case against
him.

As the appeal judges acknowledged, the background to Ackroyd's
article was an inquiry into Ashworth hospital by Peter Fallon, QC, a
retired senior circuit judge. The Fallon Report, published in January
1999, concluded that the management culture of the hospital was
'dysfunctional'. Senior managers were 'secretive, out of touch and totally
unable to control this large institution'. Pornography was widely available on the ward, patients were running their own businesses, hospital
policies were ignored and security was grossly inadequate. Finding that
critical internal reports had been suppressed and ministers misled, the
Inquiry recommended that the hospital should close. It did not.

Lord Justice May, who had also been a member of the Court of
Appeal in *Ashworth Hospital Authority v MGN Ltd*, believed he had not
been told about the Fallon Report when the case was argued towards
the end of 2000. This seems plausible: there is no mention of it in the

detailed history that appears on the hospital's website. Lord Justice May's decision in *Ackroyd v Mersey Care NHS Trust* was clearly influenced by evidence that Ackroyd was a responsible investigative reporter whose earlier efforts to expose incompetence at the hospital and expose it to public scrutiny had led directly to the establishment of the Fallon Inquiry.

Ackroyd explained in a witness statement that he had been approached by sources at the hospital and told that Brady's move and his force-feeding 'represented very serious failings on the part of those responsible, even by the standards of Ashworth as described so graphically in the Fallon report'. He continued: 'However evil Mr Brady is, Ashworth is responsible for his proper treatment. It is grotesque for a manager to stand behind a patient who is being force fed while making gagging noises to mock him.'

The journalist pointed out that the Fallon Report would never have been set up without disclosures by patients and other sources at Ashworth. The money paid by the *Mirror* had gone to him, not the sources. They had been acting not for financial gain but in the public interest. So the agreed facts on which the law lords had based their decision were wrong: the source was not guilty of the venality that both the Court of Appeal and the House of Lords had assumed. Accepting these arguments, Lord Justice May added that Ackroyd could challenge the earlier finding that leaks of information 'had the effect of creating a highly detrimental effect on the security of the hospital, the treatment of the patients and the morale of the staff': he would maintain that they were a symptom of discontent with its secrecy and had helped patients and staff by opening up Ashworth's practices to outside scrutiny.

And then there was the *Norwich Pharmacal* principle, that where a blameless person gets 'mixed up' in the wrongful acts of others so as to facilitate their wrongdoing, he comes under a duty to assist the person who has been wronged by giving him full information and disclosing the identity of the wrongdoer. But what if Ackroyd's source at the hospital was not a wrongdoer at all, because he (or she, or they) had a public-interest defence? 'A claim for breach of confidence, including a claim for breach of a contract requiring confidentiality, may in law be defended if the public interest in disclosure outweighs the right of the [claimant] to protect his confidence,' the judge pointed out, predicting that such a claim by Ackroyd's supposed source would have 'a real prospect of success' and that the journalist would have an equivalent public-interest defence to any claim that he was in breach of confidence by passing the information to the *Mirror*. If that proved to be the case, the judge was prepared to assume that the *Norwich Pharmacal* principle would not apply.

In concluding that Ackroyd should be allowed to defend the case at a full hearing, Lord Justice May delivered a resounding defence of free speech. 'I consider that Mr Ackroyd has a real prospect of successfully defending this claim notwithstanding the decisions in the *MGN* case,' he said. 'If that might be regarded as expressing an unduly rosy view of his prospects of success in what is undoubtedly a difficult defence . . . there is another compelling reason why this case should be disposed of at a trial. Protection of journalistic sources is one of the basic conditions for press freedom in a democratic society. An order for source disclosure cannot be compatible with Article 10 of the European Convention unless it is justified by an overriding requirement in the public interest. Although there is a clear public interest in preserving the confidentiality of medical records, that alone cannot, in my view, be automatically regarded as an overriding requirement without examining the facts of a particular case. It would be an exceptional case indeed if a journalist were ordered to disclose the identity of his source without the facts of *his* case being fully examined . . . His defence may not perhaps succeed in the end, but I think that he is entitled to a trial.'

Lord Justice Carnwath added that the case had gone all the way to the House of Lords on the mistaken assumption that success for the hospital would lead to identification of the culprit. Time had passed, the primary source had not been identified and the 'cloud of suspicion' that Lord Woolf had thought was hanging over the hospital's staff no longer appeared to be blighting activity there. Even if there proved to be no public-interest defence, it was arguable that the court's discretion should not be exercised in favour of identifying the perpetrator of 'something which happened so long ago and, as far as we know, has not been repeated'.

Finally, Lord Justice Ward thought that there was a 'palpable tension between the judiciary and elements of the press'. If that was so, it was 'all the more important, not that judges should pander to perceived pressure from the press, but only that judges should be vigilant to protect the freedom of the press where it is legitimate to do so'. Cutting short the evidence gathering when there were real differences between this case and *MGN* sent a 'chill of apprehension' down his spine.

It was a fine judgment by three independently minded judges who were not afraid to admit that the courts had previously got it wrong. They sent a clear message to Ashworth: back off, or risk losing the case. Just to emphasize the point, Mersey Care NHS Trust was ordered to pay Ackroyd's costs in the Court of Appeal and the High Court, with £20,000 to be paid on account within fourteen days.

Good win for journalism

As the Court of Appeal seemed to accept when it overturned Mr Justice Gray's ruling in *Ackroyd v Mersey Care NHS Trust*, his decision had been hard to reconcile with *Goodwin v UK*, decided by the European Court of Human Rights in 1996. In its submissions on that case, the Government had argued that 'a journalist's express promise of confidentiality or his implicit undertaking of non-attributability may have to yield to a greater public interest'. The UK's view was that 'the journalist's privilege should not extend to the protection of a source who has conducted himself [in bad faith] or, at least, irresponsibly, in order to enable him to pass on, with impunity, information which has no public importance.' This argument, which anticipated the claimants' position in *Interbrew* and *Ashworth*, was rejected by the European Court.

The case involved Bill Goodwin, a trainee journalist on a trade paper called *The Engineer*. In November 1989, three months after he had started work there, Goodwin was phoned by a source who told him that a leading private company was raising a loan to cover unexpected financial problems. A few days later, he telephoned the company to check the story, which had come from a leaked copy of its corporate plan.

The company—later identified as Tetra Ltd—went straight to court and Mr Justice Hoffmann (as he then was) granted an immediate injunction preventing the media from reporting the plan's contents. A few days later, he ordered Goodwin and his employers, Morgan-Grampian Ltd, to disclose their source. They refused, but Mr Justice Hoffmann's orders were upheld by the Court of Appeal and the House of Lords in *X Ltd v Morgan-Grampian Ltd*. Goodwin had been an innocent party, the courts acknowledged, but he was caught by the *Norwich Pharmacal* principle (discussed earlier in this chapter).

Section 10 of the Contempt of Court Act applied to the case but all the judges agreed that it was in the interests of justice for a private company to be able to keep its business private. Otherwise—who knows?—the company might have gone out of business and jobs would have been lost. 'The importance of protecting the source,' according to Lord Bridge in the House of Lords, was, however, 'much diminished by the source's complicity, at the very least, in a gross breach of confidentiality which is not counterbalanced by any legitimate interest which publication of the information was calculated to serve'. But Goodwin still refused to comply with the order to disclose his source and he was fined £5,000 for contempt of court.

At Strasbourg, the case of *Goodwin v UK* turned on whether the interference with the reporter's freedom of expression under Article 10 had been 'necessary in a democratic society'. The court pointed out that Mr Justice Hoffmann's initial order had been sufficient to prevent anyone from discovering that the company was in difficulties. That order, by itself, would not enable the company to prevent further leaks, obtain compensation or sack a disloyal member of staff: for that, it needed to identify the source. But the aim of tracking down a disloyal employee did not outweigh 'the vital public interest in the protection of the applicant journalist's source'. As the Court explained, there was not 'a reasonable relationship of proportionality between the legitimate aim pursued by the disclosure order and the means deployed to achieve that aim. The restriction which the disclosure order entailed on the applicant journalist's exercise of his freedom of expression cannot therefore be regarded as having been necessary in a democratic society.'

This was how the Human Rights Court summed up the law in 1996:

Protection of journalistic sources is one of the basic conditions for press freedom . . . Without such protection, sources may be deterred from assisting the press in informing the public on matters of public interest. As a result the vital public-watchdog role of the press may be undermined and the ability of the press to provide accurate and reliable information may be adversely affected. Having regard to the importance of the protection of journalistic sources for press freedom in a democratic society and the potentially chilling effect an order of source disclosure has on the exercise of that freedom, such a measure cannot be compatible with Article 10 of the Convention unless it is justified by an overriding requirement in the public interest.

Goodwin was fully entitled to be proud of achieving this 'important statement of principle', as Lord Justice May called it in *Ackroyd*, even though he was not awarded compensation and the judgment did not lead to any new legislation. The journalist never disclosed his source although his counsel, Geoffrey Robertson, QC, narrowed down the field considerably when he revealed in the fourth edition of his book *Media Law* that the English courts had been wrong to infer 'that the source had been involved in stealing a copy of the business plan or else must have been a high executive deserving exposure and punishment for corporate disloyalty'.

Next time the English judges are asked to order some young reporter to betray his sources, they should remember how much they rely on journalists to uncover dark doings in government, industry and elsewhere. As the Court said, there needs to be an 'overriding requirement in the public interest' before disclosure can be ordered. If the price of a free press is letting a few whistleblowers keep their jobs, it is a price well worth paying.

The tables turned

Journalism is not an occupation for those who wish to preserve their personal privacy. Television news reporters, in particular, soon realize that they risk being recognized anywhere in the world they may go, an inhibiting factor for anyone who might otherwise be tempted to pick a fight with a waitress, drive aggressively or slip discreetly into a place of ill-repute.

In this context I am, of course, adopting a broad definition of privacy. Some might argue that the things we do in public—such as visiting a restaurant, sitting behind the wheel of a car or walking down the street—can never be truly private. However, unless you happen to be near your home, your work, your pub or club or your place of worship, the chances of being seen by anyone who knows you are quite low. And unless your car is reasonably distinctive, it is even less likely that anyone will recognize you while driving, provided you are some distance away from your normal haunts. Being seen by a stranger, though, is little deterrent to low-level misbehaviour; what makes you think twice is the risk of being seen by someone who knows your name—someone, indeed, who might tell your friends or even a tabloid newspaper. Though we know we are being photographed by security cameras as we walk down a city street or enter a shop, we may still enjoy a sense of invisibility, a feeling that we are blending into an anonymous crowd. But losing that privilege is the price of fame. Even newspaper columnists whose photographs appear above their words are not exempt from the risk of being spotted by a sharp-eyed reader.

And this is as it should be. Specialist correspondents should not make themselves too remote from individuals who may have some news to give them. But it must be news: I have become increasingly impatient with members of the public who ring up out of the blue and proceed to tell me in great detail about their long-running dispute with a neighbour, or with their former solicitors. What can I do? Write about their case and all the others? Hardly: I would soon have no readers left. Give them legal advice? Not my job; and, if I do break my own rule, I invariably advise them to settle.

Perhaps all journalists should know what it feels like to have their privacy invaded in this way. My wife, a writer and commentator, has sometimes been the subject of newspaper profiles; I make the occasional appearance in these pieces as a footnote. One article, in particular, purported to describe our domestic arrangements. Since almost none of it was true, it could not have been an invasion of our privacy. On the other hand, readers could hardly have been expected to know that the piece was largely false. Though defamatory, it did not strike us as particularly damaging (few people saw it and even fewer would have believed it) so we decided to let matters rest. But there was at least a body to complain to if the magazine had been unwilling to publish a letter in response to the offending article. That, of course, is the PCC.

Complaining about the press

As we have seen, the PCC is an industry-funded body that deals with complaints from members of the public about the editorial content of newspapers and magazines. Established in 1991 to replace the much-criticized Press Council, it provides what it describes as a 'free, quick and easy' service to people who complain that publications have breached its Code of Practice (set out in full in the appendix).

The Commission completed its investigation into 2,630 complaints in 2002, of which nearly one in four related to intrusion into privacy. Its main aim is to resolve the complaint as quickly as possible, preferably by publishing a correction, an apology, or a letter from the complainant. Alternatively, an editor may offer to publish a follow-up piece or send a personal private acknowledgement and apology for a breach of the Code. Crucially, the PCC does not award compensation.

Since editors are naturally keen to settle complaints, the Commission had to adjudicate on only thirty-six complaints in 2002, the lowest number ever. It considered that to be a sign not of the weakness of self-regulation, but of its strength. Of the thirty-six complaints, seventeen were upheld. All adjudications that were critical of a newspaper were published in full and with due prominence, it points out. The adjudication process operates 'with great speed', as the Commons Culture, Media and Sport Committee found in June 2003. It took the PCC an average of thirty-two days to complete its handling of a complaint (those rejected took eleven days, on average, while complaints upheld after an adjudication took seventy-seven days). Nine out of ten complaints come from members of the public.

The aim of the PCC is to stave off moves towards what it describes as 'any form of legal or statutory control'. It believes that 'legal controls would be useless to those members of the public who could not afford legal action and would mean protracted delays before complainants received redress'. However, a complaint to the Commission does not preclude subsequent legal action. Sara Cox, the Radio 1 disc jockey, complained to the PCC after the *People* published pictures showing her and her husband naked. An apology duly appeared, but the couple decided to take legal action anyway, claiming 'breach of privacy': we saw in Chapter 1 that the newspaper paid them £50,000 to settle.

As the Commons Media Committee said:

The rationale argued for the PCC is that to maintain the freedom of the press —vital in an open and democratic society—the industry has to regulate itself; otherwise the door is open to Government influence, censorship, even control . . . For self-regulation to work, however, it has to command the confidence of a split constituency . . . As it has no authority, nor indeed resources, other than what is ceded voluntarily to it by the press industry, the PCC must command the confidence of that industry. In view of past threats to replace self-regulation with a statutory system, a proposal described as 'repugnant' by the PCC and the press industry, the commission must also command the confidence of Government and Parliament. Crucially, to meet its objectives and to be effective, the PCC must command the confidence of the public.

In its report on *Privacy and Media Intrusion*, the Commons select committee found that the PCC had, broadly speaking, the confidence of the newspaper industry. Whether it had the Government's trust as well was more in doubt, but in any event ministers had no plans to put newspaper regulation on to a statutory footing. However, what MPs appeared unsure of was whether the PCC had the public's confidence. On the one hand, its staff were praised for helping complainants through the process. On the other hand, some complainants would have preferred a formal adjudication rather than what one of them dismissed as the newspaper's offer of 'an apology on page 31'.

A new broom

In May 2003, Sir Christopher Meyer made his first major speech since taking over from Lord Wakeham as chairman of the PCC. He called on the Commission to make eight improvements:

- Increase the number of lay members on the Commission from nine to ten, while retaining the number from the press at seven—as 'a clear, tangible, forceful sign of the PCC's independence and objectivity'.
- Advertise openly for all new lay members.
- Hold an independent annual audit of its customer service.
- Give adjudications 'a clear, common branding' to ensure they are 'consistently and prominently labelled as PCC criticisms of a newspaper'.
- Hold open meetings around the United Kingdom where Commission members could talk about its work and answer questions.
- Arrange an annual audit of the Code of Practice to see whether changes are necessary, perhaps because of new technology or public concerns.
- Issue a users' handbook for all newsrooms, setting out the back-

ground to the Code's provisions, and highlighting current PCC case law.

- Appoint a Charter Commissioner who could look at procedural complaints. This would be tantamount to creating the PCC's own internal system of judicial review.

Sir Christopher's remarks were timed to take some of the sting out of the expected criticism from the Commons Media Committee. To some extent, they overlapped with the views of Tessa Jowell, the Secretary of State. Even so, the MPs considered that the PCC was still 'slightly too "softly, softly"' in its approach. It should 'flex its muscles a bit', perhaps setting up a system whereby those complainants who did not want mediation could seek an adjudication on their case. The Committee also suggested the creation of a PCC 'pre-publication team' to handle inquiries from the public about possible stories and liaise with the editors concerned. This would not amount to 'prior restraint' or 'press censorship', the MPs insisted. This team could also take a more proactive approach, intervening in advance to seek compliance with the Code of Practice rather than waiting for complaints after it had been breached.

The Code itself should be updated, the Committee believed. Its ban on intercepting telephone calls should be extended to e-mails and other electronic communications. Journalists should be allowed to refuse an assignment if it breached the Code. There should be an explicit ban on direct or indirect payments to police officers for information. A publication that was required to publish a formal adjudication should refer to it prominently on the front page. The offending article and all references to it should be removed from public databases.

Finally, there was the issue of money. The MPs recommended two innovations, 'one gently punitive and the other modestly compensatory'. The punitive one would be to gear the fee paid to the PCC's funding body by each publication to the number of adverse adjudications it received in the previous year. The compensatory one would be a fixed scale of awards to be paid to complainants (or a charity of their choice) 'in serious cases'. In addition, complainants' outgoings (though not legal fees) should be reimbursed where, for example, they had needed to purchase the transcript of a trial.

Sir Christopher Meyer issued a holding response to the Committee's recommendations when they were published in June 2003, promising no more than to read them in detail. 'It is important to remember,' he added, 'that as an independent body—independent from newspapers, politicians, lawyers and any other interest group—the PCC is not obliged to accept any of them.' This approach may have been intended to keep the newspapers on side in response to the battering they had just received from the MPs. Certainly, publishers would be reluctant to pay any more for the PCC at a time when newspaper advertising was still in recession. But perhaps the PCC chairman was reflecting the confidence felt by the industry in the light of the Government's firm commitment to self-regulation. If legal controls are not an option, there is little incentive to make radical changes. Even the threat of a possible privacy law might have persuaded the PCC to implement some of the Committee's more moderate reforms.

Tony Martin

Little more than a month after the Commons Media Committee called for statutory controls on the press, a popular newspaper demonstrated the limits of self-regulation. Tony Martin was the man who shot two burglars at his isolated farmhouse in Norfolk in 1999, killing one and wounding the other. His murder conviction was reduced to manslaughter after the Court of Appeal heard evidence about his state of mind. Nevertheless, he became something of a national hero.

When he was released from prison in July 2003, the *Daily Mirror* paid him a reputed £125,000 for his story, despite the provision in the PCC's Code of Practice which says that 'payment or offers of payment for stories, pictures or information, must not be made directly or through agents to convicted or confessed criminals or to their associates . . . except where the material concerned ought to be published in the public interest and payment is necessary for this to be done'. To explain what might be considered in the public interest, the Code gives the example of 'detecting or exposing crime or a serious misdemeanour'. What it means by a 'serious misdemeanour' is somewhat opaque: in English criminal law, the distinction between felony (a serious crime) and misdemeanour (a less serious crime) was abolished in 1967. However, 'exposing' a crime must mean writing about it for the first time: it cannot mean simply writing once again about a crime that has already been the subject of a trial and an appeal.

Even so, Piers Morgan, the *Mirror* editor, claimed that the public-interest argument in Martin's case was 'very obvious and easily definable'. He said Martin would be dealing with issues such as the rights of householders to defend themselves against criminals and the rights of criminals to seek compensation if they were injured. 'There are fundamental principles of British law which he will be addressing,' Morgan said. 'If these aren't matters of public interest, I don't know what are.'

Quite apart from subsuming the entirely separate systems of English and Scots law into one non-existent concept, Morgan—like Lord Woolf in Flitcroft's case—was making the classic mistake of confusing what was *of* public interest with what was *in* the public interest. It was no more in the public interest to report Martin's views on these issues than it was to recount the opinions of any other saloon-bar bore. The PCC promised to investigate.

Commentators predicted an adverse ruling, while suspecting it would make no difference to the *Mirror*. 'Piers Morgan will have published and moved on to some other yarn and some other chequebook,' Peter Preston, the former *Guardian* editor, wrote in the *Observer*. 'The PCC will get its verdict printed in his pages, but with a defiant shrug.' Better, said Preston, simply to allow criminals to sell their stories. 'There is, pragmatically, no great harm to Martin's £125,000. It doesn't incite Norfolk hermit farmers to go out and shoot a burglar for cash.'

That was not how the Government saw it. Speaking to reporters shortly after Martin's deal with the *Mirror*, Lord Falconer, the Constitution Secretary, argued that the law should prevent criminals profiting from their crimes. But surely 'everyone has the right to freedom of expression' under Article 10? No problem, according to Lord Falconer—under Government plans, the killer would still be able to *tell* his story, though not sell it. He strongly suspected Martin would have been willing to speak for nothing if payments had been banned.

What if the newspaper had instead offered a payment to a charity of Martin's choice? That would be less undesirable, Lord Falconer conceded. And what about benefits in kind? Are ministers really going to tell newspapers that they cannot install their buy-ups in plush hotels, perhaps in exotic locations abroad, while interviewing them? Banning that sort of arrangement would reduce the chances of keeping a story exclusive and risk breaching the newspaper's rights of free expression under Article 10.

A moment's thought should have shown the Government how unenforceable such a law would be. While it might be possible to inspect the criminal's bank statements or watch for signs of new-found affluence after his release from prison, there would be no way of preventing newspapers from making payments some months later to a favourite nephew or a willing stooge—unless newspaper editors themselves were to face prosecution. Surely, the Government's aim was to punish the criminal, not the messenger?

Lord Falconer should have recalled what happened when his predecessor, Lord Irvine, promised to make it an imprisonable offence for reporters to pay witnesses in criminal prosecutions. Martin was a witness at his own trial, so payments to someone in his position would presumably have been covered by the proposed ban. In March 2002, Lord Irvine said unambiguously: 'The Government has decided to introduce legislation to make it a criminal offence to make, or agree to make, or to receive, a payment to a witness or a potential witness in criminal proceedings for their story with a view to publication.' There was to be consultation, but only on 'the details of that legislation'. In August 2002, Lord Irvine changed his mind. While committed to banning payments to witnesses, he conceded that 'it might be possible to achieve this objective through tougher media self-regulation'. In March 2003, his junior minister confirmed it would be 'unfair to press ahead with forced change'.

Contrary to expectations, the PCC found in favour of the *Mirror*. Explaining in October 2003 why it believed there had been no breach of its Code after all, the Commission made the following points:

- The payment was necessary: Martin's representative had asked for payment on his behalf and indeed had received a number of offers from other newspapers.
- The issue upon which Martin had a unique perspective concerned a matter of great public interest and the PCC considered it legitimate to seek his views at the moment of his release.
- It was clear that there was a considerable public appetite to engage in a debate about the issues highlighted by the Martin case, and the Commission did not consider that it was its task to restrict that debate.
- It would have put the newspaper publishing industry in an unfair

position to have concluded that the public had no right to read material in a newspaper that they could access through other media, which had also paid Martin for his story.

- It was clearly in the public interest to expose Martin to public scrutiny so that members of the public could conclude for themselves whether his popular image was deserved.
- The articles did not glorify Martin's crime.

These findings were clearly in line with the Commission's case law, it maintained. This made it clear that the PCC would still censure payments to criminals when they were for information about romance, sex or gossip, or where the material glorified crime. 'None of those factors was inherent in this case,' the PCC concluded.

But its arguments were far from convincing. While not exactly mad at the time that he killed 16-year-old Fred Barras, Martin was suffering from a 'long-standing paranoid personality disorder which can be classified as an abnormality of the mind'. That was the view of Dr Philip Joseph, the defence psychiatrist who examined him after his trial and conviction. His expert evidence enabled the Court of Appeal to reduce Martin's murder conviction to manslaughter on the grounds of diminished responsibility.

Martin was still paranoid in 2001, according to the psychiatrist, and there is no reason to suppose he would have got much better after spending another two years in prison. Dr Joseph also believed that Martin 'suffered from a genuine period of amnesia' at the time that he shot Barras and his accomplice, Brendon Fearon. The jury at his trial did not believe Martin's claim that he could not see the intruders clearly because he was still coming down the stairs when he fired all three shots at them. All the expert evidence suggested that Martin's account was not true. So in reality his interview in the *Daily Mirror*—far from being something that, in the words of the Code, 'ought to be published'— was worthless.

The least worst option

However critical I may be of the PCC's ruling in individual cases, I still believe that self-regulation is better than any of the alternatives on offer.

The reasons were aptly summed up by Sir Christopher Meyer in a lecture to the Society of Editors in October 2003, six months into his term of office as chairman of the PCC:

I took this job on the basis of a few simple beliefs, forged initially as a government press secretary in that age of innocence before spokesmen became spin doctors. That a press free from any interference by the State is fundamental to democracy; and that self-regulation, though imperfect like any human endeavour, is a manifestation of this truth; and that without it, no press anywhere in the world can truly claim to be free.

Sir Christopher confirmed that the newspaper industry had largely accepted the improvements he had proposed four months earlier.

Self-regulation does not, of course, exclude the courts. The PCC is subject to judicial review, like any other decision-making body, and its rulings on privacy can always be overridden by the judges. Nobody, least of all the media, is above the law. But even with the ever-present threat of judicial oversight self-regulation is still better than a statutory scheme. This is because regulation by the courts is preferable to regulation by Parliament.

If I accept that the law has a role in regulating relations between individuals and the press, then surely I must prefer Parliament to draw the line? That way, as Lord Bingham argued in Chapter 1, the rules 'would carry the imprimatur of democratic approval'. The problem with this argument, put to me by a lawyer who saw an early draft of this book, is that it does not recognize the overriding importance of protecting press freedom from government interference. Leaving it all to the judges may result in piecemeal lawmaking, with inconsistencies that cannot easily be rectified until a suitable appeal comes before the courts months or even years later. It may be less effective at subjugating the press than an all-encompassing statute—though that is unlikely to cause me any sleepless nights.

But you have to remember whose side the judges are on. They have no interest in silencing the press, whatever conspiracy theorists may think. On the contrary, once they no longer have a Lord Chancellor to stick up for them in Cabinet or a platform for senior judges to speak out in the House of Lords, they will be as reliant on the press to fight their corner as any other beleaguered section of society. Although politicians sometimes talk of judges as an 'arm of government', the courts' job is often to hold the line between government and governed, between ministers and the press. If freedom of expression is at stake, I would rather take my chances with one of Her Majesty's judges than one of Her Majesty's ministers.

An invasion of privacy

Peter Foster was the confidence trickster who helped the Prime Minister's wife Cherie Blair, a close friend of his then girlfriend Carole Caplin, to buy two flats in Bristol at a discount. Before that, Foster had served prison sentences in Australia, Britain and the United States for fraudulently advertising bogus weight-loss products. In December 2002, after Downing Street had initially denied Foster's involvement in the investment scheme, Mrs Blair was forced to make a humiliating public apology. She may well have wondered why she was not entitled to keep her business transactions private. The answer, of course, is that we are entitled to know if the Prime Minister and his wife are investing their savings on the advice of a fraudster.

As part of its investigations into this extraordinary affair, the *Sun* obtained and published details of private telephone conversations between Foster and his mother. On the face of it, that would amount to a breach of clause 8 of the PCC's Code of Practice. However, that clause is one of several that must be read subject to the public-interest exception at the end of the Code. The *Sun* maintained that publication of the transcripts was in the public interest because it helped to ensure that the public was not further misled by those involved in the saga, and because the transcripts established a clearer picture of events surrounding what inevitably became known as 'Cheriegate'.

This was denied by Foster, who maintained that their publication did not contradict anything he had said that might have misled the public. Indeed, he had made no public statement. The simple fact that the story was high profile did not justify the newspaper's intrusion into his privacy, he argued.

Foster's complaint was upheld by the PCC. In reaching its decision, the Commission started from the premise that eavesdropping on private telephone conversations—and then publishing transcripts of them—was one of the most serious forms of physical intrusion into privacy.

Publication could, of course, be justified when the public interest was clearly served.

But in view of the serious nature of such intrusion . . . the commission must set the public interest hurdle at a demonstrably high level. In this case, the commission considered that the text of the telephone conversations generally served merely to illustrate the story in a manner which was already well known. Although it is arguable that some elements of the story might, presented on their own, have contributed to the development of 'Cheriegate', the commission did not consider that new information, of the significance required to justify breaching the strict terms of the code, was revealed. The commission expects a very strong public interest justification for breaching this clause—and the newspaper's defence did not meet it.

This seems to be the correct approach. Foster may be a con man and a rogue, but that does not give the newspapers a free hand to act as they wish.

Privacy in rape cases

What happens though when someone's privacy is invaded by almost the entire British media? John Leslie, a former daytime television presenter best known for being very tall, found himself under siege by reporters in the summer of 2003.

This modern immorality tale began a year earlier when Ulrika Jonsson, also a television personality, alleged in her autobiography that, many years earlier when she was a teenage weather forecaster on breakfast television, she had been date-raped in a hotel by a well-known television presenter as a result of which she spent four days in hospital. She did not name her alleged assailant at the time and always refused to do so subsequently. However, Leslie's name began to circulate widely among media gossips and Matthew Wright, a former *Daily Mirror* show-business reporter turned TV presenter, 'accidentally' named him on his live television programme. Once one media outlet had taken the plunge, several newspapers felt safe in following up the story—though by no means all of them chose to publish Leslie's name. He chose not to issue a denial, his lawyers having presumably advised him that this would have allowed the remaining papers to identify him. What might otherwise have been a shrewd move backfired spectacularly when Leslie promptly lost his job presenting *This Morning*. Granada Television said it had received no response from Leslie for a week, despite repeated requests for information. 'Given his silence, it became impossible for him to continue to present the live daily show.' Perhaps another factor was the decision of a Sunday newspaper to print footage from a home video that was said to show Leslie snorting cocaine through a rolled-up banknote at his London home.

Meanwhile, the publicity that followed Wright's programme prompted a number of women to make allegations against Leslie in the press; a few were even willing to go to the police. In June 2003, Leslie was charged with two offences of indecently assaulting a woman in May 1997. He denied the charges and was preparing to argue that the publicity was so great that he could not have had a fair trial.

A month later, however, the alleged victim gave the police further information. What she said has not been revealed, but it was enough to persuade the Crown Prosecution Service to drop the charges against Leslie. It was to her credit that she had volunteered the new information, the CPS said. 'To say any more,' it continued, 'would in our view be apt to mislead and would be unfair to the complainant.' Accordingly, Leslie left court 'without a stain on his character', in the judge's hackneyed phrase. As newspapers interviewed other women who accused Leslie of sexually assaulting them, he complained about press invasion of his privacy while selling his story to the *Daily Express*. Some of its more traditional readers were said to have complained subsequently about its salaciousness.

We do not know the identity of the woman concerned. Even if a case is dropped, an alleged victim of sexual assault is generally entitled to lifelong anonymity—although this may be waived by the complainant or lifted by the judge. Victims can however be named if they themselves are charged in connection with the allegations. Thus it may be reported that Alison Welfare, 26, from Orpington, Kent, was sentenced to twelve months' imprisonment in August 2003 for making false allegations of rape against her former boyfriend. He spent eight weeks in prison on remand before detectives established that the evidence had been fabricated. Welfare had sent abusive text messages to her own phone. In addition, CCTV pictures helped establish that she had not been kidnapped and dragged into a branch of McDonald's, as she had alleged.

Name and shame

There is no blanket restriction on naming an adult *accused* of rape—or, indeed, of any other crime—although such restrictions did exist between 1976 and 1988. Every time a high-profile figure is acquitted of rape, there are calls for this anonymity to be restored in the interests of equality. It is said that individuals tried for alleged sexual offences frequently suffer disproportionate publicity and, if acquitted, suffer serious consequences when they try to rebuild their lives. A clause to give defendants the same life-long anonymity as complainants was even inserted by the House of Lords into the Sexual Offences Bill in the summer of 2003 as result of a backbench amendment moved by Lord Ackner, the former law lord. That amendment was rejected by the Commons during the Bill's committee stage. In November 2003, the Conservatives called for a ban on identifying individuals accused of sexual offences unless or until they were formally charged. The Home Office minister, Paul Goggins, generally supported this objective while arguing that it would be best achieved by self-regulation. The Tory amendment was also defeated.

As Leslie's case itself demonstrates, a ban on naming people suspected of sexual offences is effectively unenforceable. As soon as anybody of the slightest public interest becomes involved with the police, officers will tip off their contacts on the tabloid newspapers. It is hard to believe that the reporters and newsdesks do not show their appreciation in some way to the officers concerned. Even if newspapers do not publish the name of a high-profile suspect, it will soon begin to circulate among colleagues and rivals who move in the same circles. Before long, somebody will post it on a website where it may be found by anybody who knows how to use a search engine such as Google. It may of course turn out to be entirely the wrong name, in which case some poor unfortunate will find it very hard to quash such defamatory rumours unless the real defendant is publicly identified.

A ban on naming defendants is also undesirable because it prevents news of the charges reaching potential witnesses who may come forward and give alibi or other evidence. The defendant may not know who may have spotted him at the crucial time; equally, witnesses may not know that he is the one facing charges. This problem was explicitly recognized by the Sexual Offences (Amendment) Act 1992, which provided that the existing ban on identifying the alleged victim could be lifted by the court if the accused needed to find witnesses and there would be serious prejudice to the defence if the ban was not lifted. Lord Ackner's proposed ban would also have prevented the naming of an alleged rapist who absconds while awaiting trial, leaving potential victims unaware of the danger they face.

Furthermore, a ban on identifying defendants is wrong in principle because of the paramount need for open justice. The state should not be able to charge people with criminal offences, jeopardizing their livelihood and liberty, without this fact being publicly known. The fear of publicity is also something of an incentive to obey the law. And it is hard to justify anonymity for alleged rapists while refusing it for the more serious offences of murder and manslaughter. Anonymity for defendants in rape cases alone would also give the impression that there was more doubt about a complainant's credibility than in other types of case. That might discourage victims from coming forward.

Supporters of the move say that defendants could be named if and when they were found guilty, although this was not provided for in the poorly drafted Lords amendment to the Sexual Offences Bill—which would anyway have still allowed anyone under investigation for rape to be identified until he or she was formally charged. In any event, allowing defendants to be named once convicted would do nothing to quash initial rumours, attract witnesses or ensure an open trial.

Even so, there were two high-profile cases in October 2003 when the media held back from identifying men accused of sexual assault. One involved members of a football club who were alleged to have raped a young woman at a London hotel. The media went to extraordinary lengths to avoid identifying them, fading down the sounds of crowd chanting at a subsequent match in case the club's name was shouted out. On this occasion, the main concern seemed to be libel; anyone wrongly accused of rape would be in line for substantial damages from the media organization involved. There were also dire warnings from the Attorney General, Lord Goldsmith, about impeding the administration of justice. His main concern was identification: the complainant was subsequently asked to pick out the faces of her alleged assailants, a task that would have been harder if some of them had already been pictured in the press.

But that could not have been a problem in the case of a young civil servant working for Lord Falconer's Department of Constitutional

Affairs, who was said to have assaulted a woman at an office party. Again, libel seems to have been the main reason his name was not published, together with a somewhat hazy approach to the contempt laws. But since the police had tipped off the press in the first place, it is hard to see how he could have succeeded in a claim for defamation.

CHAPTER 6

A Chilling Effect

'Heed Their Rising Voices' was the headline on a full-page advertisement published in the *New York Times* on 29 March 1960. It was to have profound repercussions on press freedom in the United States and, some decades later, on the ability of our own media to report on matters of public concern.

'As the whole world knows by now', the advertisement began, 'thousands of Southern Negro students are engaged in widespread non-violent demonstrations in positive affirmation of the right to live in human dignity as guaranteed by the US Constitution . . . They are being met by an unprecedented wave of terror by those who would deny and negate that document . . .'

Some examples followed:

In Montgomery, Alabama, after students sang 'My Country, 'Tis of Thee' on the State Capitol steps, their leaders were expelled from school, and truckloads of police armed with shotguns and tear-gas ringed the Alabama State College Campus. When the entire student body protested to state authorities by refusing to re-register, their dining hall was padlocked in an attempt to starve them into submission . . .

The advertisement claimed that unnamed 'Southern violators of the constitution' were 'determined to destroy the one man who, more than any other, symbolizes the new spirit now sweeping the South—the Rev Dr Martin Luther King'.

Again and again the Southern violators have answered Dr King's peaceful protests with intimidation and violence. They have bombed his home almost killing his wife and child. They have assaulted his person. They have arrested him seven times—for 'speeding', 'loitering' and similar 'offenses.' And now they have charged him with 'perjury'—a *felony* under which they could imprison him for *ten years* . . .

The text concluded with an appeal for funds signed by sixty-four sponsors and 'warmly' endorsed by another twenty individuals, mainly black clergymen. Within a short time, according to Anthony Lewis in his book *Make No Law*, the Committee to Defend Martin Luther King and the Struggle for Freedom in the South had raised many times the $4,800 that the advertisement had cost.

Unfortunately, not all its allegations were accurate. Although black students had staged a demonstration on the State Capitol steps, they sang the US National Anthem and not 'My Country, 'Tis of Thee'. Nine students had been expelled by the State Board of Education, but for demanding service at a lunch counter in the Montgomery County Courthouse on another day. Not the entire student body, though most of it, had protested against the expulsion—not by refusing to register, but by boycotting classes on a single day. The campus dining hall was not padlocked on any occasion, and the only students who may have been barred from eating there were the few who had neither signed a pre-registration application nor requested temporary meal tickets. Although the police were deployed near the campus in large numbers on three occasions, they did not at any time 'ring' the campus, nor were they called to the campus in connection with the demonstration on the State Capitol steps. Dr King had not been arrested seven times, but only four; and although he claimed to have been assaulted some years earlier in connection with his arrest for loitering outside a courtroom, one of the officers who made the arrest denied that there was such an assault. The maximum penalty for perjury was five years rather than ten; although Dr King faced two charges in all (of which he was later acquitted) and so he could, in theory, have served consecutive terms.

Did any of that matter? It must have been in the public interest to raise these allegations, even if some details were wrong. There must surely be issues of such public concern that responsible journalists may safely write about them, even though some of the initial allegations may turn out to be erroneous. But when will it be in the public interest for reporters to be granted the privilege of writing false and potentially defamatory articles about others? In what circumstances should our press enjoy the same level of free speech as was allowed by the US Supreme Court in 1964—what English lawyers now call 'QP' (short for qualified privilege) or '*Reynolds*-privilege'? That is the question this chapter seeks to answer.

Libel, of course, is not the same as privacy. It is possible to defame people without revealing anything about their private lives, just as it is possible to invade their privacy without revealing anything that damages their reputation. But an exposé of a public figure runs the risk of offending both laws. If journalists are wary of the libel courts, they may also think twice about potential invasions of privacy.

Sullivan and the *New York Times*

In the early 1960s, the *New York Times* (circulation 650,000) was hardly the paper of choice in the Southern states—it sold fewer than 400 copies in Alabama and only 35 in Montgomery County. A few days after 'Heed Their Rising Voices' had appeared, however, the advertisement was spotted by a keen young reporter on the *Alabama Journal* who wrote it up in his paper, pointing out that some of the statements it contained were not strictly true. As a result, it came to the attention of one L B Sullivan, the elected commissioner responsible for Montgomery's Police Department (as well as for the Fire Department, the Department of Cemetery and the Department of Scales). Sullivan believed that the paragraphs quoted above were defamatory of him, arguing that anyone reading them would know that the city's police came under his control and direction and therefore consider him responsible for their actions. When the *Times* failed to publish an immediate retraction, he sued for libel.

Those too young to remember the sixties will find it hard to believe it was a time when apartheid was still practised in the Southern states of America. Lunch counters were segregated in Alabama, as were taxis and libraries. Although six years had passed since the US Supreme Court ruled (in *Brown v Board of Education*) that racially segregated schools were unconstitutional, not a single black student attended a publicly run school or university with white students in Alabama, Mississippi, Georgia, Louisiana or South Carolina. Less than five years earlier, a black woman had been arrested in Montgomery for refusing to give up her seat on a bus to a white man. Only 14 per cent of Alabama's black citizens were registered to vote. Black attorneys were even denied the honorific 'Mr' in court.

In this atmosphere, it must have come as little surprise when an all-white jury found in Sullivan's favour and awarded him the $500,000 he had claimed. On appeal, the verdict was upheld by the Alabama Supreme Court. Subsequently, another of the city's three commissioners lodged his own claim for libel arising from the same advertisement: he, too, won half a million dollars. Eleven further claims were lodged against the newspaper by local and state officials, seeking a total of $5,600,000. No newspaper could sustain losses on that scale. Nor would a free press survive if gagging writs could be used to deter publication.

The *New York Times* appealed to the US Supreme Court in Washington, arguing that the state courts in Alabama had acted unconstitutionally. The newspaper's lawyers relied on the First Amendment to the US Constitution, approved in 1791, which says 'Congress shall make no law . . . abridging the freedom of speech, or of the press.' Although this provision refers to Congress, it is now considered to apply equally to states because, under the Fourteenth Amendment, states must not 'deprive any person of . . . property without due process of law'.

Relying on the First Amendment was a brave move by the newspaper. Libel had always been seen as a matter of state law, and therefore outside the ambit of the federal courts. The US Supreme Court had repeatedly said in past rulings that libellous publications were not protected by the First Amendment. It had never accepted that a case such as this raised constitutional questions. All that was challenged in a 95-page argument filed by the *New York Times*.

At the time Sullivan brought his claim, there was no need to prove that a defendant in such cases had acted in bad faith: a publication was intrinsically libellous in Alabama if it injured a person's reputation or brought him into public contempt. The jury needed to find that the words were published 'of and concerning' the claimant, but his position as a public official was considered enough to support a finding that his reputation was affected by statements that reflected upon the agency of which he was in charge. As in England, the burden then shifted to the defendant. Unless he could persuade the jury that the allegations were true, it could award unlimited damages.

Clearly, the *New York Times* could not persuade the jury that the words complained of were 'true in all their particulars'. But Sullivan was a public official. He was suing critics of his official conduct. Did that make any difference?

Freedom of expression on public questions has been long secured by the First Amendment, the US Supreme Court noted. 'We consider this case against the background of a profound national commitment to the principle that debate on public issues should be uninhibited, robust, and wide-open, and that it may well include vehement, caustic, and some-times unpleasantly sharp attacks on government and public officials,' said Justice Brennan, delivering the opinion of the Court in 1964. That prin-ciple, as he explained, had been given its classic formulation in 1927 by Justice Brandeis in *Whitney v California*, a case brought by a communist who claimed that her conviction in 1919 for 'criminal syndicalism'— advocating the use of force to achieve political change—had been unconstitutional. On that occasion, Justice Brandeis delivered this resounding message:

Those who won our independence . . . valued liberty both as an end and as a means . . . They believed that freedom to think as you will and to speak as you think are means indispensable to the discovery and spread of political truth; that without free speech and assembly discussion would be futile; that with them, discussion affords ordinarily adequate protection against the dissemina-tion of noxious doctrine; that the greatest menace to freedom is an inert people; that public discussion is a political duty; and that this should be a funda-mental principle of the American government. They recognized the risks to which all human institutions are subject. But they knew that order cannot be secured merely through fear of punishment for its infraction; that it is hazardous to discourage thought, hope and imagination; that fear breeds repression; that repression breeds hate; that hate menaces stable government; that the path of safety lies in the opportunity to discuss freely supposed griev-ances and proposed remedies; and that the fitting remedy for evil counsels is good ones. Believing in the power of reason as applied through public discus-sion, they eschewed silence coerced by law—the argument of force in its worst form. Recognizing the occasional tyrannies of governing majorities, they amended the Constitution so that free speech and assembly should be guaran-teed.

In 1927, Justice Brandeis went on to explain why 'fear of serious injury cannot alone justify suppression of free speech and assembly':

Men feared witches and burnt women. It is the function of speech to free men from the bondage of irrational fears. To justify suppression of free speech there must be reasonable ground to fear that serious evil will result if free speech is practiced. There must be reasonable ground to believe that the danger appre-hended is imminent. There must be reasonable ground to believe that the evil to be prevented is a serious one . . . The fact that speech is likely to result in some violence or in destruction of property is not enough to justify its suppression. There must be the probability of serious injury to the State.

However, in the *Whitney* case the Court found evidence to show that members of the International Workers of the World had conspired to commit serious crimes, and that such a conspiracy would be furthered by the activity of the society of which Miss Whitney was a member. For this reason, her petition to the Supreme Court was dismissed—though in the light of Justice Brandeis's comments she was pardoned a month later.

After citing Justice Brandeis in *Whitney v California*, Justice Brennan went on to explain that the constitutional protection for free speech did not depend on any test of truth. Erroneous statement was inevitable in free debate, as he himself had said in an earlier judgment, and must be protected if freedom of expression was to have the breathing space it needed to survive. 'Injury to official reputation error affords no more warrant for repressing speech that would otherwise be free than does factual error,' he continued. 'If judges are to be treated as "men of forti-tude, able to thrive in a hardy climate", surely the same must be true of other government officials, such as elected city commissioners.' So the factual errors in the advertisement and Sullivan's official position were no longer sufficient to exclude the court's jurisdiction.

Justice Brennan's conclusion was clear. 'The constitutional guarantees require, we think, a federal rule that prohibits a public official from recovering damages for a defamatory falsehood relating to his official conduct unless he proves that the statement was made with "actual malice"—that is, with knowledge that it was false or with reckless disre-gard of whether it was false or not.' This was a considerable advance, though three of the judges would have gone even further in holding that the First Amendment required critics of official conduct to enjoy absolute privilege—even if their criticism was intentionally false.

To make sure that Sullivan could not seek a retrial in Alabama, the Supreme Court took the unusual step of holding that the facts as proved did not support a finding of actual malice. After all, there was no evidence that the newspaper had not acted in good faith. 'We think the evidence against the *Times* supports at most a finding of negligence in failing to discover the misstatements, and is constitutionally insufficient to show the recklessness that is required for a finding of actual malice,' the Court concluded. And, just in case there was still any doubt, the justices said that the evidence did not support the jury's finding that the statements were made 'of and concerning' Sullivan himself.

The effect of *Sullivan*

The effect of this and the cases that followed was to shift the burden of proof in US libel cases involving public figures or matters of public concern. In such cases, it is now for the claimant to prove that the statement in issue was made with 'actual malice'. If the claim is to succeed, the defendant must have been at fault: he must have knowingly published a false statement or been reckless as to whether the statements were true or false. As we shall see, this is very different from English libel law, where a defendant who seeks to justify his comments must prove their accuracy.

'The allowance of room for honest mistakes of fact encouraged the press, in particular, to challenge official truth on two subjects so hidden by government secrecy, Vietnam and Watergate, that no unauthorised story can ever have been "absolutely confirmable",' says Anthony Lewis in *Make No Law*. On the other hand, the unlimited and apparently arbitrary awards of damages by US juries mean that libel actions remain highly popular in the United States. Their attractiveness to claimants is enhanced by the way in which American claimants specify the sum they are claiming—one million dollars, or whatever it may be—when they file suit.

Binding local councils

An important test of the *Sullivan* principles in Britain came thirty years later, when the House of Lords was asked to consider the case of *Derbyshire County Council v Times Newspapers* in 1993. David Bookbinder, Labour leader of the Council, had already won substantial damages from the *Sunday Times* over articles relating to the investment policies of the council's pension fund. In addition, though, the County Council had sued in its own name.

Striking out the Council's claim against the newspaper, five law lords agreed that under common law a local authority or central government department had no right to maintain an action in damages for defamation. Explicitly following the reasoning in *New York Times v Sullivan*, Lord Keith said:

It is of the highest public importance that a democratically elected governmental body, or indeed any governmental body, should be open to uninhibited public criticism . . .

What has been described as 'the chilling effect' induced by the threat of civil actions for libel is very important. Quite often the facts which would justify a defamatory publication are known to be true, but admissible evidence capable of proving those facts is not available. This may prevent the publication of matters which it is very desirable to make public . . .

I regard it as right for this House to lay down that not only is there no public interest favouring the right of organs of government, whether central or local, to sue for libel, but that it is contrary to the public interest that they should have it. It is contrary to the public interest because to admit such actions would place an undesirable fetter on freedom of speech.

The question of whether individual politicians should be equally restricted was deliberately left open. That had to wait for the next test case to come before the House of Lords.

The Gombeen Man

Though the *Derbyshire* case was good news for reporters, it did not protect news organizations from libel actions by individual politicians. It was for this reason that Albert Reynolds, the former Prime Minister of Ireland, was able to launch proceedings against the *Sunday Times* over an article headed 'Goodbye Gombeen Man: Why a Fib too Far Proved Fatal for the Political Career of Ireland's Peacemaker and Mr Fixit'. In response, the newspaper tried to persuade the English courts to follow *New York Times v Sullivan* by allowing it to publish responsible reports of issues that concerned the public, even if these turned out not to be true.

The *Sunday Times* article, published in 1994, told the story of the political crisis in Dublin that had just culminated in Reynolds's resignation as Taoiseach of Ireland and leader of the Fianna Fáil party. Because of his role in the Northern Ireland peace process, his fate was of some importance to readers in the United Kingdom. This is how the piece began:

In another age Albert Reynolds could have been the classic *gombeen* man of Irish law—the real fixer with a finger in every pie. His slow fall last week, his finger-nails scratching down the potential cliff-face, has been welcomed with a whoop of delight by many Irish people who want to see their country dragged out of the past. The full story of this eclipse, however, has sullied Ireland's reputation, damaged its Church, destroyed its peacemaking and provided its unionist neigh-bours with a fistful of new reasons to avoid the contamination by the South.

The article appeared only in England, Scotland and Wales: a different and much less defamatory piece appeared in the editions circulating in Northern Ireland and the Republic, no doubt because Reynolds was a well-known libel claimant in the Irish courts. So the former Prime Minister came to London, a familiar figure as, week after week, he strolled into the law courts for what turned out to be a 24-day hearing in the autumn of 1996. Reynolds argued that the 'sting' of the article was that he had deliberately and dishonestly misled the Irish Parliament and his coalition Cabinet colleagues by withholding vital information.

If you want to bring a case under English libel law, you need prove only that words have been published about you that would make reasonable and respectable people think less of you. This could be by exposing you to 'hatred, contempt or ridicule' or by lowering you 'in the estimation of right-thinking people generally'. So it is not enough for a statement about you to be false: if you are to win a libel claim, it has to damage your reputation in the eyes of society generally. Whether a statement is capable of bearing such a defamatory meaning is a ques-tion of law to be decided by the judge, rather than a matter for the jury. Views have changed over the years of what may be defamatory but the test remains how the words would have been understood by the ordi-nary reader, taken in the context of the article as a whole.

Once you have proved that a specific person or company is respon-sible for publishing words about you that have a defamatory meaning in this sense, the burden of proof shifts to the defendants. They must convince the court, on the balance of probabilities, that they have a defence. This is a major and much-criticized imbalance in the law of libel that does much to protect the reputation (and, as a result, the privacy) of the rich and famous. Since juries are naturally reluctant to believe the worst about television stars and sporting heroes, newspapers must think carefully about whether they should publish stories based on little more than unattractive sources, instinct and supposition—however true they may be. Until *Reynolds*, newspapers were at grave risk of being sued by the nearest plausible rogue unless they could prove the truth of what they had published. I should add that libel lawyers of my acquaintance—and at least one former libel judge—see no imbalance at all here. In my view, the burden of proof should rest on the claimant; my friends argue that the burden should fall on the person who harmed the claimant's reputation by publishing defamatory words; they point out that it is harder for the claimant to prove he is *not*, say, a child molester than it is for the journalist to prove he is. Difficult though it may be to prove a negative, I find my friends' arguments unconvincing. It is much easier for the alleged child molester to establish in court how he spends his time than it is for the journalist. But, as I have already hinted, help may be at hand.

In response to Reynolds's claim, two defences were put forward by the *Sunday Times*. The first, straightforwardly enough, was *justification*—that what it had reported was true. Truth is a complete defence to libel—provided you can prove it. You need establish only that the 'sting' of the allegation was substantially correct, though it is not enough to show that you have correctly reported an incorrect rumour unless it is to demonstrate that the rumour has no truth. Justification was rejected as a defence by the jury in the *Reynolds* case: the article in question was simply not true.

Qualified privilege

The second defence put forward by the *Sunday Times* was *qualified privilege*. In English libel law, there are two types of privilege. Statements made by MPs in Parliament or by judges in court have *absolute privilege*—meaning that these comments cannot form the basis of a libel action, even if they are untrue (and even if they are made recklessly or dishonestly). This type of privilege is also available to MPs making statements in select committee hearings and reports; and to lawyers and witnesses in court.

In December 2002, the validity of absolute privilege was upheld by the European Court of Human Rights when it ruled on the case of

A v UK. Louisa McNeil, from Bristol, complained that she and her children had been forced to move house in 1996 when Michael Stern, then the local Conservative MP, referred to her family in a Commons adjournment debate as 'neighbours from hell'. Mentioning her full address and the fact that her brother was in prison, the MP repeated neighbours' claims about threatening behaviour and 'alleged drug activity'. McNeil told the Court that none of the allegations was substantiated or upheld and claimed that many of them came from neighbours who were motivated by racism and spite. But the Strasbourg judges rejected her claim that she had been denied her human rights because she had been unable to sue Stern for libel. While acknowledging that the MP's allegations about her were 'clearly unnecessary' in a debate about municipal housing policy and that his repeated references to her name and address were 'particularly regrettable', the Court held that a general rule of Parliamentary immunity could not be regarded as imposing a disproportionate restriction on the right of access to court under Article 6 of the Human Rights Convention. Indeed, the Court pointed out, legislators in other countries enjoyed much wider immunity, covering press releases and comments even if they were made outside their respective parliaments.

Absolute privilege is also granted to reports of court proceedings that are fair, accurate and contemporaneous. Section 14 of the Defamation Act 1996 gives a wide meaning to 'court' for these purposes. To be 'contemporaneous', a report must be published as soon as practicable. A weekly magazine could claim absolute privilege for fair and accurate news reports of trials held the previous week, but a book like this would find it harder to establish.

Statements that do not attract absolute privilege may still enjoy qualified privilege. Such comments, though untrue, cannot be the subject of a libel action if they are made honestly and without malice. Better still from the defendant's point of view, if the person sued can raise a defence of qualified privilege then the burden of proving malice bounces back to the claimant. *Malice* generally refers to dishonest or reckless writing or reporting—the publication of words known to be false or opinions that are not genuinely held.

Qualified privilege does not apply to all statements: only those made on a protected or privileged occasion. It certainly applies to all reports of Parliamentary proceedings and accounts of trials that are not published contemporaneously. So, an otherwise libellous law report in this book cannot land the author and publisher in the libel courts unless the person claiming to have been defamed can prove that those responsible for its publication did not believe the statement was true or that they had an improper motive in publishing it. Qualified privilege was originally developed by the judges to protect references passed from one employer to another; it also covers complaints to bodies with supervisory powers. The reason for allowing qualified privilege as a defence to libel is, to quote from Baron Parke's judgment in the splendidly named case of *Toogood v Spyring* in 1834, 'the common convenience and welfare of society'—in other words, the public interest.

As defined by the courts during the twentieth century, qualified privilege exists when the maker of a statement has a *duty* to communicate it to a person who has a material *interest* in receiving the information (the so-called 'duty/interest test'). In *Reynolds*, the *Sunday Times* wanted to extend this defence to cover political information, defined as 'information, opinion and arguments concerning government and political matters that affect the people of the United Kingdom'. In effect, the newspaper argued that it was in the public interest for it to report a defamatory and factually false statement that its reporters honestly believed to be true.

Not particularly smooth

The High Court hearing 'was on any view not particularly smooth', to borrow Lord Bingham's laconic phrase. Despite rejecting the newspaper's defence of justification, the jury awarded Reynolds no damages. That made little sense, since in their view he had effectively won; as a result, the judge substituted an award of one penny. That raised the question of who should pay both sides' legal costs: under the normal rule, a loser pays all.

The newspaper had prudently lodged some money with the court. A 'payment into court' amounts to an offer to settle for that sum: the defendant is welcome to take the cash at any time if he thinks it is enough. However, if he chooses not to take the money on offer and is awarded a lower figure at the end of the case then he will have to pay his own costs from the date the money was paid in by the defendant. It's a bit like betting on the horses.

Clearly, the *Sunday Times* must have paid more than a penny into court, so Reynolds could not claim his costs from the date the payment was made. But what about the period leading up to that date? As we have seen, the *Sunday Times* relied on the defence of qualified privilege. The jury also decided that the journalists responsible for the article had not been acting maliciously. So, if the occasion was privileged—and that was a question of law for the judge to decide—then the defence of qualified privilege would succeed. That, in turn, would have given the newspaper a complete defence to the action, and the judge would have ordered Reynolds to pay all its costs.

So the *Sunday Times* had more than an altruistic reason for arguing that there was a wide qualified privilege at common law for 'political speech'. In the event, though, Mr Justice French ruled that publication of the article was not privileged after all. David Hooper, in his book *Reputations Under Fire*, said that Mr Justice French 'was not up to the rigours of a five-week trial': he retired shortly afterwards on health grounds. Hooper also described the judge's summing-up to the jury as 'wholly inept'.

If Sir Christopher French had taken exception to that remark when it appeared in 2000, Hooper could have relied on the defence of *fair comment*. This protects the honest expression of opinion, even if unfair or exaggerated, on any matter of public interest. Though a broad defence, it protects only opinions—not facts. The comment must also have some factual basis, which in this case would have been the subsequent judgment given by Lord Bingham in the Court of Appeal (itself protected by qualified privilege). In practice, it can sometimes be difficult to establish whether the words used are to be read as bald facts or as comments on those facts. Like qualified privilege, the defence of fair comment can also be negated if the claimant can establish malice— that the defendant did not genuinely hold the views expressed.

Sara Keays

A good example of fair comment was an article about Sara Keays published in the *Observer* in January 2002. Keays was Lord Parkinson's mistress while he was a Conservative politician; her decision to reveal her pregnancy to *The Times* in 1983 led to his resignation as Trade and

Industry Secretary, though he was brought back into the Thatcher Government four years later.

Injunctions against publicity were obtained after their daughter, Flora, was born but these expired once she turned 18; Keays sold her story to the *Daily Mail* for £100,000, plus syndication rights. A week later, the *Observer* carried a piece by Carol Sarler that began: 'What a preposterous piece of work is Miss Sara Keays, prowling print and airwaves with the finest furies of a woman scorned as, nearly two decades after the event, she manages to excise yet another pound of Parkinson flesh. Or, as Edwina Currie once put it, rather more succinctly: "What a right cow!"'

Could Keays sue the *Observer* and Sarler for libel? Giving judgment on a preliminary issue in June 2003, Mr Justice Eady held that the article could amount only to fair comment, rather than facts that the newspaper could be required to justify. The judge said: 'Miss Sarler's article is *par excellence* a comment piece, and was indeed so labelled. She was obviously drawing an inference from the subject-matter of her observations, namely the media coverage promoted by Miss Keays. Where a journalist draws such an inference about a state of mind which she cannot, in the nature of things, verify, then it will generally be clear to any reasonable reader that it does not purport to be an objective statement of fact capable of verification . . . Anyone who chooses to enter the public arena invites comment and often this will include scrutiny of and comment about motives. Such persons cannot expect as of right to be taken at face value. It is sufficient protection in such circumstances for personal reputation that any adverse comments should be made in good faith, and that the words should be subjected, at the appropriate stage, to the objective test of whether the inferences or deductions could be drawn by an honest person with knowledge of the facts.'

The judgment was followed by an announcement in October 2003 that Keays had dropped her libel claim against the *Observer* and agreed to pay what it called 'an undisclosed sum' towards its costs. The newspaper noted that this was the first time Keays had lost a libel action. 'She has sued a number of times in the past when false allegations have been made against her about her attitude to Lord Parkinson,' it added, 'and each time she has succeeded.'

Reynolds continues

Sir Christopher French, the trial judge in the *Reynolds* case, died in 2003 at the age of 77. His death leaves me free to write what I wish about him: the ultimate defence to a claim for libel is that the claimant is no longer alive. However, all I shall say is that there needs to be a better way of ensuring that judges whose powers are in decline through age or illness do not carry on sitting. At present, it is only when that decline becomes painfully obvious that a judge is prevailed upon to stand down. And why should the parties have to bear the costs of a substandard service from the judiciary?

It was inevitable that *Reynolds* would go to the Court of Appeal. The former Prime Minister himself must have been heavily out of pocket on costs, despite winning his case. He complained to the Court of Appeal that Mr Justice French had read out large tracts of the written evidence to the jury with no attempt to summarize it or relate it to the issues or highlight the more significant passages. Reynolds had also complained that the judge's summing up was confusing and unstructured, so much so that the jury asked for a transcript of Reynolds's entire evidence.

'We see considerable force in these criticisms,' said Lord Bingham and his fellow appeal judges in July 1998. 'The summing up was indeed long, and the judge did little to relate the evidence to the specific issues . . . But defects of form or presentation would not entitle Mr Reynolds to the relief he seeks unless the misdirections complained of, singly or cumulatively, lead us to the opinion that "some substantial wrong or miscarriage has been thereby occasioned". In approaching that question our task is not to decide whether the jury gave the right answers to the questions put to them but to consider whether the misdirections complained of, singly or cumulatively, were such as to deny Mr Reynolds a fair trial of his claim. With very great regret, because we are mindful of the consequences, we conclude that the misdirections which we have identified above were, cumulatively, such as to have that effect. Having reached that conclusion, we have no effective alternative but to set aside the verdict, finding and judgment of the court below and order a new trial of this action.'

More damagingly for the newspaper, the Court of Appeal ruled against the *Sunday Times* on the crucial question of whether the defence of qualified privilege should be allowed for political speech. On this point, the newspaper then appealed to the House of Lords. Giving the leading judgment in October 1999, Lord Nicholls summed up the issues with admirable clarity:

This appeal concerns the interaction between two fundamental rights: freedom of expression and protection of reputation. The context is newspaper discussion of a matter of political importance. Stated in its simplest form, the newspaper's contention is that a libellous statement of fact made in the course of political discussion is free from liability if published in good faith. Liability arises only if the writer knew the statement was not true or if he made the statement recklessly, not caring whether it was true or false, or if he was actuated by personal spite or some other improper motive. Mr. Reynolds' contention, on the other hand, is that liability may also arise if, having regard to the source of the information and all the circumstances, it was not in the public interest for the newspaper to have published the information as it did. Under the newspaper's contention the safeguard for those who are defamed is exclusively subjective: the state of mind of the journalist. Under Mr Reynolds' formulation, there is also an objective element of protection.

Lord Lester, QC, for the *Sunday Times*, had argued that—in the absence of malice—publication of political information should be privileged regardless of the status and source of the material and the circumstances of the publication. In rejecting that argument, Lord Nicholls explained the case for protecting the individual's good name against unjustified criticism:

Reputation is an integral and important part of the dignity of the individual. It also forms the basis of many decisions in a democratic society which are fundamental to its well-being: whom to employ or work for, whom to promote, whom to do business with or to vote for. Once besmirched by an unfounded allegation in a national newspaper, a reputation can be damaged for ever, especially if there is no opportunity to vindicate one's reputation. When this happens, society as well as the individual is the loser . . . It is in the public interest that the reputation of public figures should not be debased falsely. In the political field, in order to make an informed choice, the electorate needs to be able to identify the good as well as the bad. Consistently with these considerations, human rights conventions recognise that freedom of expression is not an absolute right. Its exercise may be subject to such restrictions as are prescribed by law and are necessary in a democratic society for the protection of the reputations of others. The crux of this appeal, therefore, lies in identifying the restrictions which are fairly and reasonably necessary for the protection of reputation.

Lord Nicholls pointed out that when dealing with alleged facts, rather than comments, it was harder for members of the public to know where the truth lay. It was notoriously difficult for the aggrieved claimants to prove that a newspaper had acted with malice, particularly as the journalists involved would be unwilling to disclose their sources. That would leave newspapers 'free to publish seriously defamatory misstatements of fact based on the slenderest of materials'.

The *Sunday Times* had suggested leaving it up to the 'ethics of professional journalism'. Lord Nicholls was clearly not born yesterday. 'Unfortunately, in the United Kingdom this would not generally be thought to provide a sufficient safeguard,' he said. 'The sad reality is that the overall handling of these matters by the national press, with its own commercial interests to serve, does not always command general confidence.'

The Nicholls points

The law lords agreed that the existing law remained sound. Qualified privilege would be available on the established common-law test of whether there had been a duty to publish the material to the intended recipients and whether they had had an interest in receiving it, taking into account all the circumstances of the publication. But when would this happy state of affairs exist? Lord Nicholls gave ten examples of the factors that courts might take into account when deciding whether qualified privilege would be available:

(1) The seriousness of the allegation. The more serious the charge, the more the public is misinformed and the individual harmed if the allegation is not true.

(2) The nature of the information, and the extent to which the subject matter is a matter of public concern.

(3) The source of the information. Some informants have no direct knowledge of the events. Some have their own axes to grind or are being paid for their stories.

(4) The steps taken to verify the information.

(5) The status of the information. The allegation may have already been the subject of an investigation which commands respect.

(6) The urgency of the matter. News is often a perishable commodity.

(7) Whether comment was sought from the claimant. He may have information others do not possess or have not disclosed. An approach to the claimant will not always be necessary.

(8) Whether the article contained the gist of the claimant's side of the story.

(9) The tone of the article. A newspaper can raise queries or call for an investigation. It need not adopt allegations as statements of fact.

(10) The circumstances of the publication, including the timing.

Lord Nicholls stressed that 'the common law does not seek to set a higher standard than that of responsible journalism, a standard the media themselves espouse'. He concluded with this splendid passage:

Above all, the court should have particular regard to the importance of freedom of expression. The press discharges vital functions as a bloodhound as well as a watchdog. The court should be slow to conclude that a publication was not in the public interest and, therefore, the public had no right to know, especially when the information is in the field of political discussion. Any lingering doubts should be resolved in favour of publication.

Even so, a majority of the law lords decided after applying these principles that qualified privilege was not available to the *Sunday Times* on the facts of this case. Lord Nicholls said that 'a most telling criticism' of the article was its failure to mention Reynolds's own explanation to the Dáil. The reporter had omitted this from the article because he had rejected Reynolds's version of the events and concluded that the former Prime Minister had been deliberately misleading. 'It goes without saying that a journalist is entitled and bound to reach his own conclusions and to express them honestly and fearlessly,' observed Lord Nicholls. 'He is entitled to disbelieve and refute explanations given. But this cannot be a good reason for omitting, from a hard-hitting article making serious allegations against a named individual, all mention of that person's own explanation'. Readers had been left to suppose that Reynolds had offered no explanation. 'Further, it is elementary fairness that, in the normal course, a serious charge should be accompanied by the gist of any explanation already given. An article which fails to do so faces an uphill task in claiming privilege if the allegation proves to be false and the unreported explanation proves to be true.'

This was disappointing for the *Sunday Times*, but not for the press as a whole. Though the law lords in *Reynolds* had professed to be doing little more than applying the existing law, their ruling introduces a radical change and provides valuable protection for journalists. It establishes the important principle that in certain circumstances the media may be protected from liability for publishing false information if the public has a right to know that information. Defamatory statements that cannot be 'justified'—proved to be true—may still be '*Reynolds*-privileged' if they are broadly in line with Lord Nicholls's ten points.

But there is always a balance to be struck as Jonathan Coad, a prominent media solicitor, pointed out early in 2002. He thought the loss of the right to refute untrue and defamatory allegations against oneself could prove 'catastrophic'—not only for individuals such as MPs and for senior figures in education, industry and the Church but for society as a whole. In his view, a defence that was created for the common convenience and welfare of society risked becoming one for the common convenience and welfare of the media.

After *Reynolds*

So far, the courts seem to have been striking a fair balance between claimants and the media. Not all claims of qualified privilege have been allowed, but the Court of Appeal has been sympathetic to the concept of 'responsible journalism'—a novel concept, at least to the courts.

In *Al-Fagih v H H Saudi Research & Marketing (UK) Ltd* the Court of Appeal went even further than *Reynolds*. Giving judgment in November 2001, Lord Justice Simon Brown began by summarizing the effect of the law lords' ruling in *Reynolds*:

In essence, the case held that the question whether a particular publication attracts qualified privilege at common law should be decided simply by asking whether in all the circumstances 'the duty-interest test, or [what Lord Nicholls called] the right to know test' is satisfied. Amongst the relevant circumstances are likely to be the ten specific factors [he] identified. This approach reflects the European Court of Human Rights jurisprudence under Article 10 of the Convention and is designed to enable a proper balance to be struck between, on the one hand, the cardinal importance of freedom of expression by the media on all matters of public concern and, on the other, the right of an individual to his good reputation. Neither right is absolute but the former, particularly in the field of political discussion, is of a higher order, a constitutional right of vital importance to the proper functioning of a democratic society. That is why [Lord Nicholls said] 'any curtailment of freedom of expression must be convincingly established by a compelling countervailing consideration, and the means employed must be proportionate to the end sought to be achieved', and why 'any lingering doubts [as to how the balance should be struck] should be resolved in favour of publication'.

The case before Lord Justice Simon Brown concerned 'reportage'— neutrally reporting allegations attributed to their authors, rather than taking sides and adopting them as true. A newspaper that sold 1,500 copies a day in London to members of the Saudi Arabian community had reported what two prominent Saudi political dissidents had been saying about each other. Lord Justice Simon Brown said the trial judge had been wrong to hold that the publication could not be regarded as being in the public interest. The newspaper, he concluded, had been entitled to publish without attempting to verify the allegations:

I am not, of course, saying that verification (or at least an attempt at verification) of a third party's allegations will not ordinarily be appropriate and perhaps even essential. In rejecting the general claim for qualified privilege for political discussion Lord Nicholls said in *Reynolds*: 'One difficulty with this suggestion is that it would seem to leave a newspaper open to publish a serious allegation which it had been wholly unable to verify. Depending on the circumstances, that might be most unsatisfactory.' I am saying, however, that there will be circumstances where, as here, that may not be 'most unsatisfactory'—where, in short, both sides to a political dispute are being fully, fairly and disinterestedly reported in their respective allegations and responses. In this situation it seems to me that the public is entitled to be informed of such a dispute without having to wait for the publisher, following an attempt at verification, to commit himself to one side or the other.

The claimant, incidentally, was complaining about remarks made by Dr Mohammed al-Masari, who was given exceptional leave to remain in Britain in 1996. A year earlier, al-Masari had used the courts to defeat an attempt to deport him to Yemen when a tribunal ruled that he would be in danger there. The Government then persuaded the Caribbean island of Dominica to offer him sanctuary, allegedly with an offer of banana-trade concessions, but Judge Pearl, the Chief Immigration Adjudicator, said the Government's tactics were 'not a course of action

I either support or consider to be within the humanitarian spirit within which the convention should be interpreted'. One does not have to support al-Masari's views to thank him for establishing that newspapers, acting more as watchdogs than bloodhounds, will receive the protection of qualified privilege at common law if they adopt a position of neutral reportage.

Gleaning the meaning

In June 2002, Lord Nicholls found himself asked once again to consider the standards of responsible journalism. Some Commonwealth countries still find it convenient to allow appeals to the Judicial Committee of the Privy Council—a court consisting of law lords and other senior judges from the United Kingdom and Commonwealth—despite frequent claims that they want nothing more to do with colonial justice. So it was that Hugh Bonnick's appeal in his libel case against the Jamaican *Sunday Gleaner* came to be heard in London by Lord Nicholls and four other judges.

Bonnick had been managing director of a Government-owned company that imported basic foodstuffs into Jamaica. A dispute had arisen over two contracts for the supply of milk powder and, according to the newspaper, 'Mr Bonnick's services as managing director were terminated shortly after the second contract was agreed.' Bonnick complained that, in context, this suggested that he had been sacked for impropriety. The trial judge agreed but, by a majority of two to one, the Jamaica Court of Appeal decided that this was not how the ordinary reader would have understood the story. He appealed to London.

The Privy Council shared the trial judge's view that the words were defamatory. But would qualified privilege apply? If the article had expressly stated that Bonnick had been sacked because of dissatisfaction with the way he had handled the disputed contracts, the newspaper would have had no defence. 'By not making further enquiries and omitting Mr Bonnick's own explanation the article would have fallen short of the standards to be expected of a responsible journalist,' Lord Nicholls explained. 'But the article contained no such express statement. The defamatory imputation was a matter of implication. Plainly, there is room for different views on whether the article contained such an implication. [The reporter] seems to have thought she was not making a statement to this effect in her article. Rather more relevantly and importantly, one of the members of the Court of Appeal was of the same view.'

Should the court assign a meaning for these purposes, as it would in deciding whether words are to be treated as defamatory? No, said the Privy Council:

The *Reynolds* privilege is concerned to provide a proper degree of protection for responsible journalism when reporting matters of public concern. Responsible journalism is the point at which a fair balance is held between freedom of expression on matters of public concern and the reputations of individuals. Maintenance of this standard is in the public interest and in the interests of those whose reputations are involved . . . To be meaningful this standard of conduct must be applied in a practical and flexible manner . . . A journalist should not be penalised for making a wrong decision on a question of meaning on which different people might reasonably take different views.

This should not be pressed too far. Where questions of defamation may arise ambiguity is best avoided as much as possible . . . In the normal course, a responsible journalist can be expected to perceive the meaning an ordinary, reasonable reader is likely to give to his article. Moreover, even if the words are highly susceptible of another meaning, a responsible journalist will not disregard a defamatory meaning which is obviously one possible meaning of the article in question. Questions of degree arise here. The more obvious the defamatory meaning, and the more serious the defamation, the less weight will a court attach to other possible meanings when considering the conduct to be expected of a responsible journalist in the circumstances.

The judges thought that the defamatory meaning was not so 'glaringly obvious' that any responsible journalist would be bound to realize this was how an ordinary reader would understand the words used. Although near the borderline, this article was a piece of 'responsible journalism' for which the new *Reynolds* defence of qualified privilege was available.

This area of the law is still being developed by the courts and practitioners find it hard to advise clients when the courts will allow 'QP'. Some lawyers say it is misleading to categorize it as a form of privilege, arguing instead that it is a unique defence which other legal systems would regard as 'reasonable publication'.

Responsible journalism

Newspapers in England and Wales have not yet reached the level of protection that the *New York Times* achieved in *Sullivan*. But *Reynolds* and the cases that followed it have demonstrated an acceptance by the judiciary that responsible journalism is worth protecting. The more that judges in this country come under pressure from governments, the more they will begin to realize that the media, on the whole, do a worthwhile job in telling them what is going on. If a journalist makes an honest but relatively unimportant mistake, the judges are less willing than previously to restrain that reporter's freedom of speech. This is as it should be: remember the remarks of Lord Justice Simon Brown, quoted above, that freedom of expression is 'a constitutional right of vital importance to the proper functioning of a democratic society'. But what, precisely, is 'responsible journalism'? That is what we shall consider next.

CHAPTER 7

Responsible Journalism

'This scarecrow of a suit has, in course of time, become so complicated, that no man alive knows what it means.' That was Dickens, of course, writing about *Jarndyce and Jarndyce* in *Bleak House*. But his description could equally well have applied to the real-life case of *Loutchansky v Times Newspapers Ltd*, a series of claims dating from 2001 that give us a valuable insight into what the courts regard as 'responsible journalism'. As we saw in Chapter 6, newspapers that meet this standard will be able to defend themselves in the libel courts by claiming qualified privilege, an important safeguard for the press against the 'chilling' effect of a libel action.

Loutchansky sues

The claims were brought by Dr Grigori Loutchansky, a businessman born in Tashkent and subsequently based in Latvia, who alleged that he had been libelled by two articles published by *The Times* in September and October 1999. He brought a second action a year later, complaining that both reports remained accessible on the newspaper's website.

The articles alleged that Loutchansky was a 'mafia boss', running a major Russian criminal organization. Through Nordex, a company he owned and controlled, he was said to have been involved in smuggling nuclear weapons. The first article claimed that, either personally or by means of companies that he owned or controlled, he was involved in the criminal laundering of billions of dollars from Russia—or, at the very least, that his conduct had given people reasonable cause to suspect him or his companies of such involvement—although it did add that he had 'repeatedly denied any wrongdoing or links to criminal activity', a position he continued to maintain.

Although the two articles had been published a few weeks before the law lords' ruling in *Reynolds*, the newspaper relied on the defence of qualified privilege established by that case. But before Loutchansky's claim could be heard by a jury, *The Times* unsuccessfully sought permission to rely in court on facts it had discovered after the original publication. Whether such evidence should be admissible had been left undecided by *Reynolds*. However, *The Times* was refused permission to amend its defence by the trial judge, Mr Justice Gray. In March 2001, his decision was upheld by the Court of Appeal, Lord Justice Brooke ruling that 'it was at the moment of publication that the defendants had to decide whether, given the information available to them then and the extent of the inquiries they had then made, they could properly consider they were under a duty to tell the public what they wrote about Mr Loutchansky in their articles'.

This somewhat artificial ruling was a setback for the newspaper, which had wanted to explain why Loutchansky had been excluded from Britain by the Home Office since 1994 and why he had been refused a visa to visit the United States in 1995. It also wanted to produce intelligence reports on his companies and a statement giving the Israeli Government's reasons for opposing the renewal of his Israeli passport. However, the Court of Appeal saw its ruling as consistent with the discipline of *Reynolds*. 'If a defendant acts on the basis of facts which he honestly believes to be true but which are later found to have been, through no fault of his own, untrue,' said Sir Martin Nourse, one of the judges, 'he will not be deprived of his defence. Equally, facts which are unknown to him at the time of publication cannot have any bearing on the question whether he is under the requisite duty at that time.'

This seems logical enough, although it does not allow for the possibility that reporters may strongly suspect something adverse at time of publication while not having detailed proof. *The Times*, however, hit back as only a newspaper can, attacking the appeal judges' decision in a leading article headed 'Loutchansky versus *Times*: a most bizarre case of libel'. An understandably furious Mr Justice Gray considered discharging the jury, which had been sworn in and was waiting for the Court of Appeal's ruling before beginning to hear Loutchansky's case. In the end, he decided to allow the case to go ahead. The judge also decided against referring the case to the Attorney General as a possible contempt of court.

The judge's ruling

A week later, the case came to trial. It became clear that the jury would not have long enough 'within the available timeframe' to decide on the size of any damages as well as liability, so Mr Justice Gray decided that they should deal with liability alone. Since qualified privilege was in issue—and it is for the judge to decide whether an occasion is privileged—the jury were asked a series of fifteen questions from which he could make his rulings on the law.

Did a source tell *The Times* reporter that Loutchansky or his company were mentioned in a British police report? 'Yes,' said the jury. Did an author called Jeffrey Robinson tell the reporter that Loutchansky was being investigated by the FBI? Yes again. Did the reporter try to contact Loutchansky for comment through his company? 'No,' the jury concluded. After hearing evidence, the jury answered ten questions in favour of the reporter, two against and were undecided on the remaining three. That 'vindicated' its reporter, according to *The Times*. But it was not enough to justify a claim of qualified privilege, Mr Justice Gray decided in April 2001. His judgment—though overturned on appeal because he interpreted qualified privilege too stringently—is worthy of quoting at some length because it demonstrates just what judges now expect of the press.

'Although *Reynolds* has rightly been perceived as enlarging the ambit of qualified privilege, the conceptual foundation for the defence remains the existence of a reciprocity of duty and interest on the part of the publisher and the publishees respectively,' explained the judge.

It follows that the mere existence of a legitimate interest on the part of the readership of a newspaper to have the information imparted to them will not of itself suffice to establish the privilege. It is possible to visualise cases where it can be said that the readership has a legitimate interest in knowing the information (perhaps because of the status or nature of the information in question) but where the claim to privilege will fail because the requisite duty to publish is not made out (perhaps because of the newspaper's failure to report the gist of the answers of Dr Loutchansky to the accusations against him).

After many years practice in the libel courts, Mr Justice Gray showed he understood all too well how newspapers operate. Having considered the reliability of the reporter's admitted sources, three of whom were anonymous, the judge assessed the extent to which *The Times* had tried to track down the claimant and the urgency of the story:

To be truly urgent, there has to be some quality about the story itself which makes it imperative or at least highly desirable that the information in question should be made public without delay . . . I am not persuaded that the story about Dr Loutchansky was truly urgent in that sense. It is to be noted that, although the *Times* was in possession of evidence which [its Foreign Editor] felt was strong enough to publish the story by September 3, 1999, publication did not in the event take place until September 8. [The Foreign Editor] explained that she did not feel the story was suitable for publication in the *Times* on a Saturday.

In my view the story was far from being so urgent that it needed to be published before diligent efforts had been made to obtain Dr Loutchansky's side of the story. It is common ground that no comment was obtained from Dr Loutchansky or from anyone else in a position to speak on his behalf . . . Fairness and good journalistic practice required such a comment, providing that Dr Loutchansky or a spokesman on his behalf could be traced.

There will be occasions where it is impossible to make contact with the claimant in advance of publication. I do not accept that this was such an occasion. The place of business of Nordex had been Austria, where Dr Loutchansky had (and continues to have) a residential address. [The reporter] gave evidence that he called international directory enquiries and asked them whether there was any listing for Nordex in Moscow. He did not claim to have asked about a listing for Dr Loutchansky . . . [The reporter] also communicated with a *Times* 'stringer' in Moscow . . . All he asked her to do was to find a telephone number for Nordex in Moscow (something which according to his evidence he had already done himself) and to try to find Dr Loutchansky in Moscow.

That was the sum total of the efforts made by the defendants to contact Dr Loutchansky before publication. Contrary to the evidence of [the Foreign Editor], 'layers and layers of effort' were not made. In my judgment more strenuous efforts could and should have been made to contact him and obtain a comment. For example the suggestion could have been made to [the stringer] that she carry out an internet search in Russian or check the register of companies registered in Moscow. Efforts could and should have made to trace Nordex and Dr Loutchansky in Austria, where Nordex remained incorporated. The defendants could and should have carried out a Dun & Bradstreet [company database] search on Nordex.

Failing contact with Dr Loutchansky himself, there was the possibility of obtaining a comment on his behalf from a spokesman. Although in his witness statement [the reporter] stated that he had looked through the cuttings in the hope of finding a lawyer who might put him in touch with Dr Loutchansky, in his oral evidence [the reporter] said that he had seen reference in American reports to a lawyer named Thomas Spencer Jr . . . The attempts to trace Mr Spencer were in my judgment deficient.

[The reporter] had been provided by Mr Robinson with the name of an English solicitor who acted for Dr Loutchansky, namely Mr David Cooper who was a senior partner of the London firm Gouldens. [The reporter] gave evidence . . . that he made searches for Mr Cooper by means of cuttings and by looking in Crawfords and PriceWaterhouseCoopers directories. But these directories list the names of firms rather than individual solicitors and so were of no use. The cuttings did not help either. So Mr Lister was unsuccessful in such attempts as he made to track down Mr Cooper.

I consider that it should have been straightforward for the defendants to find Mr Cooper. He was a partner in a well-known London firm. The name of his firm could without difficulty have been obtained from the Law Society. There are directories which list individual solicitors by name. The legal department of the defendants could have been asked to assist. In my judgment the attempts to contact Mr Cooper were insufficient . . .

The article of September 8 contained a single paragraph which read: 'Mr Loutchansky has repeatedly denied any wrongdoing or links to criminal activity.' Given the seriousness of the (unproven) allegations to be published about Dr Loutchansky, it does not appear to me that the inclusion of a bare denial of that kind was a sufficient statement of Dr Loutchansky's case. There were exculpatory comments which Dr Loutchansky could have made if he had been invited to do so, for example that he had never dealt with the Bank of New York or maintained any account with that bank. Even if neither Dr Loutchansky nor any spokesman could be contacted, there was more which the *Times* could and, in my opinion, should have published by way of answer to the allegations. For instance the article could have stressed that Dr Loutchansky has never been convicted or even charged with any of the offences said to have been the subject of investigations. It could have repeated the statement of Dr Loutchansky's US lawyer, Mr Spencer, reported in a *Washington Post* article which [the reporter] had read, that everywhere in Europe that the allegation that Dr Loutchansky had ties to organised crime had been reported, he had either sued and won or it had been retracted.

The Times should have proceeded with great caution, Mr Justice Gray concluded. It was particularly important to obtain Loutchansky's side of the story, given the limited corroboration that the newspaper had obtained. *The Times* was entitled to publish the story, but it was not under any *duty* to do so. For this reason, it was 'not entitled to the immunity from liability in libel which, subject to malice, is provided by the defence of qualified privilege'. Still less was qualified privilege available for the second article, which was based on unchecked and anecdotal evidence from an unreliable source.

The judge granted an injunction restraining further publication of the allegations complained of. In a statement issued through his solicitors, Loutchansky said he was delighted to have been vindicated by an English court. 'I brought my claim against *The Times* to clear my name and I have succeeded. I am pleased that *The Times*'s shoddy journalism has now been exposed.'

The Times fights back

The newspaper hit back in an ill-judged leading article. '*The Times* had to demonstrate due diligence in its reporting. Under merciless and often contemptuous cross-examination, its reporter did so to the almost complete satisfaction of the jury.' Really? That 'almost' conceals a finding by the jury that the newspaper had not tried to approach Loutchansky through his company, something it should clearly have done if it was serious about printing his response. 'The libel law of England and Wales, which seemed to be slowly emerging from the dark ages, has been set back a decade', thundered the newspaper. What, by one first-instance judgment?

Alan Rusbridger, editor of the *Guardian*, praised this as an 'elegant' *Times* leader that had 'persuasively analysed' the court's ruling. The effect of Mr Justice Gray's judgment, he said, would be 'to cement a trend, created by the recent *Reynolds* case, whereby the function of the libel laws is as much to police journalistic standards as to protect the reputation of the claimant'. This might or might not be a desirable thing, Rusbridger conceded, but it did not have much to do with either the law of libel or free speech.

In fact, it has everything to do with both. Qualified privilege allows free speech to trump the libel laws. Provided we are going to keep a defamation law, the defence of privilege cannot be made available in all cases. Lord Nicholls's ten points should give us a pretty good idea when *Reynolds* privilege will be granted. *The Times* fell down on almost all of them.

Writing for *The Times* in May 2001, Rusbridger pointed out that American publications such as the *Washington Post* and *Time* magazine were free to make allegations about Loutchansky: the Supreme Court decision in *Sullivan v New York Times* protected them against libel actions unless a claimant could prove malice or reckless disregard for the truth. Even then, there was a drawback: 'Critics of *Sullivan* sometimes argue that it has become a tool for claimants who—seeking to prove malice or carelessness—use court powers to get inside newsrooms and turn the legal microscope on journalistic methods. Gray's judgment in *Loutchansky* has imported the same tyranny into British newsrooms—but without the robust balancing protection of the rest of *Sullivan* or of the First Amendment. It is a worrying turning point for the British press.'

Requiring reporters to check stories thoroughly may be seen as 'tyranny' in the *Guardian* newsroom, but any newspaper that seeks to rely on its journalistic integrity should be answerable in court for its newsgathering methods.

Indeed, Debbie Ashenhurst, Loutchansky's solicitor, was given space in *The Times* to argue that Mr Justice Gray's judgment was not, as the newspaper had argued in court, 'the death knell of freedom of expression' but a proper illustration of its limits. *Reynolds* qualified privilege was 'alive and well and available to any defendant who acts fairly and responsibly', she explained. 'Rights carry responsibilities and a press which takes advantage of its right to freedom of expression must do so responsibly.' Ashenhurst continued: 'Most media lawyers accept that the traditional English approach to libel law was too restrictive of freedom of speech and that the House of Lords decision in *Reynolds* was a decisive step towards bringing the UK into line with the European Convention. If the pendulum were to swing still further and allow irresponsible newspapers unlimited freedom to make false allegations, that would not be consistent with the European approach to freedom of expression—nor would it be in the public interest.'

A couple of years later, Rusbridger's competitive instincts largely overcame his sympathy for a fellow editor. Sir Peter Stothard, editor of *The Times* until 2002, had been speaking on the *Today* programme about its defence correspondent, Andrew Gilligan, whose interview with the Government weapons inspector Dr David Kelly in May 2003 was followed by Kelly's suicide. Gilligan had just admitted to the public inquiry conducted by Lord Hutton that he had made some errors of detail when reporting Kelly's allegation that the Government had exaggerated the case for war against Iraq, though he stood by the substance of his story. 'Journalism is about telling the truth as well as doing good,' Stothard commented. 'At the end of a catalogue of errors some good may come but, for a journalist, that certainly does not justify the fact that these falsehoods were put out and really not corrected properly.' Rusbridger enjoyed a 'small chuckle' at the parallels between *Loutchansky* and Gilligan. Writing in his own newspaper in September 2003, he professed not to be criticizing '*The Times*, its able reporter or Stothard'. But he continued: '*The Times*—in Gray's stringent opinion—committed most of the errors of the BBC's Gilligan. Virtually no one in the outside world noticed; the directors of *The Times* held no panic meetings; the reporter wasn't sacked; and Stothard wasn't hauled over the coals. Mr Murdoch appears, on the contrary, to have been entirely supportive, backing an appeal all the way to Europe. The usual argument offered at this point is that a public service broadcaster has an obligation to act according to higher standards than those of a mere newspaper. But it is hard to imagine *The Times* or *Telegraph* advancing such a case. They would scarcely offer the BBC such stern ethical lessons unless they believed themselves to be at least its equal.'

It was hardly surprising that no one noticed Mr Justice Gray's 'stringent' criticism, since *Times* readers had to plough through the front-page report and four full inside pages in order to find the word 'lost'. But the ruling was clear. Since the newspaper's only defence had failed, judgment was entered for Loutchansky. That left the question of his compensation. He had told *The Times* he would not continue to demand damages if he received a proper apology. He was also happy for any damages to be assessed by a judge, and to allow that to happen under recently introduced rules he agreed to limit his claim to £10,000 in each case. *The Times*, on the other hand, claimed the court had no jurisdiction to order damages at all, let alone to assess them. That argument was rejected by Mr Justice Gray in May 2001. The Defamation Act 1996 was worded in such a way as to allow 'summary disposal' and he was 'firmly of the view that the fair, economic, expeditious and proportionate way of dealing with the issue' was to have the issue of damages decided by a judge sitting alone.

The Court of Appeal

But a fair, economic, expeditious and proportionate disposal of the case seemed to be the last thing *The Times* was looking for, and it brought five challenges to Mr Justice Gray's rulings in the Court of Appeal. In December 2001, Lord Phillips, Master of the Rolls, sitting with Lords Justices Simon Brown and Tuckey, allowed one appeal by the newspaper—on the standards to be met by journalists—and dismissed the rest.

As Lord Nicholls had explained in *Reynolds*, a claim to qualified privilege generally stands or falls according to whether it passes the traditional 'duty/interest' test—whether there was a duty to publish the material to the intended recipients and whether they had had a corresponding interest in receiving it—or, to put it more simply, 'whether the public was entitled to know the particular information'. But, said the Court of Appeal, 'duty' and 'interest' now have to be understood in the entirely new context of *Reynolds* privilege. 'The interest is that of the public in a modern democracy in free expression and, more particularly, in the promotion of a free and vigorous press to keep the public informed . . . The corresponding duty on the journalist (and equally his editor) is to play his proper role in discharging that function. His task is to behave as a responsible journalist. He can have no duty to publish unless he is acting responsibly any more than the public has an interest in reading whatever may be published irresponsibly . . . That is not the case with regard to the more conventional situations in which qualified privilege arises. A person giving a reference or reporting a crime need not act responsibly: his communication will be privileged subject only to relevance and malice.'

However, the appeal judges decided that Mr Justice Gray had defined 'duty' too stringently. He had thought the duty had to be 'such that a publisher would be open to legitimate criticism if he failed to publish the information in question'. But that was too high a test: there would be occasions when one editor would decide to publish and another, no less properly, would decide not to do so. The standard required was that of 'responsible journalism'. Having explained the standards to be met, the appeal judges sent the case back to Mr Justice Gray so that he could apply the new test to the facts of the case.

Internet publication

The Times was unsuccessful on its other four grounds of appeal. The first dealt with the important question of publication on the Internet. Under the Limitation Act 1980, as amended, a libel action cannot normally be started more than a year after the offending article was published. However, each individual act of publication gives rise to a fresh cause of action. The nineteenth-century case of *Duke of Brunswick v Harmer* provides a striking example of this. An article was published in the *Weekly Dispatch* in 1830, at a time when the limitation period for libel was six years. It allegedly defamed the Duke of Brunswick and Lüneburg—one duke, two titles—though he seems not to have complained at the time. Some seventeen years later, in 1847, the same magazine published a second article which meant, according to the Duke, that he had been guilty of 'such acts of outrage and oppression as justified his deposition by his subjects' in northern Germany. Prompted by this, the Duke sent his man to buy a back number of the magazine containing the original 1830 article from the publisher's office. Another copy was obtained from the British Museum. When the Duke sued over the 17-year-old article, Harmer, the paper's proprietor, argued that the claim was out of time, the limitation period having expired in 1836. But Lord Denman, the Lord Chief Justice, overruled Harmer's objection and the Duke was awarded the colossal sum of £500 by the jury. On appeal, the Court of Queen's Bench agreed that the delivery of a copy of the newspaper to the claimant's agent amounted to a separate publication in respect of which an action could be brought within six years. The Court also saw no reason to overturn the jury's verdict on damages, even though the only publication proved in 1847 had been to the Duke's servant. Sadly, the law report by Adolphus and Ellis does not tell us what exactly was alleged by the *Weekly Dispatch*.

The consequences of this nineteenth-century ruling for twenty-first century online newspaper archives are obvious. Each time a story is downloaded from the Internet, a new one-year limitation period will begin to run. That means, in practice, that newspapers will remain vulnerable to libel suits indefinitely—unless they remove items from their websites that might land them in court. In *Loutchansky*, Lord Lester, QC, for *The Times*, had tried to persuade the Court of Appeal to follow some twenty-seven US states in adopting the 'single-publication rule', which says that any one edition of a book or newspaper, any one radio or television broadcast or the initial screening of any film is a single publication giving rise to just one cause of action that starts to run at the time of the original publication. This was too radical for the English judges—even though Lord Lester based his argument on the freedom-of-expression provisions in Article 10 of the Convention—but they did suggest that something akin to a 'health warning' might be enough to immunize newspapers against legal action:

> We do not accept that the rule in the *Duke of Brunswick* case imposes a restriction on the readiness to maintain and provide access to archives that amounts to a disproportionate restriction on freedom of expression. We accept that the maintenance of archives, whether in hard copy or on the internet, has a social utility, but consider that the maintenance of archives is a comparatively insignificant aspect of freedom of expression. Archive material is stale news and its publication cannot rank in importance with the dissemination of contemporary material. Nor do we believe that the law of defamation need inhibit the responsible maintenance of archives. Where it is known that archive material is or may be defamatory, the attachment of an appropriate notice warning against treating it as the truth will normally remove any sting from the material.

This reasoning was followed in December 2002 by the High Court of Australia, the country's supreme court, in a case brought by an Australian resident named Joseph Gutnick. He claimed he had been libelled in an article headlined 'Unholy Gains' published in *Barron's* magazine by Dow Jones, the company that also publishes the *Wall Street Journal*. The article could be read online by subscribers in Australia, even though the web server was in the American state of New Jersey. In *Gutnick v Dow Jones*, the defendants argued that they published the article only when it was 'pulled' from their computer in the United States by someone who wanted to read it. On that basis, Gutnick could sue only in the American courts, where publishers have greater protection than they do in countries such as Australia. But, as the trial judge patiently explained, 'the law in defamation has been for centuries that publication takes place where and when the contents of the publication, oral or spoken, are seen and heard and comprehended by the reader or hearer.' That approach was upheld by the High Court of Australia, which allowed Gutnick to sue in his home state of Victoria. Material held on a server could not be read until someone downloaded it, the judges observed. 'It is where that person downloads the material that the damage to reputation may be done. Ordinarily then, that will be the place where the tort of defamation is committed.'

Dow Jones found itself arguing a similar point in the English courts a few months later. This time, the claimant was Harrods, the department store owned by Mohamed Al Fayed. On 31 March 2002, the store issued a press release under the heading 'Al Fayed reveals plan to "float" Harrods'. It said that an important announcement would be made the following day that might help journalists who had speculated during the last few months as to the future direction of Harrods, adding: 'The announcement will only be posted on the website until 12 noon on April 1'. Anyone interested was invited to contact 'Loof Lirpa' at Harrods. Pretty obvious, eh?

A few days later, the *Wall Street Journal* published an elaborate correction. Headlined 'The Enron of Britain?', it said: 'If Harrods, the British luxury retailer, ever goes public, investors would be wise to question its every disclosure. Harrods made "news" at the beginning of this week, when the London department store operator announced it was about to sell shares publicly. Some news organizations picked up the news item, including the *Wall Street Journal* in a news briefs column—but it was all an April Fools' joke . . . Clues that it was a joke included the fact that the contact person listed to get more information was Loof Lirpa— April Fool spelled backward.'

Harrods claimed it was 'quite scandalous' of the newspaper to have compared it to the bankrupt energy trader and issued libel proceedings in London against Dow Jones. Perhaps deliberately, the *Wall Street Journal* had not published the offending story in its European edition. Although the 1.8 million copies of the US edition are sold in the United States, only about ten of these are sent to subscribers in the UK. Once more, though, the article was put on a Dow Jones website— although it was said to have received 'a very small number of hits'.

In court, the publishers argued that the case should be thrown out because England and Wales was not the most convenient place to try the Harrods' claim. Mr Justice Eady, giving judgment in May 2003, disagreed. 'There are two important principles of English defamation law which, although they may not commend themselves to parties, courts or commentators in other jurisdictions, are well established,' he said. The first was that English law does not recognize a single-publication doctrine. 'Thus, however limited and technical it may appear, there have been publications within the jurisdiction which are arguably tortious and which give rise to a cause of action here.' The other was that damage was presumed. Even though Harrods might win little or nothing in damages because there was no evidence of any damage to its reputation in Britain, and even though the US courts were unlikely to enforce a judgment against Dow Jones because of their respect for the First Amendment, the store was still entitled to ask for its reputation to be vindicated. Though he decided that England was the most convenient place to try a case involving the reputation of a company that traded there, Mr Justice Eady pleaded with the parties to reach a 'sensible compromise' before further costs were incurred. 'My words may fall on stony ground,' he said, 'but that is no reason for not making an attempt.'

Back to *Loutchansky*

Times Newspapers had three remaining grounds of appeal against Mr Justice Gray's ruling. One related to whether qualified privilege could be claimed in respect of the offending articles as they appeared on the Internet. Mr Justice Gray had given two reasons for rejecting this. The first was that the journalists did not have an honest belief in the truth of what they published. This was not the correct test, said the Court of Appeal. The second was that the articles had been republished without any sort of health warning. That was a good reason for ruling out *Reynolds* privilege, according to the appeal judges. 'The failure to attach any qualifications to the articles published over the period of a year on the *Times* website could not possibly be described as responsible journalism. We do not believe that it can be convincingly argued that the defendants had a *Reynolds* duty to publish those articles in that way without qualification.' The stories, incidentally, are no longer on the *Times* website, although they are quoted in full in the law reports.

The next ground of appeal dealt with the arcane question of whether Loutchansky was entitled to damages for the republication of the libels in Russia. The judge said he could, since he could have sued in Russia, and the Court of Appeal agreed.

The final appeal was against whether the judge had jurisdiction to order that the damages should not be decided by a jury. The Court of Appeal decided that he did: there was no reason in principle why Parliament should have limited the jurisdiction in the way the newspaper had argued.

After *The Times* was refused permission to appeal to the House of Lords, the case went back to Mr Justice Gray. As we have seen, his definition of qualified privilege had been too restrictive, and he was asked to apply the new test provided by the Court of Appeal. It made no difference: in November 2002, the judge again decided that *Reynolds* privilege was not available. Crucially, he thought the reporter should have approached Loutchansky or his spokesman before publication. 'Implicating the claimant in misconduct of the utmost gravity was manifestly likely to be highly damaging to his reputation,' he concluded. 'Accordingly, a proportionate degree of responsibility was required of the journalist and editor before giving currency to such allegations.' *The Times* said it would be seeking permission to appeal.

Meanwhile, the newspaper had a new card to play. In the three years since the articles against Loutchansky first appeared, *The Times* had not once sought to prove that they were true. Now, it was seeking to amend its defence to include a plea of justification. The newspaper was not seeking to justify the allegation that he was the boss of a major criminal organization or that he had been involved in smuggling nuclear weapons. However, it said it could prove that he had been involved in money laundering, or at least that he had given people reasonable cause to suspect him of such activities. In December 2002, Mr Justice Gray rejected that argument too. After detailed consideration of evidence obtained from Italian prosecutors, the judge concluded that there was not enough material for the newspaper to make good its case that there had been reasonable grounds for even suspecting Loutchansky to have been guilty of money laundering. In addition, the lateness of the application would cause Loutchansky real prejudice.

After Lord Nicholls had released his ten tests, one enterprising firm of solicitors printed them on a small folding card and sent it to potential clients. A rival firm pointed out that, following the Court of Appeal's decision in *Loutchansky*, reporters need only write 'behave as a responsible journalist' on the back of their hands. Since a back-of-the-hand definition may turn out to be rather elastic, the *Reynolds* tests should prove useful still.

Guts or green ink?

By the beginning of 2003, with *Loutchansky* dormant, lawyers were wondering whether Times Newspapers was behaving as obsessively over the case as those of its readers who traditionally wrote to it in green ink, running up huge legal costs to no obvious purpose. That was not how it looked in Wapping, where the publishers of *The Times* and *Sunday Times* saw themselves as acting with the levels of determination and commitment that led them to win victories for the entire media in the Thalidomide case, *Spycatcher* and *Reynolds* itself. We should take a moment to recall those successes before deciding whether *The Times* had lost its marbles.

Thalidomide

Thalidomide was, of course, the sedative that caused birth deformities in the early 1960s when taken by pregnant women. In 1972, the *Sunday Times* mounted a campaign to persuade Distillers, the company that manufactured the drug, to increase its compensation offer to nearly 400 victims and their families. Distillers persuaded the Attorney General to seek an injunction to prevent publication of an article that the newspaper had been planning to run, and this was granted by the High Court on the ground that the piece would have put Distillers under undue pressure. A powerful Court of Appeal, headed by Lord Denning and including Lords Justices Phillimore and Scarman, demonstrated what nonsense this was: there was no reason to prevent comment on the 62 cases that had been settled in 1968 or the 123 in which formal proceedings had not been issued. In any case, the litigation was dormant and nobody expected there to be a trial; the mere issue of a writ should not stifle all comment. Sadly, the House of Lords, headed by the much-respected Lord Reid, railed against 'trial by newspaper' and reinstated the injunction so that Distillers could continue its negotiations without having to worry about what the *Sunday Times* and its editor, Harry Evans, thought about them. The injunction was finally lifted in 1976.

Meanwhile, the newspaper had taken its case to the European Court of Human Rights, where its counsel, then plain Anthony Lester, QC, argued at a hearing in 1978 that there had been a breach of Article 10. The Court agreed. Giving judgment in 1979, it said that:

The interference complained of did not correspond to a social need sufficiently pressing to outweigh the public interest in freedom of expression within the meaning of the convention. The court therefore finds the reasons for the restraint imposed on the applicants not to be sufficient under Article 10(2). That restraint proves not to be proportionate to the legitimate aim pursued; it was not necessary in a democratic society for maintaining the authority of the judiciary.

Since the Government is required by treaty to bring domestic law into line with decisions of the Human Rights Court, it introduced the Contempt of Court Act 1981. The 1981 Act restricts contempt prosecutions—unless there has been a deliberate attempt to influence the proceedings—to cases where the publication 'creates a substantial risk that the course of justice in the proceedings in question will be seriously impeded or prejudiced'.

Spycatcher

Spycatcher was another victory for the *Sunday Times*. It was not the first newspaper to report in 1986 that the Government was seeking to use the law of confidence to prevent a former MI5 officer called Peter Wright from publishing allegations of wrongdoing by the Security Service: that was the *Observer*, closely followed by the *Guardian*. Nor was it even the first to devote its entire front page to a summary of his allegations (that was the plucky little *Independent*, in 1987, just six months after its launch). However, the *Sunday Times* was the first to acquire serial rights and publish a long extract from Wright's book, *Spycatcher*.

Was this lawful? The Government had obtained injunctions against the *Observer* and *Guardian* a year earlier, and these were still in force at the time. *Sunday Times* executives knew this of course, but since there was no injunction against their own newspaper they were advised by their QC that they would not be in contempt of court if they published extracts from the book. This may have been good law at the time, but it was a trick that could be played only once; before the end of the week, the Court of Appeal had ruled, in effect, that one injunction would bind all newspapers.

The *Sunday Times* challenged that ruling (briefing Lester again) only to lose before the House of Lords in 1991. In *Attorney General v Times Newspapers Ltd*, the law lords said that the newspaper had interfered with the course of justice by nullifying any chance that the Attorney General might have had in obtaining a permanent injunction against Wright. This was a valuable precedent for the Government and, indeed, for all those seeking to prevent a breach of confidence; ever since *Spycatcher*, for an order to bind the entire media it has been necessary only to take out an injunction against one media organization and then notify the others.

However, by serializing Wright's not very good book, the *Sunday Times* had become involved in a series of cases that led to another famous victory for the media in Strasbourg. The day after extracts had appeared in the newspaper, *Spycatcher* itself was published in the United States. No attempt was made to stop copies being brought into the United Kingdom or being sold on the streets and it became the 'must-have' volume on fashionable bookshelves and coffee tables. Since the book was becoming so widely available, the *Observer* and *Guardian* asked the courts to lift the original injunction against them. But, by a majority of three to two, the law lords decided at the end of July 1987 that the injunctions should remain in force until the full hearing of the Government's application for a permanent ban. Lord Brandon, Lord Templeman and Lord Ackner upheld the temporary injunctions; Lord Bridge and Lord Oliver profoundly disagreed with them.

Lord Brandon's thinking in *Attorney General v Guardian Newspapers Ltd* went something like this. The case against the *Guardian* and the *Observer* was aimed at protecting an important public interest: maintaining, so far as possible, the secrecy of the British security service. The injunctions were temporary: they would remain in force until the hearing of the Attorney General's claim. Before the publication of *Spycatcher* in America, the Attorney General had a strong, arguable case for obtaining permanent injunctions at the full hearing. While the publication of *Spycatcher* in America had much weakened that case, it remained an arguable one. The only way of deciding whether the Attorney General's case should succeed or fail was to have it heard. If the injunctions were lifted now he would lose all opportunity of winning permanent injunctions at the full hearing. If the injunctions were not lifted now and he lost at the final hearing, the newspapers would then be able to publish Mr Wright's allegations. It followed that lifting the injunctions at this stage could cause more injustice to the Attorney General than continuing them could cause to the newspapers. Continuing the injunctions was therefore preferable.

Though logically impeccable, Lord Brandon's judgment was complete nonsense. It was based on the premise that there was still something secret in Peter Wright's allegations. This, as even Lord Brandon seemed to acknowledge, was a tenuous argument. Lord Templeman, who agreed with him, tried to anticipate the inevitable criticism: 'I reject the argument that the law will appear ridiculous if it imposes a restriction on mass circulation when any individual member of the public may obtain a copy of *Spycatcher* from abroad. The court cannot exceed its territorial jurisdiction, but the court can prevent the harm which will result from mass circulation within its own jurisdiction.'

As far as the media were concerned, it was not the law that appeared ridiculous—it was the judges. The *Daily Mirror* published photographs of Lord Brandon, Lord Templeman and Lord Ackner on its front page. The pictures were printed upside down. Taking up half the page was a pithy comment: 'YOU FOOLS'.

This left Lord Ackner incandescent. In his written judgment, delivered a fortnight after the law lords had announced their decision, he said English justice would 'have come to a pretty pass if our inability to control what happens beyond our shores is to result in total incapacity to control what happens within our very own jurisdiction'. He accused the press of 'one-sided reporting': it was 'an abuse of power and a depressing reflection of falling standards and values'. There were 'elements in the press as a whole which not only lack responsibility, but integrity'. The image of King Canute springs inevitably to mind.

Much more persuasive were the minority judgments. For Lord Bridge, the important question was whether 'there is any remaining interest of national security which [the original temporary] injunctions are capable of protecting and, if so, whether it is of sufficient weight to justify the massive encroachment on freedom of speech which the continuance of the . . . injunctions in present circumstances necessarily involves.' In his view, there was not. In a resounding judgment, Lord Bridge said:

Freedom of speech is always the first casualty under a totalitarian regime . . .
The present attempt to insulate the public in this country from information
which is freely available elsewhere is a significant step down that very dangerous road. The maintenance of that ban, as more and more copies of *Spycatcher*
enter this country and circulate here, will seem more and more ridiculous. If
the government are determined to fight to maintain the ban to the end, they
will face inevitable condemnation and humiliation by the European Court of
Human Rights in Strasbourg. Long before that, they will have been
condemned at the bar of public opinion in the free world.

He was ably supported in these prescient remarks by another judge,
Lord Oliver:

I do not for a moment dispute that there are occasions when the strength of
the public interest in the preservation of confidentiality outweighs even the
importance of the free exercise of the essential privileges which lie at the roots
of our society. But if those privileges are to be overborne, then they must be
overborne to some purpose. The argument is not perhaps assisted by homely
metaphors about empty stables or escaping cats, but I cannot help but feel your
Lordships are being asked in the light of what has now occurred to beat the air
and to interfere with an essential freedom for the preservation of a confidentiality that has already been lost beyond recall.

Even in 1987, it was surely not just journalists who thought the majority decision of the House of Lords was wrong. The speeches of Lord
Brandon, Lord Templeman and Lord Ackner betrayed a narrow, legalis-
tic approach. The three judges seemed to ignore what was happening in
the world around them as they tried to stop the incoming tide of information. Nobody was saying that MI5 officers should be free to say what
they liked, still less that they should be allowed to make money from
selling the nation's secrets. As Lord Oliver's elegant nod in the direction
of empty stables and escaping cats indicated, it was simply too late to
stop Peter Wright.

   So the Government had its temporary injunctions, but everyone
must have realized that they could never be made permanent. Lord
Bridge, who presided over the 1987 law lords' hearing but found
himself in the minority, had his own advice for Margaret Thatcher and
her Cabinet. In a section of his judgment that read more like political
comment than legal reasoning, he suggested that the Government
should 'reappraise the whole *Spycatcher* situation'. Lord Bridge bravely
dared to hope that ministers would bring to this reappraisal 'qualities

of vision and statesmanship sufficient to recognise that their wafer-thin victory in this litigation has been gained at a price which no government committed to upholding the values of a free society can afford to pay'.

Some hope. As Hugo Young wrote in his biography *One of Us*, the Prime Minister 'stood firm on her conviction that, however many courts might find against her, she had a duty to fight the case until the last drop of taxpayer's money had been expended to defend the principle that spies should not talk. What some called stubbornness, even vanity, she referred to as her bounden duty.'

Find against her the courts certainly did. The first judge to reject her plea for a permanent injunction was Mr Justice Scott. Now that *Spycatcher* was an international bestseller, he considered the arguments in favour of allowing the media to report Peter Wright's allegations were of 'overwhelming weight'. Third parties no longer owed the Government any duty of confidence, he explained. Mr Justice Scott said the ability of the press freely to report allegations of scandals in government was 'one of the bulwarks of our democratic society'. The judge also had some strong words for the Government and its chief witness, the Cabinet Secretary Sir Robert Armstrong. He said: 'I find myself unable to escape the reflection that the absolute protection of the security service that Sir Robert was contending for could not be achieved this side of the Iron Curtain.' Not only did Mr Justice Scott lift the injunctions, he also included a detailed account of Mr Wright's allegations in his judgment that the media could safely reproduce.

As if on autopilot, the Government went to the Court of Appeal in 1988. By majority rulings, the appeal judges held in *Attorney General v Guardian Newspapers Ltd (No 2)* that Mr Justice Scott had been right to say that the *Observer* and *Guardian* were not in breach of their duty of confidentiality when they published their original reports (although the *Sunday Times* had been in breach of that duty when it published an extract from the book). The judges agreed that the injunctions should be lifted.

That decision was upheld by the law lords. They decided that because of the worldwide publication of *Spycatcher,* all confidentiality had gone and permanent injunctions should be refused. As Lord Griffiths put it, 'the balance in this case comes down firmly in favour of the public interest in freedom of speech and a free press'. The Government was ordered to pay the newspapers' legal costs.

What had the Government achieved? Its perseverance was no doubt meant to deter future whistleblowers—though this clearly had no effect on David Shayler, the former MI5 officer who was convicted on secrets charges in 2002 and briefly imprisoned. Ministers insisted that they had to act to protect the Security Service and its foreign counterpart, MI6. The Government noted with satisfaction 'that the law lords have unanimously upheld the government's contention that (to quote Lord Keith of Kinkel) "members and former members of the Security Service do have a lifelong obligation of confidence owed to the Crown. Those who breach it, such as Mr Wright, are guilty of treachery".' But this was hardly a surprise. Mr Justice Millett, the first judge to have given a reasoned judgment in the case, had said two years earlier that 'The Security Service must be seen to be leak-proof.' He added: 'The appearance of confidentiality is essential for its effective functioning. Its members simply cannot be allowed to write their memoirs.'

In reality, Mrs Thatcher had achieved nothing by her stubbornness. The estimated £3m her Government had spent trying to stop *Spycatcher* being published had turned the book into a bestseller. Although the Government had won its initial injunction by a 'wafer-thin' margin, it had lost at every level in its attempt to get a permanent ban on the book. That defeat was entirely predictable: indeed, it had been predicted by Lord Bridge. He was also right in his prediction that the Government would lose a challenge at the European Court of Human Rights. Giving judgment in *Observer and Guardian v UK* and *Sunday Times v UK (No 2)* in November 1991, the Strasbourg judges agreed with Anthony Lester, QC, for the *Sunday Times*, that once *Spycatcher* had been published in the United States all confidentiality in it had been destroyed and from then until the injunctions were finally lifted by the law lords a year later there had no justification for maintaining them. The Court unanimously found a breach of Article 10: newspapers had been prevented from publishing 'information, already available, on a matter of legitimate public concern' and they were awarded £200,000 in costs against the Government.

Looking back, it seems extraordinary that Lords Brandon, Templeman and Ackner thought they could prevent information reaching a mass audience in Britain once it had become public knowledge abroad. Indeed, Lord Templeman's reference to 'mass circulation' sounds slightly patronizing to us now, as if he was saying that only those who travelled to the United States should have access to this information. One must remember that in 1987—and even as late as 1991—the Internet and e-mail were accessible only to a handful of scientists: instant universal access to written information was not yet a reality. Nowadays, judges would not dream of trying to restrict access to information that is already circulating abroad.

Sticking up for the press

Reynolds, discussed in Chapter 6, was yet another case Lester had taken for the *Sunday Times*. The newspaper's legal manager, Alastair Brett, like his predecessor, Antony Whitaker, doggedly pursued those legal causes he believed to be right. Fighting for press freedom had become a matter of principle, whatever the importance of the individual case.

Many of these battles have benefited other newspapers and, indeed, society as a whole. The Thalidomide litigation saw off the 'gagging writ'. Taking the Government to Strasbourg over *Spycatcher* established that there could be no further ban on something that is already in the public domain. And turning *Reynolds* into an English approximation of *Sullivan* was a major advance. But *Loutchansky* achieved little. The standard of 'responsible journalism' set by the Court of Appeal in that case was not so very different from Lord Nicholls's ten points in *Reynolds*.

The other side of the CFA

Until recently, libel has been a game that only the rich could play. Legal aid has never been available, and the costs of going to court may be huge. But since the turn of the millennium it has been possible for lawyers to act in defamation cases on a 'no-win, no-fee' basis, using what's called a Conditional Fee Agreement, or CFA.

The attraction for clients is obvious: they can fight a claim in the knowledge that if they lose their case they will not have to pay their lawyers' fees. If they win, most of their side's fees will normally be paid by the losing party. The incentive for lawyers is that they can charge an additional 'success fee' if they win, which again should be paid by the losing party. That mark-up can be as high as 100 per cent of their normal fees for the case, which means that the CFA lawyer stands to make up to twice as much for each case he wins. It gets a little more complicated than that, however, because a losing client on a CFA agreement still has to pay the other side's legal costs. On the other hand, it may be possible to insure against that risk. Even better from the CFA client's point of view, the premium he pays for this insurance may be recoverable from the other side if he wins. There are yet further complications relating to outgoings and those who instruct lawyers on a CFA basis should check carefully what they are letting themselves in for. But there is no doubt that CFAs have opened up the libel courts to claimants who would not otherwise have been able to afford them.

A few defendants have made use of them too. In what was believed to be the first case to be defended under such an arrangement, Richmond Pharmacology Ltd was sued for defamation by a longer-established competitor, Charterhouse Clinical Research. The solicitor-advocate David Price agreed to represent Richmond on a conditional-fee basis and his clients bought £100,000 of insurance cover from Litigation Protection Ltd, a broker, against the risk that they might lose and be ordered to pay the claimant's costs. But Charterhouse discontinued its claim in May 2003 and agreed to pay Mr Price's bill of £167,000. That included his 'success fee' of 50 per cent and reimbursement of the £22,500 insurance premium paid by his clients. Mr Price said: 'We are totally committed to conditional fee litigation as the best way of defending defamation and media claims.'

From the lawyers' point of view, taking libel work on a CFA basis can be a risky business, unlike personal-injury work where genuine claims have a good chance of success. Even if lawyers charge a 100 per cent success fee, they cannot afford to lose more than one case in two of similar size. Not all solicitors are prepared to take the risk. One large London practice that does offer CFAs is known mainly as a claimants' firm, though it also does a substantial amount of defence work and says that in appropriate cases it may also represent defendants on a CFA arrangement. The firm tells potential claimants that its 'success rate for cases conducted on this basis is high, with nearly all ending in a successfully negotiated settlement'.

That is fine, if you happen to be a CFA claimant. It is not so good if you happen to be a newspaper whose lawyers are charging by the hour. Indeed, it can amount to a significant restriction on free speech. Let us look at an example.

In December 2001 the *Sunday Telegraph* alleged that Adam Moussa, a 'white British Muslim computer expert' previously known as Louis Szondy, had links to Osama bin Laden's terrorist network. Adam Musa King, as his name appears on the court papers, sued the newspaper, which responded by entering defences of qualified privilege and justification. It also applied to strike out the claim as an abuse of the court's process. One of its grounds was that the claim was being funded on a CFA basis, the first time that the courts had been asked to consider CFA agreements in libel cases.

James Price, for the newspaper's publishers, argued that the CFA regime presupposed that lawyers would take on such cases only where the chances of success were 50 per cent or more, given that the maximum success fee was 100 per cent. That was not the case here, he maintained. Indeed, he argued that in the light of the newspaper's defences the claim should be thrown out at a preliminary stage as having no reasonable chance of success. But if the judge was not persuaded by the argument then he should at least block the case if the chances of success were less than evens.

Mr Price argued that these CFA cases created 'a real risk of a chilling effect on the activities of journalists'. Unless CFA agreements were properly supervised and controlled by the courts, they would wrongly restrict freedom of expression under Article 10. If the newspaper won, it could not be sure of recovering its own costs—unless the claimant had managed to obtain insurance, which was not the case here. If the newspaper lost, it would have to pay a success fee of 100 per cent, in addition to normal costs and any damages. 'In this case, the [*Sunday Telegraph*] could easily find itself facing a bill of the order of £1 million, with the result that a purely commercial assessment of risk might dictate a payment of £10,000 or £20,000 at an early stage.' Claimants' solicitors would be well aware of this and therefore inclined to take cases where the chances of success were less than evens, expecting that media defendants would be willing to buy themselves out of these cases before they came to court.

Giving judgment in June 2003, Mr Justice Eady took Mr Price's arguments seriously. 'There is no doubt he has highlighted a genuine cause for concern,' said the judge. 'There is certainly the potential for a chilling effect on investigative journalism and for significant injustice.' Even so, said the judge, it was hard to maintain that lawyers should never go ahead with a case because it looked unlikely to succeed. They might have convinced themselves that their client was telling the truth and that the court would be less impressed by the other side. He referred to his own judgment in *Lillie and Reed v Newcastle City Council* (discussed later in this chapter), implying that it was a CFA-funded case which the claimants' lawyers perceived as meritorious.

Crucially, though, the facts behind *King v Telegraph Group Ltd* were far from clear. Mr Justice Eady said he could not anticipate the jury's decision and refused to stop the case at this preliminary stage. But the example still holds good. It is little surprise that the CFA solicitors referred to above, who acted for the claimant in this case, were able to say that their 'success rate for cases conducted on this basis is high'. Faced with the risk of having to pay double costs if they lost, and meet their own costs if they won, which newspaper would not be cautious about what it prints?

The *Sunday Telegraph* was given permission to appeal, raising hopes that the Court of Appeal will regulate the problem of conditional fees in libel cases. It is at least arguable that the CFA system, as currently operated, is in breach of the Human Rights Convention. Richard Shillito, a libel lawyer whose firm acts for major newspapers, maintained in July 2003 that 'it would be contrary to Article 10 if defendants were prevented or discouraged from publishing true information because of the fear of having to pay a disproportionate sum in costs or having to pay their own costs even if successful'. As Shillito explained in a magazine article, the barrister Iain Christie had suggested that an uplift of 100 per cent could breach the proportionality concept (explained in Chapter 3). 'In most, if not all, cases,' wrote Christie, 'doubling a proportionate amount will render it disproportionate'. Shillito pointed out that there was nothing to stop a solicitor acting for a wealthy client with a strong case from simply doubling his fees by taking the case on a CFA basis, even though both client and solicitor would have been willing to conduct the litigation in the traditional way. 'That cannot have been what was intended by the new regime', Shillito concluded.

His thesis was endorsed by Sir Christopher Meyer, chairman of the Press Complaints Commission (PCC), who said in October 2003 that the growing use of CFAs was having a 'pernicious impact' on journalism. But Jonathan Coad, a solicitor who generally represents claimants in libel cases against newspapers, argued in response that the balance of

power was clearly on the side of the press, 'with many times the financial and investigative resources and litigation expertise of nearly every
prospective opponent'. In Coad's view, the CFA system did little more
than to 'make it a slightly more level playing field between the print
press and its subject matter'.

Can defamation protect privacy?

The libel cases discussed so far in this chapter were all brought in order
to vindicate a claimant's reputation. Bringing a claim in defamation is
the obvious way to restore someone's good name—or damn it for ever.
But what if a defamatory statement also amounts to a disclosure of
private or confidential facts? Could an action be brought for breach of
confidence instead?

Until recently, the answer was probably 'no'. That is because the law
was thought to require a pre-existing duty of confidentiality. As we saw
in Chapter 1, however, that duty is becoming attenuated to the point
where it may be inferred from the surrounding facts or even dispensed
with altogether. And that has led Tugendhat and Christie, in *The Law of
Privacy and the Media* (2002), to raise the intriguing possibility that the
law of confidence might be better suited than defamation to the protection of personal information. There are, after all, many claims relating to
matters of health and sexual life that might be both defamatory and a
disclosure of private or confidential facts.

The biggest drawback of defamation is that truth is a complete
defence: personal information about the claimant, however embarrassing, can be published with impunity provided the defendant can prove
that what he said was true. The second drawback is that to sustain a libel
case the words complained of must lower the claimant's reputation in
the eyes of right-thinking members of society. It is easy to think of
information about a person that is not defamatory but which he would
rather keep private: for example, that he suffers from piles.

But the courts have stretched the definition of libel to allow compensation for allegations that a person was gay, or had been raped. Neither
of these allegations, even if untrue, should be seen as defamatory—even
though they may come within the alternative (and less used) test covering statements that cause a person to be shunned or avoided. In the

absence of a free-standing privacy law, libel may be of some use in protecting a person's right to be left alone.

Who needs defamation?

Despite the creation of *Reynolds*-privilege, the libel laws in England and Wales still prevent newspapers and broadcasters from publishing what they wish. The rule that requires publishers to prove the truth of what they seek to justify is a powerful inhibition on free speech. Why not abolish libel altogether? There might be more half-truths appearing in print; but shouldn't newspaper readers, and not the courts, be the judges of what is published?

Those who take that view should consider the extraordinary case of Christopher Lillie and Dawn Reed, two former nursery nurses who were wrongly found by an official inquiry in 1998 to have been sexually abusing children at a nursery in Newcastle upon Tyne. In July 2002, they were each awarded maximum libel damages of £200,000 and huge costs after the High Court found the allegations against them had been entirely untrue. After a hearing lasting seventy-nine days, Mr Justice Eady concluded that they were 'entitled to be vindicated and recognised as innocent citizens . . . untouched by the stigma of child abuse'.

He added that there was no basis for allegations of a paedophile ring involving children at the nursery, Shieldfield, or of their exploitation for pornographic purposes. Lillie and Reed 'merited an award at the highest permitted level' against the four authors of the inquiry report, he added. 'Indeed, they have earned it several times over because of the scale, gravity and persistence of the allegations.'

In 1994, both had faced charges of indecent assault and Lillie was also accused of raping a girl aged two or three. However, the judge at their original criminal trial had decided that both of them should be acquitted after considering the evidence against them. The alleged victim had sought, on her own initiative, to exculpate Reed in two of her three recorded interviews. This recording was inadmissible against Lillie because the alleged victim was too young to be cross-examined almost a year after the original interviews about events that had occurred (if at all) at least fifteen months earlier.

Mr Justice Holland's decision to order their acquittal in 1994 led to uproar in court, during which Lillie and Reed were threatened and reviled. For Newcastle City Council, the acquittals seemed to make no difference: the deputy leader of the Council said they were still regarded as guilty of abusing children in their care. As Mr Justice Eady put it, 'a widespread view took hold that the criminal proceedings had come to a halt as a result of some technicality or inadequacy in the system of justice. Very little attention was paid to the comments of the trial judge as to the state of the evidence; and, in particular, to the remarks made by [the alleged victim] in two of her interviews to the effect that Dawn Reed had done nothing wrong'. Eight years passed before this misconception was finally laid to rest: in 2002, Mr Justice Eady said: 'I am entirely satisfied of Mr Lillie's and Miss Reed's innocence. No doubt others will disagree, but I hope that at least nobody will portray the outcome as turning on a legal technicality.'

After the acquittals in 1994, Newcastle City Council set up an independent review. Holding that the review team's four members had forfeited the right to claim qualified privilege by acting maliciously, the judge said they had included claims in their report that they must have known were untrue and which could not be explained on the basis of incompetence or mere carelessness. After 'three years of supposedly rigorous and impartial analysis', for which they were paid almost £365,000, the review team consciously 'set out to misrepresent the state of the evidence available to support their joint belief that Mr Lillie and Miss Reed and other local residents were child abusers—and indeed abusers on a massive scale—and to give readers the impression that statements by parents and/or children had been corroborated by police inquiries'.

The review team had fallen under the spell of a witness who the judge found to have been 'unbalanced, obsessive and lacking in judgment'. She was Dr Camille San Lazaro, a consultant paediatrician at the Royal Victoria Infirmary, Newcastle, and senior lecturer in paediatric forensic medicine at Newcastle University. Dr San Lazaro examined more than fifty children from Shieldfield seeking signs of sexual or other abuse. Faced with physical findings that were negative or equivocal in establishing sexual abuse, she 'was prepared to make up the deficiencies by throwing objectivity and scientific rigour to the winds in a highly emotional misrepresentation of the facts', according to the judge. Under cross-examination, she admitted that her reports, which had helped parents   recover   compensation   from   the   Criminal   Injuries

Compensation Board, had been 'exaggerated and overstated in the past'. As the judge said, 'many thousands of pounds of public money were paid out at least in part as a result of her assertions.' Adopting the role of 'advocate' for the children's compensation claims had 'seriously compromised her professional independence and integrity'.

Mr Justice Eady was highly critical of Dr Richard Barker, leader of the inquiry team and head of child and family studies at Northumbria University at the time of his appointment to the team. 'His evidence was rambling and defensive . . . Much of it was waffle. More significantly, however, I am afraid that there were certain respects in which I found it impossible to believe what he was saying.'

The judge was devastating about the 'impressionistic' approach taken by Barker and his three colleagues. 'The issue of whether any given individual has raped or assaulted a small child—or, for that matter, upwards of 60 small children—is not a matter of impression, theory, opinion or speculation. It should be a question of fact.' A 'Humpty Dumpty' approach to words pervaded the review team's entire report and its evidence to the High Court, said the judge.

He gave examples of the team's mindset. If a child says she has been raped, and there are no signs of abnormality, one just resorts to the proposition that the absence of physical findings does not mean abuse has not taken place. If a child makes no allegations of abuse, it can probably be explained on the basis that he or she has been terrorized by the supposed abuser. If a child exonerates a person voluntarily, despite pressure and leading questions, then she is probably saying that the person exonerated actually did abuse her.

'The fault cannot be laid entirely at the door of the review team since none of them was legally qualified and I concluded at an early stage that it was mainly the council's fault for sanctioning an inquiry into the commission of acts tantamount to criminal offences, with a view to the ultimate publication of a report, but without the appropriate safeguards for the "accused",' said Mr Justice Eady. 'The exercise has cost a vast amount of money for the citizens of Newcastle and I have no doubt years of unnecessary heartache for many of those directly involved.'

Although Lillie and Reed had sued Newcastle City Council as well as the review team, that action failed as the Council had not acted maliciously and was therefore entitled to rely on the defence of qualified privilege.

Relying on this devastating libel judgment, David Blunkett, the Home Secretary, announced that Lillie and Reed would be exonerated and would receive compensation for their ordeal. Reed had spent fourteen weeks in custody while Lillie was held for ten months awaiting trial.

Mr Justice Eady's judgment is surely one of the most crushing ever delivered. But it was not the first of its kind: like Mr Justice Gray's powerful ruling in David Irving's case against Penguin Books in April 2000, it shows how a single judge trying a libel case can cut through conflicting accounts to establish the truth. Describing the author as an anti-Semite and a falsifier of history, Mr Justice Gray decided that Deborah Lipstadt, an American academic, had justified her assertion in a book published by Penguin that Irving was discredited as a historian because of his denial of the Holocaust.

At first blush, these two cases have little in common. Lillie and Reed regained their good names by winning their claims; Irving lost what little reputation he may have had by losing his. Neither case was brought by wealthy claimants: Lillie and Reed's lawyers knew they would be paid nothing for their work if the claim was unsuccessful; Irving represented himself in court. But both cases established, entirely convincingly, the truth or otherwise of the facts in issue.

Reputation

Even the threat of a libel action may be enough to restore a reputation. Donal MacIntyre, a television reporter, took the apparently unprecedented step of suing Kent Police for libel. Their spokesman had briefed the press in June 2000 about a programme MacIntyre had made on a care home in Kent for adults with learning difficulties. The spokesman said: 'On the basis of the claims made we anticipated charging people with substantive offences. However, we ended up with two cautions for minor assaults.' Detectives, he added, felt 'virtually nothing they [the programme] claimed was substantiated'. The force even went so far as to say it was considering suing the BBC to reclaim the £50,000 it had spent on its own investigation into MacIntyre's allegations. In response, MacIntyre accused the force of defaming him by asserting that he had 'persistently, deliberately and dishonestly distorted' undercover recordings he had made at the home so as to mislead viewers, and that he had told a lie in the course of presenting the programme.

The BBC supported MacIntyre's libel action, and in July 2002 it reached the Court of Appeal on a preliminary issue. The police challenged case-management decisions that had been made by Mr Justice Gray, arguing that the judge should have considered their claim of qualified privilege in advance of the trial. That argument was rejected and, by October, the force was ready to settle. It apologized unreservedly in the High Court for remarks which it accepted were 'not correct and were, therefore, unjustified'. Kent Police were also reported to have paid MacIntyre £15,000 in damages, on the understanding that he would donate the money to charities caring for people with learning difficulties. The force withdrew its 'untrue' remarks and agreed to pay the costs, estimated at £600,000,

As Lord Nicholls said in *Reynolds*, 'reputation is an integral and important part of the dignity of the individual. It also forms the basis of many decisions in a democratic society which are fundamental to its well-being: whom to employ or work for, whom to promote, whom to do business with or to vote for. Once besmirched by an unfounded allegation in a national newspaper, a reputation can be damaged for ever, especially if there is no opportunity to vindicate one's reputation. When this happens, society as well as the individual is the loser. For it should not be supposed that protection of reputation is a matter of importance only to the affected individual and his family. Protection of reputation is conducive to the public good. It is in the public interest that the reputation of public figures should not be debased falsely.'

Clearly, the principles established by Lord Nicholls in *Reynolds* are to be welcomed. They provide improved protection for responsible journalism, without permitting character assassination or the launching of vendettas against political enemies. In supporting the high standards of proper investigative journalism, the courts may be encroaching on personal privacy. But that is not a reason for muzzling the watchdogs and bloodhounds of the media, as the law once used to do.

In deciding that it is not the business of the libel laws to create millionaires or close down responsible newspapers, the judges have gone some way towards fashioning a libel law that is fair to both writers and their subjects. What is needed now, as Robertson and Nicol say in their book *Media Law*, is a speedy and effective procedure for securing the publication of corrections and counter-statements, with damages reserved for cases where claimants have suffered financial loss or been the victims of malice.

Abolishing the libel laws or even setting the standards of journalistic responsibility too low would allow lies to be published without redress. That would not be in anyone's interests, not even the media's. As the Court of Appeal said in *Loutchansky*, 'once untruths can be published with impunity, the public will cease to believe any communications, true or false'.

CHAPTER 8

Looking to the Future

The relationship between privacy and the press has now reached a critical point. For the best part of two centuries, judges have moulded and
modified the old law of confidence to cope with the changing needs of
society. As we have seen, it survived the introduction of the European
Convention on Human Rights—a treaty that has been part of our
domestic law since 2000, that individuals have been able to enforce
against the British Government since 1966 and that came into force as
long ago as 1953. The Convention introduced into our law the concept
of respect for private and family life—balanced, as always, against freedom of expression. Will the courts now use the Convention to transform the old law of confidence into a modern law of privacy? In this
chapter, we shall look at how other countries protect personal privacy
before considering whether we ought to have a new statute—or a
judge-made tort—here in England and Wales.

The need for a ban on unwarranted intrusion must depend to some
extent on how well the media here are regulated by existing law and
practice. We have seen encouraging signs that the courts are beginning
to understand the need for journalists to protect their sources against
disclosure, though some judges still fail to grasp that the free flow of
information will cease if informers feel at risk. A new standard of
'responsible journalism' has been developed by the judges, adherence to
which should protect the press from libel claims. The Press Complaints
Commission (PCC), despite its faults, has staved off the spectre of state
regulation. Against all that, though, is the 'firm recommendation' by the
Commons Media Committee that the Government should introduce
privacy legislation in Parliament.

In this chapter, I shall argue that a Privacy Act would be both dangerous and wrong. For similar reasons, I would also have misgivings about
a significant extension to the common law of privacy.

Europe and beyond

When senior judges speak enthusiastically about creating a law of privacy in England and Wales, they take their inspiration from legal systems just across the Channel. Speaking to me in February 2003, the Master of the Rolls, Lord Phillips, remarked that technological advances had greatly increased the potential for intrusion in people's private lives.

'When you get changes like that, the law needs to react,' he said. 'In some countries, France and Germany, the law has intervened by statute to protect individuals from intrusive photography. Here the Press Complaints Commission has its own code, which aims to do the same thing. But if self-regulation does not work then there must be scope for the courts to develop the law, particularly having regard to the provisions in relation to private life of the Human Rights Convention.'

Other judges are equally enthusiastic. In July 2002, some eighteen months after his single-handed and (at least, initially) unsuccessful attempt to create a law of privacy, Lord Justice Sedley noted ruefully that other judges had not followed his lead. Writing in the foreword to Tugendhat and Christie's *The Law of Privacy and the Media*, the judge recalled that Professor Ronald Dworkin had likened the common law to a chain novel, in which each contributor writes a chapter and then hands the script on. 'Contrary to my sanguine prognostication in the *Douglas v Hello! Ltd* case, the courts so far have not done substantially more than revisit the earlier chapters,' said Lord Justice Sedley. 'Do they need to? Is the common law, with its vaunted flexibility, at risk of being left behind by the reputedly rigid civil law systems of France and Germany which have long since developed sophisticated balances between privacy rights and legitimate media interests?' It was clear he feared the answer was 'yes'.

Privacy in France

Being left behind does not look such a bad idea if the alternatives lead us towards France and Germany. Article 9 of the French Civil Code says:

Everyone has the right to respect for his private life. The court may—without prejudice to compensation for injury suffered—prescribe any measures, such as sequestration, seizure and others appropriate to prevent or put an end to an invasion of intimate private life. These measures may, if there is urgency, be ordered under emergency interim proceedings.

This provision, enacted in 1970, did not attempt to define private life: that has been left to the courts. There is an assumption that 'intimate private life' should be more narrowly defined than private life pure and simple; otherwise—since *any* measures may be ordered—there would be too great an intrusion into press freedom. Even so, the definition remains unclear and the French courts have therefore tended to follow older statutes.

The Republic also prohibits republication: the right to privacy in France extends to information already in the public domain. Even the dead have private lives, it seems: in 1998 *Paris Match* fell foul of this law, not for the first time, when it published a picture of President Mitterrand on his deathbed. Perhaps the magazine was trying to get its own back on him for concealing—during most of his presidency—both the cancer from which he was suffering and the daughter who was born to his long-term lover.

French judges often give short shrift to public-interest considerations, even where politicians and other public figures are concerned. The Human Rights Convention is part of the law in France, as it is throughout Europe, but French courts tend to take more notice of the exceptions in Article 10(2) than the principles in Article 10(1). As a result, crooked businessmen and dubious politicians are more likely to escape public scrutiny.

In France, there can even be a right to privacy in a public place—such as a beach. The 'right to one's image' makes it generally unlawful to publish pictures of people without their express consent. So a newspaper that printed a picture of Princess Caroline of Monaco watching the Grand Prix race from a balcony together with a well-known actor was found to have breached the actor's privacy. The newspaper argued that the picture was an illustration of the race, but the court pointed out that it did not show any cars or competitors. Even in France, though, there are some limits: a person who appeared in a photograph taken after a bomb blast was unable to sue because the courts held that his appearance was merely incidental to the picture.

French courts can award both injunctions to prevent publication of prohibited material and damages if publication goes ahead, even if no harm has been caused and even if none of the parties has any link to France. In September 1986, the *Mail on Sunday* published two articles by the gossip columnist Nigel Dempster about a 14-year-old European prince. The article gave details of his schooling and information about his father, also a prince. Because the newspaper was available in France, the princely family was able to take action against its publishers and writers in the French courts even though none of the parties had any links with that country. Dempster and his editor were ordered to pay 50,000 francs (about £5,000) to each of the two princes for the attack on their private lives. After taking into account Articles 8 and 10 of the Human Rights Convention, the *Cour de Cassation*, France's highest court, upheld the ruling in October 1990. The French law reports deliberately omitted the names of the parties involved, but the only expatriate European prince born in 1972 was the Italian Prince Emanuele Filiberto of Savoy, son of Prince Vittorio Emanuele.

In November 2003, three French paparazzi who took photographs at the scene of the car crash in which Diana, Princess of Wales, died were found guilty by a French court of invading her privacy. Jacques Langevin, Christian Martinez and Fabrice Chassery were alleged to have been among a group of photographers pursuing the car carrying the Princess and her friend Dodi Fayed when it crashed in a Paris underpass at the end of August 1997, killing the couple and the driver, Henri Paul. They were said to have taken photographs of the dead and dying in the wreckage of the crashed Mercedes, as well as having caused an infringement of privacy a short time earlier by taking pictures of the couple's car as it left the Ritz Hotel. Langevin said he arrived at the scene of the crash fifteen minutes after it happened. He was not part of the group pursuing the car and maintained he was performing his job amidst the emergency services as in any other road crash.

The charges were brought despite the fact that no photographs had ever been published showing the couple's last minutes. Photographers had not previously been convicted in France for taking unpublished pictures, and the French courts were asked to consider whether the mere photographing of the Princess's car amounted to a breach of privacy. An earlier action brought by the French pop star Michel Sardou had established the principle under French law that the inside of a car should be regarded as just as private as the inside of a house.

Privacy in Germany

In Germany, the modern law of privacy dates back to 1949. According to Articles 1 and 2 of the German constitution, the Basic Law:

The dignity of the human being is inviolable. Everyone has the right to free development of his personality, insofar as he does not injure the rights of others or violate the constitutional order or the moral law.

This must inevitably be balanced against Article 5, which says: 'Everyone has the right to express and disseminate his opinion freely by word, writing and picture and to inform himself from generally accessible sources without restraint.' Neither provision has automatic priority over the other.

The right to restrict publication of one's likeness also exists in Germany. As long ago as 1898, two paparazzi (as they were not yet called) photographed the body of Prince Otto von Bismarck. The German courts granted his children an injunction against publication, deciding the case on the basis of unjust enrichment. In 1907 this was put into statutory form, when a law was passed saying that a person's image or likeness may not normally be published without that person's consent. There is an exception for 'figures of contemporary history', but even they may have a legitimate expectation that their privacy will not be invaded if they are in private surroundings. The courts will deem some people 'absolute figures of contemporary history', which seems to mean they are fair game for the photographers.

However, the situation is far from clear. Many of the leading cases appear to involve Princess Caroline of Monaco, with whom the Continental press has been obsessed. She sued a publisher over pictures showing her enjoying a candlelit dinner with her boyfriend in a quiet corner of a garden restaurant in provincial France. The Princess lost her claim and the subsequent appeal. But the German Federal Supreme Court took a different view. The table in a dark corner was 'typically private', even though the restaurant was open to the public. It might have been different if the Princess had been sitting nearer the entrance. And it was hard to argue that it was in the public interest for us to be told what she had for dinner. The less need there was for the public to know about the event, the more justification there was for protecting the Princess's privacy. That ruling was later upheld by the Federal Constitutional Court.

In an earlier case, a newspaper published a completely fabricated interview with Princess Caroline. The Supreme Court ordered the publisher to withdraw what it had said, adding that anyone who intentionally invaded someone else's privacy to make money should be deprived of the profits.

The Princess, by now married to Prince Ernst August of Hanover, took Germany to the European Court of Human Rights in November 2003. She complained about a ruling from the Federal Constitutional Court in 1999, that, as a contemporary 'public figure', she had to tolerate the publication of photographs showing her in public—even if the scenes were of her daily life rather than official engagements. The German court based its ruling on the freedom of the press and the public's legitimate interest in knowing how such a person generally behaved in public. This, she complained, was a breach of her right to respect for private and family life under Article 8. A ruling is expected in 2004. Since the courts of the United Kingdom are required under the Human Rights Act to 'take into account' judgments of the Human Rights Court, it would be a worrying precedent if Princess Caroline were to win. Incidentally, astute readers will have remembered from Chapter 3 that descendants of Princess Sophia, Electress of Hanover, have to give up their right of succession to the United Kingdom monarchy if they marry a Roman Catholic. This does not seem to have deterred Prince Ernst.

The *Mail on Sunday* seemed to enjoy testing European privacy laws. In January 2003, it alleged that the four-times-married German Chancellor, Gerhard Schröder, 58, was having an affair with Sandra Maischberger, 36, a political journalist. That week's edition of the British newspaper was not distributed in Germany but the story was still followed up in the German press. The Chancellor took legal action and a court in Hamburg issued an injunction under which the *Mail on Sunday* would face a fine of €250,000 (£164,000) if it repeated the allegations.

'Following a hearing in a German court which we were not even informed about until it was over,' the *Mail on Sunday* reported later that month, 'we are threatened with heavy penalties if we repeat the story in Germany, though we never published it there in the first place. But, for now at least, we can ignore this blustering and these threats. Because of our different tradition and our robust democracy, we can publish this sort of material and believe we have every right to do so.'

In what appears to have been an unfulfilled hope of finding more about the story it had launched, the newspaper published a note, in German, inviting readers in Germany to ring a 'German-speaking member of our Schröder Investigations Unit' in London. It also launched a campaign against the introduction of German-style privacy laws in Britain—not that there was much risk of this happening.

But others see the broader picture. 'German case law shows that a balancing act can work without resulting in a flood of claims or the suppression of free speech,' said Professor Basil Markesinis in 2001. 'It also shows how it can be done on the basis of logical criteria rather than by relying on accidents of history and litigation, which is how English law in this area developed in the past.'

What will Strasbourg say?

In *Douglas v Hello! Ltd*, you may recall from Chapter 3, Mr Justice Lindsay referred to the recently delivered ruling by the Strasbourg judges in *Peck v UK*, the case of the would-be suicide who was filmed in the street holding a knife. Explaining that the judgment demonstrated the inadequacy of English law, he made a bold prediction. 'That inadequacy will have to be made good and if Parliament does not step in then the courts will be obliged to,' he said. Some lawyers feel that the effect of *Peck* will be rather less profound. However, another case that was pending before the European Court of Human Rights in 2003 may still force the Government's hand.

It was brought by Janette Martin, from Nottingham, who—like Peck—also found that the local authority had made a video recording of her against her wishes. Martin was living with her four children in a house rented from the council. Her next-door neighbours, Mr and Mrs Davies, owned the freehold of their property. For whatever reason, the two families did not get on. In 1998, the Davieses lodged a number of complaints with the council about Martin and her children. In 1999, Martin allegedly assaulted Mrs Davies, grabbing her hair and banging her head on the top rail of the fence. In 2000, the Davieses complained that eggs had been thrown at their property, excrement had been placed on their door handle and bleach had been poured into their letterbox.

To find out who was responsible for this behaviour, the council installed a video camera on a nearby wall. This was set up to monitor the passageway between the two properties, although it was also just possible for it to see into Martin's hall when her front door was open. The camera was disguised as a junction box, and Martin knew nothing about it until the council told her nearly a month later that it had obtained video evidence of her. Even though the surveillance was no longer secret, the council continued to monitor the scene for another four months. Meanwhile, council officers began proceedings to have Martin evicted on the grounds of her behaviour. She denied the incidents about which her neighbours had complained, maintaining that Davies had assaulted her in 1999 rather than the other way round. Martin gave an undertaking not to assault the Davieses or trespass on their land; as a result, the council withdrew its application for her eviction, destroying its surveillance recordings and promising not to make any more.

But that was not the end of it. Davies lodged a series of complaints against the council. She said she had suffered distress and inconvenience because she and her family had been under surveillance for nearly five months. It was not merely feelings of injustice: once she became aware of the camera, their way of life had been curtailed. They avoided being near the front of the house, she was embarrassed to entertain visitors and she could not let her children out to play. Davies decided to spend time away from her home to avoid being observed when entering or leaving the premises. She no longer used the front door. She alleged that she became distressed by the surveillance to such an extent that she became depressed and sought medical advice and assistance as a result. She was tearful and found it difficult to cope with her normal daily activities. In the end, she complained to Strasbourg about a breach of her right to respect for private and family life under Article 8.

However, the Human Rights Court will not hear claims if there are still options available to a complainant in the national courts: applicants must 'exhaust domestic remedies' before going to Strasbourg. So the British Government set about trying to prove that Martin could have found some redress under English law for the council's invasion of her privacy. In this, the Government was entirely unsuccessful—proof that, at least until the Human Rights Act took effect, there was little protection for personal privacy in England and Wales.

Judicial review? No use, said the Strasbourg Court, as Martin would not have been entitled to claim compensation. Breach of the Data Protection Act? Again, no use as a remedy: compensation is available only where an applicant has suffered 'damage' rather than simply distress—and the Government had not persuaded the Court that she had reasonable prospects of success in this either. What about breach of confidence, then? Here the problem was the third of Mr Justice Megarry's conditions, mentioned in Chapter 1: there must be some unauthorized use to the detriment of the applicant. But in this case there was no unauthorized disclosure or use of confidential information, so no joy there.

That leaves privacy. In its submissions to the Court, the Government accepted that there was no specific right to privacy under English law. The Strasbourg judges regarded that admission as significant. They were well aware of Lord Justice Sedley's remarks in the original *Douglas v Hello! Ltd* case. But he was in a minority of one, his comments had not been binding and in any case they applied to events that took place after the Human Rights Act had come into force—unlike Martin's case. The Human Rights Court was also influenced by *Wainwright v Home Secretary*—a case 'in which the Court of Appeal clearly stated that no tort of privacy was recognised by English law'—and the view expressed by Lord Justice Buxton, one of the judges in *Wainwright*, that if any such tort were to be introduced into English law it would be a matter for Parliament and not for the courts. So the Strasbourg Court's conclusion was clear:

The Government have not discharged their burden of proving to the court that the applicant had available to her an accessible domestic cause of action for breach of privacy, at the material time, which was capable of providing redress in respect of her complaints and offered reasonable prospects of success. Furthermore, the court does not find that there was a sufficient doubt as to whether a tort of invasion of privacy existed under English law that obliged the applicant to submit the issue to the domestic courts for resolution.

So the way was clear for Martin to proceed with her application under Article 8. She claimed that CCTV should not be used in an indiscriminate way without procedural safeguards; the Government maintained that there had been 'no real intrusion' into her privacy from a camera that recorded only what could be seen by anyone from a public area. She claimed that the interference was 'not in accordance with the law', since the Regulation of Investigatory Powers Act 2000 had not been in

force at the time; the Government argued that local authorities must
have the power to obtain evidence in support of an anti-social behaviour order or a possession order. She claimed that the intrusion was not
'necessary in a democratic society' since it was part of what lawyers call
a 'fishing expedition' and there had been other courses of action open
to the council; the Government insisted that the council's decision to
use surveillance was proportionate to the problem of anti-social behaviour, and within the state's 'margin of appreciation'.

In March 2003, all that the Court was willing to say was that Martin's
claim of interference with respect for her private and family life was not
'manifestly ill-founded' and therefore admissible. Having set out the
arguments on both sides, it put off any decision on the merits of her case
until 2004. But the Human Rights Court does not go to the trouble of
issuing a reasoned 'admissibility decision' in every case. The ruling was
another warning to the Government and the courts that Human Rights
law will not allow people's personal privacy to be invaded by the state
without some means of obtaining redress.

The EU Constitution

Just when you thought you had understood the European Convention
on Human Rights, they come along and change it all. As we have seen,
the Convention is a long-established treaty that must normally be
followed by judges in the United Kingdom and is ultimately enforceable by the European Court of Human Rights in Strasbourg. You will
also have grasped that this court is effectively run by the Council of
Europe, a body of 44 member states (at the last count) that is entirely
separate from the 25-member European Union.

One commitment contained in Article 7(2) of the draft EU
Constitution published in July 2003 is that the EU will sign the
European Convention on Human Rights. This is known as 'accession'.
Once this takes effect, it should give individuals a remedy for any breach
of their human rights by the EU institutions—including the European
Commission in Brussels and the Council of Ministers drawn from
member states—in the same way that people currently have remedies
for breaches of the Human Rights Convention by Council of Europe
member states.

Presumably, an individual would have to 'exhaust domestic remedies' before taking an EU institution to Strasbourg. In practice, that must mean challenging a Brussels Directive in the domestic, or national, courts. And those courts may request an authoritative ruling on European law from the EU's own court, the European Court of Justice in Luxembourg. So a claim may go from London to Luxembourg, back to London for the Luxembourg Court's negative ruling to be implemented, and then off to Strasbourg for what amounts to a final appeal.

The strongest argument in favour of this move is that it will preserve human rights at a time when member states are planning to transfer some of their powers—or 'competences' in Eurojargon—to the new EU. Clearly, there is no point in taking a government to the Human Rights Court if that government has lost the power to put matters right: much better to take action against the EU body that has taken responsibility on a Europe-wide basis. On the other hand, critics say that the move will undermine the authority of the EU Court in Luxembourg, adding that the EU should not come under the sway of a 'foreign' court whose judges are not all EU nationals. But the answer to that is to be found in the limited functions of the Strasbourg Court: lacking the power to overturn decisions by member states, it merely declares that there has been a breach of the Human Rights Convention and leaves the relevant government—or, now, the EU body—to find a politically acceptable way of 'abiding' by the Court's ruling.

This is all rather hard to grasp, and it may be some years before we learn how it will work in practice. But there it is, in Article 7(2) of the draft Constitution: 'The Union shall seek accession to the European Convention . . .' And if it seeks, it will certainly find: the Council of Europe itself has long urged the EU to come on board. So if your privacy or my free speech are breached by an EU Directive, we may find ourselves battling it out in Strasbourg rather than Luxembourg.

The Charter

Even more important is Article 7(1) of the draft Constitution for the new EU. That says: 'The Union shall recognise the rights, freedoms and principles set out in the Charter of Fundamental Rights which constitutes Part II of this Constitution'.

This Charter turns out to be something of a rival to the European Convention on Human Rights. It was 'solemnly proclaimed' by EU governments meeting at Nice in December 2000, and it is now to become an integral part of the new Constitution rather than simply an advisory declaration. Again, we shall have to wait to see what this means in practice. However, readers of this book will want to know what the Constitution says about privacy and freedom of expression. We must turn, then, to Part II of the Constitution.

There are two provisions that stand out. Article II-7 says:

Everyone has the right to respect for his or her private and family life, home and communications.

We can see immediately that this is simply a politically correct restatement of Article 8(1) of the Human Rights Convention, with 'correspondence' updated to 'communications' to reflect the fact that people no longer write letters.

Article II-11 of the Constitution says:

1. Everyone has the right to freedom of expression. This right shall include freedom to hold opinions and to receive and impart information and ideas without interference by public authority and regardless of frontiers.
2. The freedom and pluralism of the media shall be respected.

We can also see that the first sentence in Article II-11(1) of the EU Constitution is identical to the first sentence in Article 10(1) of the Human Rights Convention. The third sentence of the Convention's Article 10(1)—allowing states to license broadcasting—is missing from the Constitution, but perhaps that is not much of a loss. And we have a completely new provision in Article II-11(2) of the Constitution— requiring respect for the freedom and pluralism of the media—that at first sight seems so broad as to be meaningless.

But what has happened to the caveats in Articles 8(2) and 10(2) of the Human Rights Convention? Where are the get-out clauses allowing interference with these rights for the protection of the rights of others, and so on?

Scroll down to Article II-52(3) of the Constitution, and you will find a rather strange provision. In so far as the Charter contains rights that correspond to rights in the Human Rights Convention, it says, their meaning and scope shall be the same as those in the Convention.

So that must bring in the caveats in Articles 8(2) and 10(2). The EU has published explanatory notes to the Charter that, while not strictly binding, clearly carry considerable weight. These say that the meaning and scope of corresponding rights, *including authorised limitations*, are the same as those laid down by the Human Rights Convention. Those limitations must presumably include the second part of Articles 8, 10 and similar provisions in other parts of the Convention. So it turns out that the Charter is no more generous than the Convention after all. But neither is it any less generous: Article II-53 says that nothing in the Charter restricts the human rights granted by the European Convention.

What's more, the notes make it clear that the case law of both the Strasbourg Court and the Luxembourg Court must be taken into account in interpreting the EU Constitution. And, to remove any lingering doubts, the notes list several articles of the Charter where both the meaning and scope are the same as the corresponding articles of the European Convention (and others, such as the right to marry, where the meaning is the same but the scope may be wider). Article II-7 of the Constitution corresponds to Article 8 of the Convention, it says. And Article II-11 of the Constitution corresponds to Article 10 of the Convention, but without prejudice to any restrictions which Community Law may impose on the right of member states to introduce the licensing arrangements referred to in the third sentence of Article 10(1).

Just to confuse matters further, Article II-52(2), after providing that rights in the Constitution mean the same as corresponding rights in the Convention, goes on to say: 'This provision shall not prevent Union law providing more extensive protection.' So the limitations in the Convention represent the high-water mark of restrictions: there is nothing to prevent the Constitution giving us more rights. It is only by looking at the notes to Article II-52 that we can find out which articles have the same meaning and scope as the corresponding articles of the Human Rights Convention and in which ones the meaning is the same but the scope is wider.

What an extraordinary way to draft a constitution! Brevity is an admirable aim, but not at the expense of clarity. It is true, of course, that nobody can understand the true meaning of the Human Rights Convention without an appreciation of the surrounding case law. But reading the Convention gives us a much clearer idea of our human rights than reading the EU Constitution. It is only by reading the notes to Article II-7 of the Constitution—which are not included in the published text—that we find that the limitations on the right to respect for private and family life are the same as those allowed by Article 8 of the Convention.

When we reach Article II-11 of the Constitution, we are told that it 'corresponds' to Article 10 of the Convention. But we are also told that the mysterious Article II-11(2) of the Constitution—'the freedom and pluralism of the media shall be respected'—is based on the case law of the Court of Justice in Luxembourg. This, of course, is the EU Court— which does not have much of a reputation for defending press freedom against commercial interests. We would be wise not to put much faith in this provision.

The New World

Giving his Bentham lecture in March 2003, Lord Phillips, Master of the Rolls, found both Australia and New Zealand moving towards a judge-made tort of privacy.

He cited the possums case, *Australian Broadcasting Corporation v Lenah Game Meats*. As you may recall from Chapter 2, Lenah was a company that killed, processed and sold game, including the Tasmanian brush-tail possum. Campaigners secretly installed cameras in its abattoir and filmed the way in which the possums were slaughtered. They passed video recordings to the Australian Broadcasting Corporation, which wanted to broadcast them. The meat producer argued that this would be a breach of its privacy. That argument was rejected by the High Court of Australia, the country's highest court, but only because the claim had been brought by a company. As Lord Phillips put it, the Court was prepared to contemplate the development in Australia of a tort of invasion of privacy but the majority held that this would be for the benefit of individuals, not corporations.

The New Zealand courts are also moving towards a privacy tort, Lord Phillips noted. The claimant in *Bradley v Wingut Films Ltd* was very upset to find that a horror film that had been shot on location in a graveyard clearly showed the tombstone over his own family plot. He unsuccessfully sought an injunction, arguing that this was a breach of his privacy.

Mr Justice Gallen, the New Zealand judge, identified earlier judgments in favour of the existence of a tort. Its three elements, he said, were that there must be a public disclosure; that disclosure should be of private facts; and that the matter disclosed should be highly offensive and objectionable to a reasonable person of ordinary sensibilities. These were, in effect, the three factors identified by Dean Prosser in 1960—as we saw in Chapter 1. The judge held that, on the facts, only the first element was made out. As to the second, he remarked that there could scarcely be anything less private than a tombstone in a public cemetery. As to the third he found that it was not the depiction of the tombstone that the plaintiff found offensive, but the activities going on in the vicinity of the tombstone which arguably included sexual intercourse with a corpse. The judge ruled that it was not necessary for him to resolve that particular issue.

In Canada, a 17-year-old woman called Pascale Aubry complained that a picture of her sitting on the steps of a building in Montreal had been taken without her knowledge or consent and published in an arts magazine called *Vice-Versa*. She was teased about it at college after being recognized by a friend. In 1998, by a majority of five to two, the Supreme Court of Canada upheld an award of $2,000 compensation against the publisher and photographer. Justices L'Heureux-Dubé and Bastarache, for the majority, based their ruling on the Quebec Charter of Human Rights. The right to one's image was an element of the right to privacy under section 5 of the Charter, they said. If the purpose of the right to privacy is to protect a sphere of individual autonomy, it must include the ability to control the use made of one's image. That was infringed as soon as an identifiable image was published without consent.

However, the right to respect for one's private life had to be balanced against the right to freedom of expression protected by section 3 of the Charter. That included freedom of artistic expression. But an artist's right to publish his or her work was not absolute and, on this occasion, did not outweigh Aubry's right to protection of her image.

Chief Justice Lamer, dissenting, agreed that there had been a violation of Aubry's privacy but said she had failed to prove that she had been harmed in any way. 'If the respondent had stated, "I felt humiliated when

I saw the photograph published in *Vice-Versa* magazine", there would have been sufficient evidence of damage in this case, provided that Judge Bourret believed her,' the Chief Justice ruled. 'However, in my view the statement "people laughed at me" does not in itself constitute sufficient evidence of damage.'

The judge drew an interesting contrast between the law in Quebec and the laws of France. 'According to one French author, damage in the case of an infringement of the right to one's image "may consist simply in the annoyance felt by a person at becoming a celebrity" . . . With respect, this statement cannot mean that the infringement of a personality right on its own results in civil liability in Quebec in the absence of evidence of prejudice, contrary to what seems to be possible in France.'

We surely cannot have laws in this country preventing photographers from taking pictures of people in the street. Television news reporters frequently broadcast from public areas, speaking to camera as passers-by are seen walking behind them. Is it really to be suggested that any one of these individuals could prevent the item from being broadcast or claim compensation for breach of privacy if the report was going out live?

We all know that our towns and cities are constantly monitored by CCTV. Even would-be suicides like Geoffrey Peck must know that they are likely to be filmed if they walk down the streets carrying a knife. We are photographed as we enter shops and public buildings: even the smallest village newsagent has a security camera recording pictures of its customers. Cable and satellite television networks constantly show US-made programmes consisting entirely of CCTV recordings made as police cars chase suspect vehicles and robbers attack shopkeepers, although identities are sometimes obscured. Pictures are taken of every vehicle entering the central London congestion charging zone; further shots are taken of each vehicle that enters the City of London 'ring of steel'; and drivers are photographed through the open window as they collect admission tickets at car parks.

Most of us do not give this a second thought: indeed, we rely on the authorities to ensure that the cameras are working properly. There was much embarrassment at the BBC when its security cameras failed to record pictures of the Real IRA terrorists who exploded a car bomb outside its own television newsroom in March 2001. And Scotland Yard was heavily criticized after its officers failed to respond to CCTV images of an intruder who gatecrashed Prince William's twenty-first birthday party at Windsor Castle in July 2003.

In a perfect world, photographers would seek permission before taking pictures of a dead German prince, a living Monegasque princess or even a pretty young woman sitting on the steps of a building. Ideally, we would not find ourselves under surveillance as soon as we enter a public building or step into a busy street. But we all look at pictures in newspapers and magazines, just as we all want terrorists to be thwarted and caught. Some loss of privacy is merely the price we must pay.

California, here I come

If the future is to be found anywhere, it is on the west coast of America. Warren and Brandeis might have written the most influential article ever to appear in a legal journal when they argued for a privacy law on the grounds that 'the latest advances in photographic art have rendered it possible to take pictures surreptitiously' (as we saw in Chapter 1). But their contribution to the *Harvard Law Review* in 1890 is unlikely to have been as well thumbed—initially, at least—as an article by David Kremenetsky that appeared 110 years later in the less well-known *McGeorge Law Review*, published by the University of the Pacific. Intriguingly entitled 'Insatiable "Up-Skirt" Voyeurs Force California Lawmakers to Expand Privacy Protection in Public Places', it mentions at least one website where readers may continue their researches into surreptitious pictures taken as the result of new advances in low-light, close-up photography.

The problem had been pithily encapsulated in a headline taken from the *Orange County Register* in 1998, 'Cyber-Peeping: It's Growing, It's Frustrating, and It's Legal: Officials Say There's Nothing They Can Do to Stop Men from Filming up Skirts in Public Places'. These men would apparently spend hours wandering round parks and shopping malls with cameras hidden in carrier bags that they would try to slide under women's legs, especially when the unknowing victims were standing on moving walkways. Kremenetsky's article is mainly about the attempt by California in 1999 to deal with this menace through the criminal law. It was already an offence in

California to look into the interior of a 'bathroom, changing room, fitting room, dressing room, or tanning booth, or the interior of any other area in which the occupant has a reasonable expectation of privacy, with the intent to invade the privacy of a person or persons inside', either through a hole or by using an instrument such as a periscope, telescope, binoculars or camera. But that, by definition, applied only to a 'private' place: it was no use if the unsuspecting victim was out shopping.

Clearly, you can't prevent someone from looking at other people in the street. The law therefore had to be narrowly targeted. To come within the definition of Chapter 231, as the California outdoor privacy crime is called, the conduct must meet five conditions:

(1) A person must use a concealed device to secretly film or record another person under or through the other's clothing (presumably using new 'x-ray' technology).

(2) The person being recorded must be identifiable.

(3) The recording must be 'for the purpose of viewing the body of, or the undergarments worn by, [the] other person'.

(4) Such a recording must be done without the consent or knowledge of the other person.

(5) The disorderly conduct described above must be done with the specific intent 'to arouse, appeal to, or gratify the lust, passions or sexual desires' of the perpetrator.

Kremenetsky points out the limitations of this definition. It excludes those who take pictures to gratify the lust of others. A voyeur need only set up his own website to take advantage of what amounts to an exemption for commercial enterprises. It also does not restrict voyeurs on balconies or ladders whose tastes are best described as 'down blouse' rather than 'up skirt'. Such pictures are not normally taken under or through a woman's clothing. But, however much we may laugh at the convolutions of Californian legislators, this was a significant step in the fight against unwarranted intrusion. For the first time, we see the criminal law explicitly recognizing a right of privacy in public places.

At the same time, California was creating a new civil law. Section 1708.8 of the state's civil code created two specific torts, physical invasion of privacy and constructive invasion of privacy. The former is committed by someone who 'knowingly enters onto the land of another without permission . . . in order to physically invade the privacy of the plaintiff with the intent to capture any type of visual image, sound recording, or other physical impression of the plaintiff engaging in a personal or familial activity and the physical invasion occurs in a manner that is offensive to a reasonable person'.

Constructive invasion of privacy takes place when a person 'attempts to capture, in a manner that is offensive to a reasonable person, any type of visual image, sound recording, or other physical impression of the plaintiff engaging in a personal or familial activity under circumstances in which the plaintiff had a reasonable expectation of privacy, through the use of a visual or auditory enhancing device, regardless of whether there is a physical trespass, if this image, sound recording, or other physical impression could not have been achieved without a trespass unless the visual or auditory enhancing device was used'.

The first of these torts is clearly aimed at a person who conceals cameras or listening devices on someone's property, or enters their property to record them without permission. The second seems to be aimed at the person who achieves the same results from afar by using a telephoto lens or a powerful directional microphone. 'Personal and familial activity' includes 'intimate details of the plaintiff's personal life, interactions with the plaintiff's family' or with what are called 'significant others'. There are exceptions for police and private investigators seeking evidence of crime or fraud—but it is not a defence to show that there was no film in the camera.

The problem with these torts is that they are far too broad. 'Interactions with the plaintiff's family' could mean just about anything. 'Physical invasion . . . in a manner that is offensive to a reasonable person' is far too subjective. One can imagine how these concepts could be stretched by a creative California lawyer.

Criminal voyeurism

Invading a person's privacy for the purpose of sexual gratification in England and Wales is now a crime under the Sexual Offences Act 2003. The maximum penalty is two years' imprisonment. Several types of voyeurism are banned under the new legislation.

First, it is an offence for a person to *observe* for his own sexual gratification another person doing a 'private act' when the observer knows that the person he is watching does not consent to being looked at for this purpose. What, then, is a private act? 'A person is doing a private act if the person is in a place which, in the circumstances, would reasonably be expected to provide privacy and [either] the person's genitals, buttocks or breasts are exposed or covered only with underwear, [or] the person is using a lavatory, or the person is doing a sexual act that is not of a kind ordinarily done in public.' As originally drafted, the 'private act' had to take place within a structure, defined broadly to include a tent, vehicle or vessel: it could also have been a temporary or moveable structure. However, a late amendment changed this to 'place', banning voyeurs from observing those individuals who enjoy sexual activity in the open air as well as those who look through windows or peepholes. As the minister, Paul Goggins, told the Commons in November 2003, the amendment widens the scope of the offence 'to protect someone engaging in a private act in any place where they could reasonably expect privacy'. He explained that it would be for the court to decide whether or not their expectation of privacy was reasonable.

It must still be a private act, of course: the sexual activity must be 'not of a kind ordinarily done in public'. Quite what sexual acts are 'ordinarily done in public' we are left to work out for ourselves. Presumably they would include kissing, but what about two men, who were not obviously related, kissing each other on the lips? This may be perfectly ordinary in some public places, though it is not normally seen in others. What is happening must be 'live': the definition is not intended to cover someone who views images recorded through voyeuristic means. On the other hand, it does not have to be direct: 'observation' can be 'direct or by looking at an image' and 'image' means 'a moving or still image, produced by any means'. That seems to cover both the use of mirrors, binoculars and CCTV.

The second offence occurs if a person (*A*) *operates equipment* with the intention of enabling another person (*B*) to observe, for the purpose of obtaining sexual gratification, a third person (*C*) doing a private act, and *A* knows that *C* does not consent to his operating equipment with that intention. This would cover, for example a landlord (*A*), operating a webcam to allow people on the Internet (*B*) to view live images for their sexual gratification of his tenant (C) getting undressed, if A knew that C had not agreed to this performance.

Thirdly, it is an offence for a person (A) to *record* another person (B) doing a private act with the intention that either A or a third person (C) will look at an image of B doing the act for the purpose of obtaining sexual gratification, and A knows that B does not consent to his recording the act with that intention. This would therefore cover the person (A) who secretly films someone (B) masturbating in a bedroom to show others (C) for their sexual gratification. Proof that the intention was the sexual gratification of others could be inferred from, for example, the fact that the image was posted on a pornographic website, or appeared in a pornographic magazine. It need only be proved that the defendant, A, knew that B did not consent: it makes no difference whether those looking at the image (C) know that the person filmed did not agree to be recorded with that intention. Merely publishing the images would not be an offence under this provision.

The fourth and final offence of criminal voyeurism occurs when a person simply *installs equipment*, or constructs or adapts a structure or part of a structure, with the intention of enabling himself or another person to commit the first offence listed above. That would cover someone who, for example, drilled a spyhole or installed a two-way mirror in a house—or made a hole in the canvas of a changing room in a market stall selling clothes—with the intention of spying on someone for sexual gratification or of allowing others to do so. The offender could be prosecuted even if the peephole or mirror was discovered before it was used.

These provisions aroused little interest as they passed through Parliament, although Lord Lloyd of Berwick, a retired law lord, described them as an 'absurdity' that would 'never be used in practice and should not be on the statute book'. They are certainly more tightly drafted than the Californian provisions. On the other hand, the element of sexual gratification may be difficult to prove if the voyeur does no more than, say, stare at the next man in a public urinal. They also make no attempt to deal with the supposed menace of voyeurs in public places.

But is this really the sort of behaviour that we should be criminalizing? Imagine your teenage son discovers that the people whose house backs on to yours sometimes get undressed at night before drawing the curtains. Does his curiosity really merit a police investigation, a criminal prosecution and the prospect of a prison sentence? Do we really want people calling in the police because they believe the man across the way has been secretly spying on them? And do we want to see detectives invading that person's privacy by searching his house for recording equipment, especially if the initial call was prompted by no more than a grudge? This may not be a 'victimless' crime, but it is an activity that almost always takes place without the supposed victims being aware of it. Of course it should not be encouraged, but does it really merit the attention of the criminal law? Shouldn't people simply draw the curtains?

A Privacy Act?

Since we now have a law protecting a person from intrusion when he or she is 'doing a private act', should Parliament go all the way and create a universal privacy law? 'Yes', said the House of Commons Culture, Media and Sport Committee in June 2003. The Committee, chaired by the former Labour spin-doctor and one-time journalist Gerald Kaufman, was uncompromising in its conclusions: it recommended that the Government should 'reconsider its position and bring forward legislative proposals to clarify the protection that individuals can expect from unwarranted intrusion by anyone—not the press alone—into their private lives'. The MPs said this was 'necessary fully to satisfy the obligations upon the UK under the European Convention of Human Rights, adding that 'there should be full and wide consultation but in the end Parliament should be allowed to undertake its proper legislative role'.

As the Committee was well aware, this was contrary to Government policy. The Department for Culture, Media and Sport, whose responsibilities the Committee shadowed, took the view that the newspaper industry should continue to regulate itself through the PCC. As the Department had said in evidence to the Committee, 'the Government's starting point is a fundamental belief that a free press is best served by unfettered self-regulation'. It added: 'The Government has no plans whatsoever to legislate in this area, or to interfere with the way the PCC operates.' That remained its position, despite the MPs' report.

Why then was the Committee rushing in where the Government—and, of course, the PCC itself—feared to tread? It was clear the newspapers themselves were not entirely of one voice. Paul Dacre, editor of the *Daily Mail*, said there were quite enough restrictions on newspapers already. Alan Rusbridger, editor of the *Guardian*, said that if there had to be a privacy law he would rather it was passed by Parliament than developed through the courts—though his preference was for no privacy law at all. Only five years earlier, the *Guardian* itself had sponsored a Privacy and Defamation Bill. However, Rusbridger was no longer in favour of legislation for a number of reasons: the PCC had subsequently toughened its Code of Practice on privacy; the Human Rights Act had come into effect; the *Reynolds* judgment had 'in the opinion of many journalists, improved the libel laws in respect of responsible reporters working on stories with a clear public interest element'; and the courts had begun redeveloping the law of confidence in the direction of privacy law.

Lawyers were also split: in oral evidence, Michael Tugendhat, who had represented the claimants in *Douglas v Hello! Ltd*, gave MPs some lessons in their limitations as legislators:

The difficulty I have with legislation is that legislation does not finally answer questions any more, because it has got to be interpreted in accordance with the Human Rights Act. But so has case law. And until there is a problem my view is: 'if it ain't bust, don't fix it'. At the moment it is not bust.

I agree you have a lot of conflicting decisions, for example you have different opinions about role models expressed in the footballer case [*A v B plc*] and in the Naomi Campbell case. But you are going to have that if you legislate as well, because the legislation can only be in general terms. So I would say that if you give it a little bit of time to settle in: it probably will come right, in much the same way as other areas of the law have.

After this 'leave it to the judges' approach it was perhaps not entirely surprising that Tugendhat took a judicial appointment soon after giving evidence to the committee. By contrast, written evidence from Eric Barendt, Professor of Media Law at University College London, displayed the academic's desire for a clear set of rules:

There is now a strong case for legislation to protect individuals against intrusion on their privacy by the media. Privacy is an important human right protected in many European and other jurisdictions (for example, France,

Germany, most states in the USA, and some Commonwealth countries). Further, it is guaranteed by the International Covenant on Civil and Political Rights and the European Convention on Human Rights . . . So it is anomalous that it is not protected under English or Scots law.

The courts have not yet held that the Human Rights Act requires them to recognise a right to privacy, either generally or in particular against the media. But judges have said that the law should be developed to respect the rights protected under the HRA, including the right to respect for private life . . . It is likely that the House of Lords, if not the Court of Appeal, will declare in an appropriate case that the law does protect a right to privacy; it is artificial to leave its protection to the breach of confidence action and other remedies.

It would be much better for Parliament to establish a right to privacy than leave this entirely to the courts. Judicial development of the law would inevitably be slow. Newspapers and other media would face a period of uncertainty in which they would not know whether it was safe to investigate or report a current scandal. Press fears about the 'chilling effect' of a privacy right may be exaggerated, but they are not entirely groundless.

Legislation can, and should, define the scope of a right to privacy. It should also provide defences for the media, including a broad public interest defence and a defence that the information is no longer private because it has already been put in the public domain. The law should probably contain provisions about the measure of damages and specify the situations in which it might be appropriate for a court to award punitive damages for a deliberate or persistent infringement of privacy rights. Although it would be silly to pretend that a privacy statute could be so precise that the result in any case would be predictable, it would give the law more certainty than could be expected from a series of court rulings.

Professor Barendt was supported by Rabinder Singh, QC, who said that the system of self-regulation was 'legally deficient', emphasizing 'that not only has the time come to say openly that there must be a right to privacy in English law, but that if the courts are not prepared to provide such recognition, the UK Government will be obliged to do so by legislative intervention if it is to meet its Convention obligations'.

The PCC was, of course, against the idea of a privacy law. Lord Wakeham, its former chairman, had argued that a privacy law would be a law for the rich and could make the press industry withdraw effective co-operation with the PCC, thus depriving ordinary people of an avenue for redress without giving them anything useful in its place.

Summing up, the Committee said it regarded 'the pragmatic arguments against introducing a privacy law to be quite seductive, especially with regard to the question of limited access to the law for people of ordinary means'. However, it seemed to the MPs that the right to respect for private life, introduced into English law by the Human Rights Act had sown the seed of privacy law. 'If so, the really pragmatic question is whether its growth should be under the care of the courts, on a case-by-case basis, or of the Government and Parliament subject to the extensive consultative processes now available for legislative proposals: Green Paper, White Paper, draft Bill, Bill and passage through the two Houses.' Their answer, as we have seen, is that, 'in the end Parliament should be allowed to undertake its proper legislative role'.

I disagree—both in practice and as a matter of principle. The practical difficulty, as expressed by Tugendhat in his evidence to the Commons Committee, is that, as a result of the Human Rights Act, legislation no longer removes uncertainty in the law. It must now be interpreted by the courts in such a way as to be compliant with the Human Rights Convention. Far from contradicting him, Barendt merely reinforces Tugendhat's objections to a new statute when he says it should include a 'broad public interest defence'. Who is to decide what is in the public interest, if not the judges? It would be easy enough to set out the law on paper, but impossible to predict how the courts would apply it to a given set of facts until there had been a substantial number of decisions from the appellate courts.

The principled objection is to any more restrictions on the media. Which government would not like to gag its critics while enhancing the privacy of its members? Nobody can be very surprised when MPs call for more restrictions on those who write about them, but that is not enough to justify further government interference with the right of free speech.

Supporters of a privacy law insist that this is not their objective. Far from seeking greater restrictions, they are merely trying to achieve certainty, while trying to defend individuals who have been the subject of unjust criticism or intrusion against an all-powerful press. These supporters also argue that we have a privacy law already, whether we like it or not. Writing in the *Entertainment Law Review*, Jonathan Coad, a lawyer whose clients include celebrity victims, argues that a privacy law exists as a result of Article 8: far better he says that its boundaries should be set by Parliament, in line with the Government's obligations under the Human Rights Convention, than by the courts. Of course it will still have to be interpreted by judges in individual cases, he acknowledges, but it is surely better to have a principle set out clearly in statute than in a series of overlapping and inconsistent decisions from the Court of Appeal or the House of Lords.

Coad says there are two ways in which the media may infringe a person's rights: by stealing that person's good name and by invading the individual's privacy. Both, he argues, may breach the right to respect for private and family life under Article 8 by making it harder for the individual to relate to family, friends and society. Reputation may be restored by the courts, although the process is far from easy. 'However privacy, once lost, can never be restored. Once material about an individual's private life has ceased to be confidential, it can never again become so.'

That is why Coad argues for a system of prior restraint, protecting the individual against irreparable damage by the media. Since that is not on offer from the PCC, it needs to be provided by the courts: the rights granted by Article 8 must be enforceable against the press.

But, to some extent, they are already. Why is Garry Flitcroft's case reported as *A v B plc* if not because his identity was protected for nearly a year? The courts have shown themselves well able to grant injunctions in appropriate cases, and these have been fully respected by the media. Coad's statute might reduce the area of uncertainty and ensure that cases were heard more quickly, but that is hardly a justification for bringing the press under state control.

He may be right to stigmatize the PCC as a creature of the newspaper industry, campaigning on behalf of its paymaster (although this is firmly denied by its chairman, Sir Christopher Meyer). But the alternative to legislation is not lawlessness. It is a continuation of the present common-law structure, as enhanced by the Human Rights Act. Our courts can and will protect personal privacy in the most deserving cases.

The willingness of judges to protect individuals against the media is fully acknowledged in Coad's article, though he says judges have suffered severe attacks from certain parts of the media when they have come down in favour of privacy. 'It would be more productive of the press to engage in constructive dialogue as to how the twin but often conflicting freedoms enshrined in Article 10 and Article 8 can be protected by means of a properly constituted privacy law,' he concludes.

I come clean

To some extent, this is what I have tried to achieve in this book. I am against legislation because it would inevitably lead to greater restrictions on the media than the courts are currently willing to impose—however much my opponents may claim it would merely put the existing common law into statutory form. I am against the 'activist' approach associated with leading judges like Lord Phillips, Lord Bingham and Lord Justice Sedley—if only because I consider that the law is restrictive enough already. That is not to say I am impressed with Lord Woolf's well-meaning but woolly attempt in *A v B plc* to keep everybody happy. I much prefer the approach taken by the Court of Appeal in *Wainwright*, when Lord Justice Buxton said there were 'serious difficulties of principle' in creating a privacy law—because it would protect not only individuals wanting to get on with their lives but also companies that wanted to keep their affairs private'—with Lord Justice Mummery wisely adding that a new tort, even one created by the judges, 'would give rise to as many problems as it is sought to solve'.

But you would expect me to say that. I am, after all, a journalist; and one who believes that the freedom of the press to write about people— even footballers and television presenters about whom I know little and care less—is more precious than their right not to read intrusive accounts of their sexual conquests or see topless photographs of themselves in the newspapers.

Of course, we are all entitled to some measure of respect for our private lives. Certainly, we should be able to speak in confidence about others without our comments being leaked to a newspaper. But you only have to look at the Hutton Inquiry, established to investigate the apparent suicide in July 2003 of the Government weapons expert Dr David Kelly, to see which is considered more important. Once Kelly was found dead, most of the confidentiality that formed such a large part of his life expired with him. The BBC acknowledged that he had been their source for allegations that the Government had enhanced the case for war in Iraq. Ministers and officials disclosed documents, dealing with both policy and personnel, that would otherwise have remained top secret for many years. And Kelly's last moments alive—perhaps the most intimate moments of his private and family life—were laid bare in the most public way imaginable.

In a properly ordered society, both privacy and the press deserve protection. When they conflict, a line must be drawn between these two immensely valuable human rights. I have made very clear which side of the line I favour. The media in Britain have a great deal to answer for but, in the end, there is no contest. Privacy good; free press better.

The PCC Code

This is the full text of the Press Complaints Commission's Code of Practice, as revised and reissued in 2003.

All members of the press have a duty to maintain the highest professional and ethical standards. This code sets the benchmark for those standards. It both protects the rights of the individual and upholds the public's right to know.

The Code is the cornerstone of the system of self-regulation to which the industry has made a binding commitment. Editors and publishers must ensure that the Code is observed rigorously not only by their staff but also by anyone who contributes to their publications.

It is essential to the workings of an agreed code that it be honoured not only to the letter but in the full spirit. The Code should not be interpreted so narrowly as to compromise its commitment to respect the rights of the individual, nor so broadly that it prevents publication in the public interest.

It is the responsibility of editors to co-operate with the PCC as swiftly as possible in the resolution of complaints.

Any publication which is criticised by the PCC under one of the following clauses must print the adjudication which follows in full and with due prominence.

1. Accuracy

(i) Newspapers and periodicals must take care not to publish inaccurate, misleading or distorted material including pictures.

(ii) Whenever it is recognised that a significant inaccuracy, misleading statement or distorted report has been published, it must be corrected promptly and with due prominence.

(iii) An apology must be published whenever appropriate.

(iv) Newspapers, whilst free to be partisan, must distinguish clearly between comment, conjecture and fact.

(v) A newspaper or periodical must report fairly and accurately the outcome of an action for defamation to which it has been a party.

2. Opportunity to reply

A fair opportunity for reply to inaccuracies must be given to individuals or organisations when reasonably called for.

3. Privacy★

(i) Everyone is entitled to respect for his or her private and family life, home, health and correspondence. A publication will be expected to justify intrusions into any individual's private life without consent.

(ii) The use of long lens photography to take pictures of people in private places without their consent is unacceptable.

Note—Private places are public or private property where there is a reasonable expectation of privacy.

4. Harassment★

(i) Journalists and photographers must neither obtain nor seek to obtain information or pictures through intimidation, harassment or persistent pursuit.

(ii) They must not photograph individuals in private places (as defined by the note to clause 3) without their consent; must not persist in telephoning, questioning, pursuing or photographing individuals after having been asked to desist; must not remain on their property after having been asked to leave and must not follow them.

(iii) Editors must ensure that those working for them comply with these requirements and must not publish material from other sources which does not meet these requirements.

5. Intrusion into grief or shock

In cases involving personal grief or shock, enquiries must be carried out and approaches made with sympathy and discretion. Publication must be handled sensitively at such times but this should not be interpreted as restricting the right to report judicial proceedings.

6. Children★

(i) Young people should be free to complete their time at school without unnecessary intrusion.

(ii) Journalists must not interview or photograph a child under the age of 16 on subjects involving the welfare of the child or any other child in the absence of or without the consent of a parent or other adult who is responsible for the children.

(iii) Pupils must not be approached or photographed while at school without the permission of the school authorities.

(iv) There must be no payment to minors for material involving the welfare of children nor payments to parents or guardians for material about their children or wards unless it is demonstrably in the child's interest.

(v) Where material about the private life of a child is published, there must be justification for publication other than the fame, notoriety or position of his or her parents or guardian.

7. Children in sex cases★

1. The press must not, even where the law does not prohibit it, identify children under the age of 16 who are involved in cases concerning sexual offences, whether as victims or as witnesses.

2. In any press report of a case involving a sexual offence against a child—

   (i) The child must not be identified.

   (ii) The adult may be identified.

   (iii) The word 'incest' must not be used where a child victim might be identified.

(iv) Care must be taken that nothing in the report implies the relationship between the accused and the child.

8. Listening Devices★

Journalists must not obtain or publish material obtained by using clandestine listening devices or by intercepting private telephone conversations.

9. Hospitals★

(i)   Journalists or photographers making enquiries at hospitals or similar institutions must identify themselves to a responsible executive and obtain permission before entering non-public areas.

(ii) The restrictions on intruding into privacy are particularly relevant to enquiries about individuals in hospitals or similar institutions.

10. Reporting of crime★

(i)   The press must avoid identifying relatives or friends of persons convicted or accused of crime without their consent.

(ii) Particular regard should be paid to the potentially vulnerable position of children who are witnesses to, or victims of, crime. This should not be interpreted as restricting the right to report judicial proceedings.

11. Misrepresentation★

(i)   Journalists must not generally obtain or seek to obtain information or pictures through misrepresentation or subterfuge.

(ii) Documents or photographs should be removed only with the consent of the owner.

(iii) Subterfuge can be justified only in the public interest and only when material cannot be obtained by any other means.

12. Victims of sexual assault

The press must not identify victims of sexual assault or publish material likely to contribute to such identification unless there is adequate justification and, by law, they are free to do so.

13. Discrimination★

(i)   The press must avoid prejudicial or pejorative reference to a person's race, colour, religion, sex or sexual orientation or to any physical or mental illness or disability.

(ii) It must avoid publishing details of a person's race, colour, religion, sexual orientation, physical or mental illness or disability unless these are directly relevant to the story.

14. Financial journalism

(i)   Even where the law does not prohibit it, journalists must not use for their own profit financial information they receive in advance of its general publication, nor should they pass such information to others.

(ii) They must not write about shares or securities in whose performance they know that they or their close families have a significant financial interest without disclosing the interest to the editor or financial editor.

(iii) They must not buy or sell, either directly or through nominees or agents, shares or securities about which they have written recently or about which they intend to write in the near future.

15. Confidential sources

Journalists have a moral obligation to protect confidential sources of information.

16. Witness payments in criminal trials

(i) No payment or offer of payment to a witness—or any person who may reasonably be expected to be called as a witness—should be made in any case once proceedings are active as defined by the Contempt of Court Act 1981. This prohibition lasts until the suspect has been freed unconditionally by police without charge or bail or the proceedings are otherwise discontinued; or has entered a guilty plea to the court; or, in the event of a not guilty plea, the court has announced its verdict.

★(ii) Where proceedings are not yet active but are likely and foreseeable, editors must not make or offer payment to any person who may reasonably be expected to be called as a witness, unless the information concerned ought demonstrably to be published in the public interest and there is an over-riding need to make or promise payment for this to be done; and all reasonable steps have been taken to ensure no financial dealings influence the evidence those witnesses give. In no circumstances should such payment be conditional on the outcome of a trial.

★(iii) Any payment or offer of payment made to a person later cited to give evidence in proceedings must be disclosed to the prosecution and defence. The witness must be advised of this requirement.

17. Payment to criminals★

Payment or offers of payment for stories, pictures or information, must not be made directly or through agents to convicted or confessed criminals or to their associates—who may include family, friends and colleagues—except where the material concerned ought to be published in the public interest and payment is necessary for this to be done.

The public interest

There may be exceptions to the clauses marked ★ where they can be demonstrated to be in the public interest.

1. The public interest includes:
   (i)   Detecting or exposing crime or a serious misdemeanour.
   (ii) Protecting public health and safety.
   (iii) Preventing the public from being misled by some statement or action of an individual or organisation.
2. In any case where the public interest is invoked, the Press Complaints Commission will require a full explanation by the editor demonstrating how the public interest was served.
3. There is a public interest in freedom of expression itself. The Commission will therefore have regard to the extent to which material has, or is about to, become available to the public.
4. In cases involving children editors must demonstrate an exceptional public interest to over-ride the normally paramount interest of the child.

Bibliography

Bingham of Cornhill, Lord, *The Business of Judging* (Oxford: Oxford University Press, 2000).

Clayton, R, and H Tomlinson, *The Law of Human Rights* (Oxford: Oxford University Press, 2000).

Coad, J, 'The Press Complaints Commission: Some Myths About Self Regulation' (2003) 14(8) *Entertainment Law Review* 211–14.

Cook, R, *Point of Departure* (London: Simon & Schuster, 2003).

Denning, Sir A T, *The Road to Justice* (London: Stevens & Sons, 1955).

Grosz, S, J Beatson, and P Duffy, *Human Rights* (London: Sweet & Maxwell, 2000).

Hargreaves, I, *Journalism: Truth or Dare?* (Oxford: Oxford University Press, 2003).

Hooper, D, *Reputations Under Fire* (London: Little, Brown, 2000).

Kremenetsky, D, 'Insatiable "Up-Skirt" Voyeurs Force California Lawmakers to Expand Privacy Protection in Public Places' (2000) 31 *McGeorge Law Review* 285.

Lester of Herne Hill, Lord, and D Pannick (eds) *Human Rights Law and Practice* (London: Butterworths, 1999; second edition, 2004).

Lewis, A, *Make No Law* (New York: Random House, 1991).

Malcolm, J, *The Journalist and the Murderer* (New York: Alfred A Knopf, 1990).

Prosser, W, 'Privacy' (1960) 48 Cal L Rev 383 (reprinted in Wacks, *op cit*).

Robertson, G, *The Justice Game* (London: Chatto & Windus, 1998).

—— and A Nicol, *Media Law*, 4th edn (London: Sweet & Maxwell, 2002).

Schilling, K, 'Public Lives and Public Interest', Law Society's *Gazette*, 7 November 2002.

Sereny, G, *Cries Unheard: The Story of Mary Bell* (London: Macmillan, 1998).

Tomlinson, H (ed), *Privacy and the Media: The Developing Law* (London: Matrix Chambers, 2002).

Tugendhat, M, and I Christie (eds), *The Law of Privacy and the Media* (Oxford: Oxford University Press, 2002).

Wacks, R, *Privacy and the Law*, vol II (London: Dartmouth, 1993; New York: NYUP, 1993).

Warren, S and L Brandeis, 'The Right to Privacy' (1890) 4 *Harvard Law Review* 193 (reprinted in Wacks, *op cit*).

Wright, P, *Spycatcher* (New York: Viking, 1987; Victoria: Heinemann, 1987).

Young, H, *One of Us* (London: Macmillan, 1989).

Table of Cases

Index